...So How Can We Make Them Scream?

"Polygons feel no pain" Volume 2

Ingemar Ragnemalm

Course book in advanced techniques for game programming

Foreword

Welcome to the 2017 version of So How Can You Make Them Scream? This is the very first version available online as print-on-demand for anyone, and with an official ISBN number. This makes it a "first edition", despite having existed since 2008, with a major revision 2012 when moving to modern OpenGL (which means 3.2 and up) and many minor revisions almost every year. The most recent additions include 3D displays, ambient occlusion, texture compression and geometry and tesselation shaders.

I am happy to say that this makes the book feel comfortably current. What I want this to be is a tight, to the point book on game related algorithms, suitable for an advanced under-graduate university course. Just like Volume 1 (Polygons Feel No Pain) I want the book to be smaller, lighter, cheaper, but most of all more informative than other, bigger text books. It want it to be well packed with interesting things, often including relevant, working, up-to-date demo code, while not wasting too much space on lengthy discussions on marginal matters. And it should be small and light enough to slip into your backpacks any time. These have been a major points since the first printing in 2008.

When I say that we use OpenGL 3.2, you may wonder why we don't move directly to OpenGL 4, the latest versions, or even Vulkan. This is because OpenGL 4 would be unus-able for many students, at least on their own computers, due to hardware or OS limita-tions. The difference from OpenGL 3 to 4 is much smaller than from 2.1 to 3.2, the big jump is to OpenGL 3, and by using 3.2 as platform (with OpenGL 4 as an option) we work with future safe, modern code, where OpenGL 4 features can easily be incorporated as needed, while we still support most hardware configurations and OSes. Vulkan, on the other hand, is not suitable for teaching, at least not at this time.

Finally, why am I using small utility source modules instead of extensive libraries, like VectorUtils rather than glm? The reason is *transparency*. These solutions were created to give you the essentials while still making the add-on source digestable, so you can go in and see how it works without being overwhelmed with complexity.

Cover image by Ingemar and Susanne Ragnemalm. (Rough hand drawing by Ingemar, neat "production quality" version by Susanne.)

Related web page: http://www.computer-graphics.se

ISBN 978-1974110650

First public edition 2017. (Earlier revisions were only locally available and had no ISBN.)

1. Introduction

This book was written as course material for the course in Advanced Game Programming at Linköping University.

1.1 Who should read this book?

Since this book is written for the course TSBK03 Advanced Game Programming at the University of Linköping, attendants of that course are the target audience. However, anyone interested in the subject is also in the target audience!

The purpose of the book is to provide a fairly broad overview of the most important game-related technologies that you should learn beyond the basics, a common base on which the students are encouraged to build further on in their projects.

1.2 What should you expect to learn from this book, and its course?

This is not one of those game programming books that spend many pages talking about what a game is and why it is fun. It is a book about technologies relevant to games, and thereby also to many related fields. The book covers a rather broad range of subjects. It has four main target areas:

- 1. Advanced computer graphics. We build on what you learned in earlier courses.
- 2. Game physics
- 3. Animation
- 4. Artificial intelligence for games

For various reasons (not least the choice of projects of former students), the course has mostly focused on graphics and animation. This has, however, varied over time.

1.3 Advanced techniques? What does "advanced" mean?

The topic of the book and the course is advanced techniques for game programming, but the term "advanced" is highly relative. The book does not claim to describe the current state-of-the art. Such knowledge quickly becomes old. Rather, it builds on the previous book with more advanced topics. It raises the level a bit, but the last chapter is written by yourself, the project you make where you go beyond this book on your favorite subject.

So "advanced" means

- More advanced than simple 2D games (e.g. Tetris)
- More advanced than Volume 1
- A more advanced "base level" from which you are encouraged to go higher.

1.4 Why is the book in English?

Why is the book in English, when the course language is Swedish? Some reasons:

- The course may be opened for international students in the future.
- The book is made available on the international market.
- Even if it was not, it would feel strange to make the first part of a series in English, and the second in Swedish. All references between the two volumes will be easier to do.

I do use my own language when I can, and I believe in making proper translations of terms. In order to make it easier for you to use the right Swedish words, despite a book in English, I put in a few footnotes for non-trivial translations.

1.5 Acknowledgments

The material for this book comes from a variety of sources, books, papers, web pages. In many cases, I have had help from students.

In particular, many of my exam workers have contributed. Johan Sjöstrand, Tomas (Zsolt) Szabo, Pär Wieslander, Lars Abrahamsson and Björn Milton did very important work on both lab material and background research. Other exam workers whose reports have been important sources include Roger Johannesson, Johannes Nilsson, Henrik Hansson, Erik Torstensson, Johan Hedström, Björn Lindahl, Markus Fahlén, Emil Jansson and John Nilsson. The list is not complete and is growing.

I have based some material on lecture notes by Peter Johansson, Kenneth Järrendahl and Johan Hedborg, and have had important feedback from them on the content of this book. Jens Ogniewski expanded the networking chapter for 2011 (later excluded), and wrote the texts on 3D displays and texture compression for 2012.

Special thanks to Arvid Kongstad for proofreading.

Finally, all previous students on the course have contributed in various ways. Your interest for certain problems have been very important for the course. A number of good projects (especially those with high quality reports) have directly influenced the book.

2. Table of contents

3. More computer graphics

This chapter starts the first part of the book, which is about advanced computer graphics. As mentioned in the introduction, "advanced" is a dangerous word that requires a clarification: In this case it essentially means "interesting topics that did not fit in Volume 1 and its course", with emphasis on topics that are relevant for game programming.

In this chapter, I will talk about concepts that are pretty central, features and functionality in the GPU, accessible through OpenGL, which are useful, and essential for much of what we will do later, but which had little or no coverage in the first book.

3.1 Notes about OpenGL 3.2(+) and auxiliary libraries

In the following chapters, examples are given as OpenGL 3.2 code. That means that it looks quite a bit different from OpenGL up to 2.1, for which most available example code you find on-line is written. It also means that the code depends on more additional libraries than before. This section briefly summarizes the differences.

You always use shaders. This means that a shader loader must always be present, which is not shown in the examples but is external code (in GL_utilities, my own code).

No more immediate mode. You never specify geometry with glBegin/glEnd pairs. Instead, you upload geometry to VAOs/VBOs (vertex array and vertex buffer objects). We use Wavefront OBJ files with our own (GL 3.2 friendly) loader.

No more built-in matrices. This means no glPushMatrix/glPopMatrix, no glRotate, glTranslate etc. Instead, you create matrices, do whatever calculations you need, and upload to the shaders. I use my own VectorUtils library, with functions like rotation (Rx, Ry, Rz, ArbRotate), translation (T), projection matrix creation, look-at matrix creation etc. The library is mainly aimed at C, but there are also some C++ extensions built in for operator overloading. The good part with this is that there are fewer calls that you are forced to use; your freedom is bigger. Also, the math and the code gets closer.

No more built-in light sources. You handle all light source data as you see fit.

Fewer states. You don't glEnable/glDisable light nor textures, you just use them or not.

Overall, the examples are fairly similar to their 2.1 counterparts, the simpler examples are slightly more complex, but we avoid low performance solution while having more freedom in selecting the tools we want, and the code really gets cleaner and more to the point than before, with less secret tricks behind your back. Just get the algebra right and that's it.

But isn't there any drawback? Sure. The biggest problem with 3.2 is that it is much easier to get a blank screen that doesn't help you at all. You need to have a certain base functionality (provided with my demos) and work from there. It is wise to backup your code often, in case you mess up something vital and need to go back.

3.2 Buffers

In Volume 1, I deliberately left out some information about OpenGL and graphics programming in order to make the presentation easier to grasp. I will start this chapter by wedding the scope, first of all by discussing all the buffers that are available on the GPU. Because there are several image buffers in a GPU, not only the one you see on the screen. Figure 1 shows a summary.

You already know of some of them:

- The frame buffer. This is the image you see on the screen.
- The back buffer (double buffer) to avoid flicker.
- The Z buffer (depth buffer), which handles low-level visible surface detection.

But there are more:

- Stencil buffer: For masking, for conditional drawing.
- Framebuffer objects, for drawing directly to a texture.

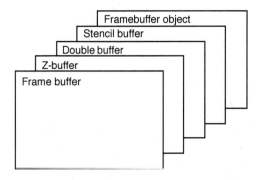

FIGURE 1. The buffers on the GPU

On these buffers, there are a few standard operations:

- Erase the buffer with glClear.
- Copy between buffers and copy to and from the CPU: glCopyPixels, glReadPixels

Beyond these basic operations, there are special-purpose functionality for some buffers, which is much of what this chapter will tell about.

3.3 Stencil buffer

A "stencil" is an old method for printing, using a sheet with holes forming the shape that should be printed.[1] The digital stencil buffer can do the same thing; it is a mask that pixel by pixel determines what pixel that may be written.

For setting the stencil buffer contents, you enable the buffer and control it with special calls, and draw with the usual drawing operations, e.g. polygons. Here follows a simple example, where I draw the Utah teapot masked with a wireframe sphere.

First of all, we must specify that we want a stencil buffer when we create the OpenGL context. When using GLUT, you add GLUT_STENCIL when calling glutInitDisplay-Mode. Thus, that call may look like this:

```
glutInitDisplayMode(GLUT_DOUBLE | GLUT_RGB | GLUT_DEPTH | GLUT_STENCIL);
```

Let us have a look at the display function. It will demonstrate most of the API, which I will comment on below.

```
void display()
{
    GLfloat mv2[16], tx2[16], trans[16], rot[16], scale[16];
        // Clear frame buffer, Z buffer and stencil buffer
    glClear(GL_COLOR_BUFFER_BIT | GL_DEPTH_BUFFER_BIT |
GL_STENCIL_BUFFER_BIT); // <- ***
    count++;
```

In typical OpenGL fashion, we have our own projection and modelview matrices, passed to the shaders as needed.

```
    glUniformMatrix4fv(glGetUniformLocation(program, "projectionMatrix"),
1, GL_TRUE, projectionMatrix);
    glUniformMatrix4fv(glGetUniformLocation(program, "modelViewMatrix"),
1, GL_TRUE, modelViewMatrix);
```

Now we enable the stencil buffer. Disabling frame and Z buffer is optional; you often draw into the frame buffer and the stencil buffer at the same time, for example when drawing a floor that you will later draw a shadow or reflection on. In this example, the stencil contents is drawn separately.

```
    // Enable the Stencil Buffer
    glEnable(GL_STENCIL_TEST);

    // Disable Color Buffer and Depth Buffer
    glColorMask(GL_FALSE, GL_FALSE, GL_FALSE, GL_FALSE);
    glDepthMask(GL_FALSE);

    // Set 1 into the stencil buffer
```

---

1. In Swedish: "schablon"

```
glStencilFunc(GL_ALWAYS, 1, 0xFFFFFFFF);
glStencilOp(GL_REPLACE, GL_REPLACE, GL_REPLACE);
// Draw the wired sphere in the stencil buffer only
DrawWireframeModel(sphere);
```

glStencilFunc and glStencilOp control the stencil buffer, both how its contents is changed and how it affects other drawing. Above, we state that the stencil buffer should always be changed to 1 whenever a pixel is drawn.

```
// Turn on Color Buffer and Depth Buffer
glColorMask(GL_TRUE, GL_TRUE, GL_TRUE, GL_TRUE);
glDepthMask(GL_TRUE);

// Only write to the Stencil Buffer where 1 is set
glStencilFunc(GL_EQUAL, 1, 0xFFFFFFFF);
// Keep the content of the Stencil Buffer
glStencilOp(GL_KEEP, GL_KEEP, GL_KEEP);
```

Before drawing the masked shape, we set the stencil buffer to demand that the stencil is equal to 1 to allow drawing.

```
Point3D axis = {1, 1, 1};
ArbRotate(&axis, 0.2 * count*0.1, rot);
Mult(modelViewMatrix, rot, mv2);
glUniformMatrix4fv(glGetUniformLocation(program, "modelViewMatrix"),
1, GL_TRUE, mv2);
DrawModel(teapot);

glDisable(GL_STENCIL_TEST); // Turn off (in case we add other stuff
that does not use it)
glutSwapBuffers();
}
```

The result of this code is shown in Figure 2.

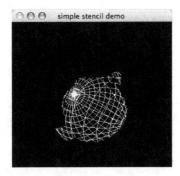

FIGURE 2. The stencil buffer used for masking; the teapot masked by a wireframe sphere.

What we see is the Utah Teapot "sampled" to be visible only in the positions where it intersects the wireframe sphere. Since the teapot is plain white, with no texture, the result is pretty much a logical AND between the two shapes. With a texture that follows the teapot, the texture will change the impression.

In the demo above, the stencil buffer is used as if it was a binary buffer, but it is not. Every pixel does not hold a bit, but an integer value, 8 or 16 bits as an unsigned integer.

3.3.1 Using the stencil buffer for masking mirrors

Two notable cases where masking is critical are planar shadows (chapter 4.1) and mirrors. Let us cover mirrors here, the simpler of the two. In Volume 1 we saw that you can easily make a matrix for mirroring geometry, but how do you implement a mirror in a scene? That takes more than just mirroring the vertices. Here are a few things to take into account:

- The mirror has to be flat. If that is not what you want, consider a real-time rendered cube map instead.
- The mirrored geometry will be located *behind* the mirror, so you want to draw in the right order to avoid problems with the Z buffer.
- Geometry behind the mirror must be excluded or it will end up in front.
- Mirroring will reverse back-face culling of your models. You need to switch the culling (by calling glCullFace(GL_FRONT)) when drawing the mirrored geometry.

We are still not talking about a rocket science effect; The resulting algorithm is nicely summarized as follows:

- 1. Clear the stencil buffer
- 2. Draw the ground *only* in stencil
- 3. Draw the mirrored teapot (behind the ground), masked by stencil buffer
- 4. Draw the ground with some transparency, to make the mirrored geometry visible. Thus, the reflectivity of the mirror is determined by its transparency.
- 5. Draw the teapot in a position matching the mirrored one

I have made a demo for this, which is shown in Figure 3. (Also available on-line.)

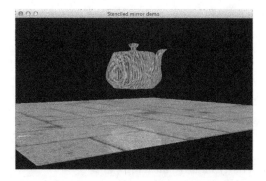

FIGURE 3. Mirrored shape with reflection masked by the stencil buffer

The planar shadows algorithm (chapter 4.1) is quite similar to this, with the addition of some extra math for making a projected shadow instead of a simple mirroring. Thus, we can do some pretty nice things only by a binary mask. But there is more.

3.3.2 Advanced stenciling

There are plenty of applications for the stencil buffer, a lot more than you may believe at first. Here are a few:

- Mask out frames, HUDs etc.
- Dissolve effects, by drawing patterns over the entire buffer.
- Limit the drawing to a specific shape in the scene. This is a common use, used for things like reflections and shadows (like above).
- Shadow volumes.
- CSG, Constructive Solid Geometry. This is a more exotic use.

My conclusion is that the stencil buffer is actually extremely important.

Let us look closer at the API. The call glStencilFunc selects the function of the stencil buffer when drawing elsewhere:

```
glStencilFunc(func, ref, mask);
```

The other side of the coin is glStencilOp, which decides how the stencil buffer itself is modified when drawing:

```
glStencilOp(fail, zfail, zpass);
```

Finally, you can fill the entire stencil buffer with an arbitrary value using glClearStencil().

The three parameters to glStencilOp refers to the three possible cases that can occur for each pixel/fragment when drawing: Stencil fail, stencil pass/depth fail, stencil pass/depth pass.

Stencil fail means that the fragment was blocked by the stencil buffer (due to the current setting of the stencil func). Stencil pass/depth fail means that the fragment survived the stencil buffer but not the depth buffer (yes, the standard Z-buffer that you use all the time). Finally, stencil pass/depth pass means that the fragment made it through and was written to the pixel (if that is allowed under current settings).

For each of these cases, we may define different operations. We may zero the stencil value, increment it, set it, leave it as it is... The total list is GL_KEEP, GL_ZERO, GL_REPLACE, GL_INCR, GL_INCR_WRAP, GL_DECR, GL_DECR_WRAP, GL_INVERT, all with fairly intuitive meanings.

The stencil and depth tests, controlled by glStencilOp, are illustrated by Figure 4 on page 17.

More computer graphics

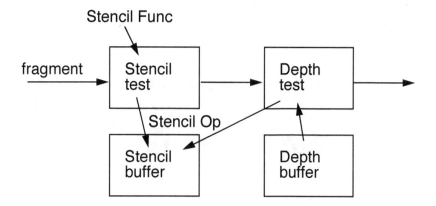

FIGURE 4. The last operations before a fragment is written to the frame buffer.

Now for an example (without code this time). For simplicity, the example is not exactly realistic, but more chosen for showing what operation the stencil buffer can handle.[1] We start with a rectangle (upper left) which is drawn with Z-buffering on, giving a rectangular area with a Z-value corresponding to a closer distance than the rest. The stencil buffer, too, has different values in the two regions, 1 and 3. See Figure 5 below.

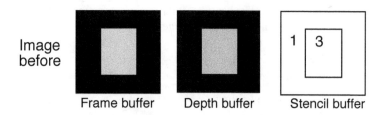

FIGURE 5. Stencil example, before drawing

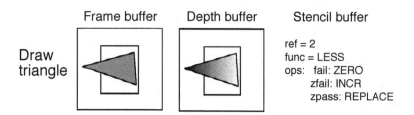

FIGURE 6. Stencil example, triangle being drawn.

Then we draw a polygon, intersecting the rectangle, as shown in Figure 6. We use different stencil operations for the three possible cases, zeroing, replacing and incrementing. The

---

1. I honestly no longer remember if I made this example myself or found it in a book or on the web. Most likely it is a variant of some nice example I found.

bottom-right image in Figure 7 shows the final values. The areas not covered by the triangle are unaffected, while the other three are, from left to right, zeroed, incremented and set to the reference value (3).

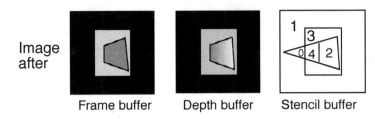

FIGURE 7. Stencil example, final result.

The importance of the freedom beyond plain masking may not be obvious now, but it has plenty of uses. One significant algorithm using it is Shadow volumes (chapter 4.2.3).

3.4 Texture mapping

In Volume 1, texture mapping was presented entirely as the technique to map 2D images onto surfaces. We did cover multi-texturing, filtering and cube mapping, but otherwise many advanced techniques were left out. Coordinates were given manually or generated with simple geometries. We will go a bit further here.

In this section, I will cover

- Textures with other dimensions than 2
- Texture matrix and projective textures
- Texture compression

while I expect you to already know much about

- Texture coordinate generation (linear, cylindrical, spherical)
- Environment mapping
- Texture settings (repeat/clamp, filtering)
- Mip-mapping
- Multitexturing

Later, we will also cover bump mapping, in chapter 5.

3.4.1 Textures with other dimensions than 2

A texture does not have to be 2-dimensional. They can also be 1-dimensional, that is a linear array of texels, or 3-dimensional, which implies volume data. These variants do not seem anywhere near as important as 2-dimensional, but they have their uses.

There are several applications for 1-dimensional textures. One that you may see some-times in older games and simpler demos is to use a 1-dimensional texture to colorize a ter-rain depending on height. It can be implemented like this (illustrated in Figure 8):

The lowest part of the terrain is given a minimum height, the water level. This extreme end of the 1-dimensional texture is blue. Immediately above, there is a green section. After some time, the green fades into grey (rock) and at the upper end, the texture is white (snow). The texture is combined with more fine-grained texture(s) to get a nice detail. While this is a simplification from making a more "designed" colorization of the terrain, and there are other tricks to consider, it does help to a certain extent.

Another, slightly more exotic example is to use a 1-dimensional texture mapped along Z from the camera, to model light attenuation in detail from a camera-bound light source.

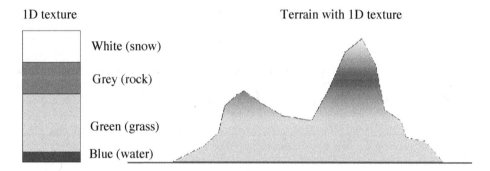

FIGURE 8. Using a 1D texture to give a terrain a height-dependent color

3D textures are less suited for most gaming applications. They are most obviously useful for medical applications, for visualizing 3D data, e.g. tomography images. However, there are other applications. One is to model objects that are volumetric by nature, like clouds. Another is to carry other kinds of information where the limitations of a 2D texture gets in the way, like a detailed lighting model like BRDF. We will return to these applications later in the book.

3.4.2 Texture matrix and projected textures

In Volume 1, texture placement could be specified by texture coordinates by vertex, or even by fragment, either from the model or generated from the geometry. But we mostly considered static textures. It isn't too hard to come up with simple shifts of textures, even rotations, but for cases when we need something even more flexible, we can use a *texture matrix*. This is something as simple as yet another matrix operation, but applied on texture coordinates rather than vertices.

All transformations that a 4x4 matrix can represent can be applied on texture coordinates - even projection! And this is where the texture matrix is the most important. Among its uses, it is a key component in shadow mapping (chapter 4.2). However, even the standard transformations can be useful. For example, you can rotate a texture using a rotation matrix.

For texture projection, we will need to create a new, alternate transformation chain, defining projection from a second point, the projection reference point for the texture projection (which we can see as the light source of the "projector"). (Figure 9)

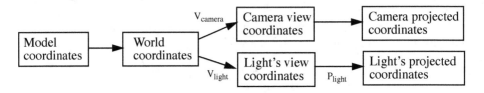

FIGURE 9. Coordinate systems involved in projective texturing

Each arrow in the figure is a transformation.

Now consider this from a shader perspective. In a vertex shader, you get the model coordinates, and you have modelview and projection transformations that you can multiply. That means that you have model coordinates (left box), and you can get to the camera view coordinates or camera projected coordinates, but you really want to get to the light's view coordinates and its projection. Working from the camera projected coordinates makes no sense at all, so we have two possible starting points.

In some texts on this subject, it is recommended that you work from camera view coordinates, using the transformation

$$P_{light}*V_{light}*V^{-1}_{camera}$$

With this approach, the model-to-world transformation can be made completely as usual, and when we reach the camera view coordinates, we transform back to the world coordinates and go forward from there.

However, we may also consider working from model coordinates, which I find simpler. You build the two chains from the ground up, with different projection and camera placement matrices, but with the same model-to-world transformation.

So we build projection (P) and camera placement (V) matrices for each path, and a common model-to-world transformation. Multiply together and upload to the shader.

When projecting a texture, there is a difference in the coordinate system produced by projection and the texture coordinates that we need. Projection produces coordinates in the interval -1 to 1, while textures are defined from 0 to 1. To correct that, we need a *scale and bias* transform. That is just a translation and a scaling:

```
GLfloat trans[16], scale[16];
```

```
trans = T(0.5, 0.5, 0.0);
scale = S(0.5, 0.5, 0.5);
```

That's plenty of halves, but what happened was that we started by a 2x2 square centered at origin, scaled it down to 1x1, which means -0.5 to 0.5. Though a translation by 0.5, 0.5, we end up at the 0 to 1 that textures should have. See Figure 10.

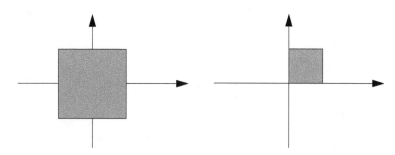

FIGURE 10. Scale and bias transformation maps between -1..1 and 0..1 ranges.

The entire texture matrix construction can then be done like this:

```
// Build the transformation sequence for the light source path,
// by copying from the ordinary camera matrices.
void setTextureMatrix(void)
{
    mat4 trans;

    textureMatrix = IdentityMatrix();

// Scale and bias transform, moving from unit cube [-1,1] to [0,1]
    trans = Mult(T(0.5, 0.5, 0.0), S(0.5, 0.5, 1.0));
    textureMatrix = Mult(Mult(trans), projectionMatrix), modelViewMa-
trix);
}
```

But the matrices are not quite done here. Any additional transformations needed while drawing the scene (usually translations and rotations) must be in the model-to-world transform of both transformation pipelines (Figure 9 on page 20). For every operation you do, you multiply them on both matrices. For example, this is one of the toruses, with a translation and a scaling as model-to-world part:

```
    // One torus
    trans = Mult(T(0,4,-16), S(2.0, 2.0, 2.0));
    mv2 = Mult(modelViewMatrix, trans); // Apply on both
    tx2 = Mult(textureMatrix, trans);
    // Upload both!
    glUniformMatrix4fv(glGetUniformLocation(projTexShaderId, "modelView-
Matrix"), 1, GL_TRUE, mv2.m);
    glUniformMatrix4fv(glGetUniformLocation(projTexShaderId, "textureMa-
trix"), 1, GL_TRUE, tx2.m);
    DrawModel(torusModel);
```

Finally, we need shaders that handle the final stages of transformations and the actual texturing. I will not handle shader loading here; we should consider that trivial by now. (See the full sample code on the course page, or Part 1.)

Here is the vertex shader:

```
#version 150

out vec4 lightSourceCoord;

in vec3 in_Position;
uniform mat4 textureMatrix;
uniform mat4 modelViewMatrix;
uniform mat4 projectionMatrix;

void main()
{
// Transform vertex to light source coordinates:
   lightSourceCoord = textureMatrix * vec4(in_Position, 1.0);
   gl_Position = projectionMatrix * modelViewMatrix
       * vec4(in_Position, 1.0);
}
```

The transformation with the texture matrix is the important feature here.

And here is the fragment shader:

```
#version 150

uniform sampler2D texture;
in vec4 lightSourceCoord;
out vec4 out_Color;
uniform float shade;

void main()
{
   vec4 lightSourceCoordinateWdivide =
       lightSourceCoord / lightSourceCoord.w;
   vec4 texel = texture(texture,lightSourceCoordinateWdivide.st);

   out_Color = texel * shade;
}
```

This is equally simple, but still unusual. We perform the perspective division, to get the final texture coordinates. Then we just multiply the texel with the surface color and we are done.

The result may look like in Figure 11.

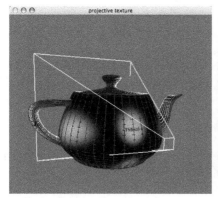

FIGURE 11. A texture projected onto the Utah Teapot, from two different views.

Most demos you find on Internet are fixed pipeline demos, where the problem is complicated by using texture coordinate generation etc. These demos are in my opinion outdated and best avoided. I have based my solution above on a shadow mapping demo by Fabien Sanglard [71], but rewritten it to a projective texture demo and ported it to modern OpenGL. We will return to this code in the shadow mapping chapter (chapter 4.2), where projective textures play a vital part.

3.4.3 Detail texturing

Detail texturing is an application of multitexturing, for texture optimization.

If you want a texture to be both large, varied and with much detail (high frequencies), then the cost in disk and memory space becomes very big, and you might find yourself limited by the maximum size of textures. A very efficient way to accomplish the same thing is to combine two textures, each of which can be a lot smaller. One is a low frequency texture, which describes the overall structure of the surface, while the other is a high frequency texture, which is repeated over the low frequency texture to provide the detail that the other lacks.

Detail textures can be created separately, where the detail texture is more or less filled with high frequency noise. An alternative is to generate low and high frequency images from the same original image. That will result in higher quality since the result has the frequency spectrum of the original. However, it must not include patterns that are disturbing when repeated.

Below follows code for one way to implement detail texturing, where two very small textures (both 32x32 texels, Figure 12) are combined to texture a cube. The result is not the prettiest detail texturing you have seen - it essentially puts some noise on top of the low-frequency texture - but still the resulting texture gives some impression of more detail.

FIGURE 12. Low-frequency (left) and detail texture (right). Both are merely 32x32 texels.

The noise texture gives noise around 50% gray.

Before drawing the surface with the detail texture, we assign the two textures to one texturing unit each, access them in the fragment shader, and combine them by a suitable function. In this case, you get a reasonable result just by addition.

You assign the textures to texture units just like with any other multitexturing:

```
// Texture 0, low frequency
    glActiveTexture(GL_TEXTURE0);
    glEnable(GL_TEXTURE_2D);
    glBindTexture(GL_TEXTURE_2D, lfTex);

// Texture 1, detail
    glActiveTexture(GL_TEXTURE1);
    glEnable(GL_TEXTURE_2D);
    glBindTexture(GL_TEXTURE_2D, detailTex);
```

When accessing the texture, you use different density for the texture coordinate access. For example, the global texture may go from 0 to 1, while the detail texture repeats, for example from 0 to some repeat number. This gives one round of the low-frequency texture (0 to 1) and a number of repeats for the detail texture.

The result looks like in Figure 13 (but would be even better with better textures):

FIGURE 13. Detail texturing, combining the two textures to a seemingly more detailed texture.

With higher quality textures, the result can be a lot better, but I hope this simple example can still convince you that this technique is quite useful. The detail texture does not have to be noise. It can also be a wood or stone texture, or even flowers and grass for terrains.

3.5 Render to texture

So far, we have considered textures to be pre-generated data that comes from somewhere else, than we can map on surfaces. However, it is also possible to generate the textures on-line, to perform a rendering that is ends up in a texture; we *render to texture*.

There are several ways to make rendered data end up in your textures:

- glReadPixels/glTexImage
- glCopyTexImage
- glCopyTexSubImage
- pBuffers (Pixel buffers)
- Framebuffer objects (FBO) - preferred!

With glReadPixels, you can read data from the frame buffer to the CPU, and then you can upload it to a texture using glTexImage. This is a poor solution that will choke the CPU. Avoid!

The calls glCopyTexImage and glCopyTexSubImage copy pixel data to textures. They may seem equivalent when copying the whole texture, but NVidia experts [15] recommend glCopyTexSubImage, since it is more likely to be well optimized than glCopyTex-Image. Using glCopyTexSubImage is probably the easiest solution, and performance is not bad. Still, it is not optimal, since it imposes a copying from one memory position to another, which does not come for free.

The solution *pbuffers* was an intermediate solution. Pbuffers were a WGL extension. It was never implemented on all platforms, so it never became a cross-platform solution. Although it does allow us to render directly to it, it has the significant drawback that the pbuffer is a separate OpenGL context. It has limited interest today in case you need to support some platform that still has problems with FBOs, not a very likely case today.

Today, *framebuffer objects* is the current, standard and preferred solution. A framebuffer object (FBO) is a collection of data in the GPU that can be used as rendering target. It contains:

- One or more textures
- A *renderbuffer*, which typically means a Z buffer.

3.5.1 Creating framebuffer objects

The task of creating a framebuffer object is surprisingly complicated that is likely to go wrong. You are best off with a working example, so that is what I have right here.

This code is fairly modern, and should work on any modern OpenGL installation. If it does not, you may have to re-introduce some ARB or EXT suffixes. If you are in that position, maybe you should ask me for the old version.

```
void CHECK_FRAMEBUFFER_STATUS()
{
    GLenum status = glCheckFramebufferStatus(GL_FRAMEBUFFER);
    if (status != GL_FRAMEBUFFER_COMPLETE)
        printf("Framebuffer error\n");
}

void initFBO()
{
// create objects
    glGenFramebuffers(1, &fb); // frame buffer id
    glGenRenderbuffers(1, &rb); // render buffer id
    glBindFramebuffer(GL_FRAMEBUFFER, fb);
    glFramebufferTexture2D(GL_FRAMEBUFFER, GL_COLOR_ATTACHMENT0,
GL_TEXTURE_2D, tex, 0);
    CHECK_FRAMEBUFFER_STATUS();
// initialize depth renderbuffer
    glBindRenderbuffer(GL_RENDERBUFFER, rb);
    glRenderbufferStorage(GL_RENDERBUFFER, GL_DEPTH_COMPONENT24, width,
height);
// attach renderbuffer to framebuffer depth buffer
    glFramebufferRenderbuffer(GL_FRAMEBUFFER, GL_DEPTH_ATTACHMENT,
GL_RENDERBUFFER, rb);
    CHECK_FRAMEBUFFER_STATUS();
}
```

The call CHECK_FRAMEBUFFER_STATUS calls glCheckFrameBufferStatus and
reports errors. In my example I only check for GL_FRAMEBUFFER_COMPLETE
(which means no error) but there are more messages to check for. (See below.)

Just like with textures, you start by creating a reference, which means nothing until you
make it refer to something.

```
glGenFramebuffers(1, &fb);
```

You attach an existing texture like this:

```
glFramebufferTexture2D(GL_FRAMEBUFFER, GL_COLOR_ATTACHMENT0,
GL_TEXTURE_2D, tex, 0);
```

We create the renderbuffer (Z buffer):

```
glBindRenderbuffer(GL_RENDERBUFFER, rb);
glRenderbufferStorage(GL_RENDERBUFFER, GL_DEPTH_COMPONENT24, width,
height);
glFramebufferRenderbuffer(GL_FRAMEBUFFER, GL_DEPTH_ATTACHMENT,
GL_RENDERBUFFER, rb);
```

Note that we use GL NEAREST filtering. That filtering is otherwise usually best avoided,
but a framebuffer object generally demands it. Such limitations may change over time, but
that is the rule I live by today.

There is much more options for creating FBOs, but we have enough to start using them.
Refer to the OpenGL documentation for more information.

More computer graphics

3.5.2 Using framebuffer objects

Using a framebuffer object is much easier than creating them. For rendering to the frame-buffer, you select it like this:

```
// render to the FBO
    glBindFramebuffer(GL_FRAMEBUFFER, fb);
    glBindTexture(GL_TEXTURE_2D, anothertex);
```

Binding another texture is not necessarily what you want to do, but somewhat typical; you often render to texture for using it as texture later, so the FBO is always used for one of the two roles (input texture or output buffer). Thus, the rendering to screen may look like this:

```
// render to the screen, using the FBO texture
    glBindFramebuffer(GL_FRAMEBUFFER, 0);
    glBindTexture(GL_TEXTURE_2D, fbotex);
```

It can be confusing to handle separate texture and FBO references when they really refer to the same data. Thus, I tend to handle them together, as a structure holding all needed information about the FBO, like this:

```
// A structure to collect FBO info
typedef struct FBOstruct
{
    GLuint texid;
    GLuint fb;
    GLuint rb;
    int width, height;
} FBOstruct;
```

Using this structure, I defined useFBO(), which assigns one FBO as output and up to two textures as input (on predefined texture units). This is merely an example of how you can handle this data. There is no universal truth to what it should contain, so you may wish to add more data depending on your problem.

Finally, a note on the renderbuffer part. I included renderbuffer creation in the code above, but that is not always needed. When you render to texture in a 3D application, the render-buffer is obviously usually needed, to include a Z-buffer with the FBO. In GPGPU applications (see page 39), you often work without renderbuffer.

3.5.3 Debugging information from FBOs

During development, you should catch error messages the your FBOs. This is done with glCheckFramebufferStatus().

A typical problem can be that you pass invalid arguments for your texture. FBOs do not necessarily support all filtering options. When in doubt, set it to nearest neighbor filtering.

Important result codes from `glCheckFramebufferStatus()` that you should check for include

```
    GL_FRAMEBUFFER_COMPLETE
    GL_FRAMEBUFFER_UNSUPPORTED
```

GL_FRAMEBUFFER_INCOMPLETE_ATTACHMENT

The first signals that all is well, the others signal problems.

Now it is time for two examples of how to use these techniques. I will do the same simple example, first with glCopyTexSubImage, and then with framebuffer objects, that is the two preferred techniques.

3.5.4 Example using glCopyTexSubImage

Here follows a complete example (display function only), using glCopyTexSubImage.

```
void display(void)
{
    printError("pre display");
    a += 0.1;

    // clear the screen
    glViewport(0, 0, width, height); // Set viewport to match texture size
    glClearColor(1,1,0.5,0);
    glClear(GL_COLOR_BUFFER_BIT | GL_DEPTH_BUFFER_BIT);
    glBindTexture(GL_TEXTURE_2D, minitexid);

    rotationMatrix2 = Rz(a/5.0);
    rotationMatrix = Rx(a);
    glUniformMatrix4fv(glGetUniformLocation(program, "rotationMatrix2"),
1, GL_TRUE, rotationMatrix2.m);
    glUniformMatrix4fv(glGetUniformLocation(program, "rotationMatrix"),
1, GL_TRUE, rotationMatrix.m);

    glBindVertexArray(vertexArrayObjID);// Select VAO
    glDrawArrays(GL_TRIANGLES, 0, 36*3);// draw object

    printError("display");

    glFlush();

    // Copy the result to the texture
    glBindTexture(GL_TEXTURE_2D, tex);
    glCopyTexSubImage2D(GL_TEXTURE_2D, 0, 0, 0, 0, 0, width, height);

    glViewport(0, 0, lastw, lasth);

// Render to screen with the generated texture

    glClearColor(0,0,0,0);
    glClear(GL_COLOR_BUFFER_BIT | GL_DEPTH_BUFFER_BIT);

    glBindVertexArray(vertexArrayObjID);// Select VAO (same - we could
skip this)
    glDrawArrays(GL_TRIANGLES, 0, 36*3);// draw object

    printError("display 2");

    glutSwapBuffers();
}
```

The interesting events here are these:

We set the viewport to a size that fits our texture. After that, we draw whatever we want to put in the texture, and copy it to the texture using `glCopyTexSubImage2D`. Then we render the final image using that texture.

The resulting scene will be a shape (in this case a cube) covered with animated teapots, like in Figure 14.

FIGURE 14. A cube animation used as texture on an animated cube

3.5.5 Example using framebuffer objects

Here follows the same example using framebuffer objects. It assumes that the framebuffer object is already created.

```
void display(void)
{
    printError("pre display");
    a += 0.1;

    // Bind FBO
    glBindFramebuffer(GL_FRAMEBUFFER, fb); // Already refers to the tex-
ture "tex"
    glBindTexture(GL_TEXTURE_2D, minitexid);

    // clear the screen
    glViewport(0, 0, width, height); // Set viewport to match texture size
    glClearColor(1,1,0.5,0);
    glClear(GL_COLOR_BUFFER_BIT | GL_DEPTH_BUFFER_BIT);

    rotationMatrix2 = Rz(a/5.0);
    rotationMatrix = Rx(a);
    glUniformMatrix4fv(glGetUniformLocation(program, "rotationMatrix2"),
1, GL_TRUE, rotationMatrix2.m);
    glUniformMatrix4fv(glGetUniformLocation(program, "rotationMatrix"),
1, GL_TRUE, rotationMatrix.m);

    glBindVertexArray(vertexArrayObjID);// Select VAO
    glDrawArrays(GL_TRIANGLES, 0, 36*3);// draw object
```

```
    printError("display");
```

```
// glFlush(); It worked for me without glFlush but consider it if you get
problems.
```

```
// The image is now rendered to the texture and we can set it as input.
    glBindFramebuffer(GL_FRAMEBUFFER, 0);
    glBindTexture(GL_TEXTURE_2D, tex);
```

```
    glViewport(0, 0, lastw, lasth);
```

```
// Render to screen with the generated texture
```

```
    glClearColor(0,0,0,0);
    glClear(GL_COLOR_BUFFER_BIT | GL_DEPTH_BUFFER_BIT);
```

```
    glBindVertexArray(vertexArrayObjID);// Select VAO (same - we could
skip this)
    glDrawArrays(GL_TRIANGLES, 0, 36*3);// draw object
```

```
    printError("display 2");
```

```
    glutSwapBuffers();
}
```

Most of the code is identical to the previous example, and the visual result is identical. All that has happened is really that we use the FBO so we don't have to copy.

The conclusion is that we can render to textures, and framebuffer objects is the best solution. The primary backup plan should be glCopyTexSubImage, which is reliable and highly backwards compatible.

Some of the applications of rendering to texture should be obvious. For example, you can make environment mapping using "live" textures, rendered from the environment mapped object for every frame. Other applications include shadow maps (see page 43) and GPGPU applications (see page 39).

3.6 Navigating on a mesh

For many problems, for example collision detection or mesh simplification, it is vital to be able to navigate over a mesh, finding neighbor parts of the mesh and being able to analyze local properties. For doing that, we must add some extra information over the usual vertex list and index list. This can be done in many ways, and it is often possible to choose a method that fits the problem at hand. We will here present one popular navigation tool, the *half-edge structure*, originally suggested by Muller & Preparata [105]. This text is partially based on a tutorial by Rutanen [106].

The half-edge structure, also known as the *doubly connected edge list*, is a structure that associates two vertices and one polygon. The name "half-edge" sounds hilarous, but the reason is that an edge usually has two neighbor polygons and therefore has two half-edge structures connected to it. Moreover, each of these two half-edges should go in the opposite direction than the other.

The complete data involved is slightly more than one structure. The actual half-edge structure may contain the following information:

• "next", pointer to the next half-edge along the polygon (possibly also previous)

• "pair", pointer to the "other half", the half-edge along the same edge belonging to the neighbot polygon

• "vert", vertex at end of the half-edge

• "face", the polygon that the half-edge borders

See Figure 15. The exact contents vary with different implementations. The faces and vertices will also need to have references to the half-edge structures (one of the ones connected to them) so that it is possible to traverse the mesh from some starting point.

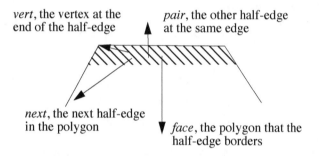

vert, the vertex at the end of the half-edge

pair, the other half-edge at the same edge

next, the next half-edge in the polygon

face, the polygon that the half-edge borders

FIGURE 15. The half-edge structure

This structure is sufficient for a lot of navigation problems on a mesh. For example, in order to loop through all edges in a polygon, you do like this:

```
firstedge = polygon->edge; // Get any edge of the polygon
edge = firstedge;
do
{
    edge = edge->next;
} while (edge != firstedge);
```

Looping through all edges around a vertex is somewhat more complicated:

```
firstedge = polygon->edge; // Get any edge of the polygon
edge = firstedge;
do
{
    edge = edge->pair->next;
} while (edge != firstedge);
```

Note that the use of pair and next depends on the half-edges sharing one edge are oriented in different directions! See Figure 16.

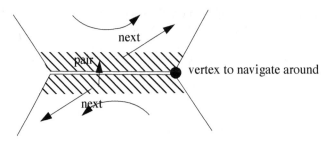

FIGURE 16. **Navigating a mesh with the half-edge**

For the purposes of this book, the most obvious use of mesh navigation is collision detection. However, there are many other applications.

3.7 Texture optimization

Another way to optimize performance is to take control over how texture data is used. This can have some importance when all textures no longer fit in the VRAM.

There are two significant texture optimization issues:

- Optimizing the choice of what textures are in VRAM
- Texture compression

For the former, OpenGL may give you a good caching by default. If not, you need to keep track of how much textures you load and glDeleteTexture as needed, following either a FIFO or LRU (least recently used) policy.

Texture compression is a more complicated subject, but it can have a great impact when the size of the VRAM is limited, or the access to it (e.g. due to a slow and/or shared bus). This is certainly the case in embedded systems, like smartphones or tablets. Unfortunately, we can't simply use standard image compression like JPEG here since we have to be able to decode the texture in real-time. Decoding speed is in fact one of the most important criteria when designing a texture compression scheme, as well as the possibility to access pixels randomly. On the other hand, encoding speed is not that important (since this will be done in advance in most cases), and a visual loss in quality is acceptable since it will be barely noticeable after rendering anyway. Current texture compression methods, like DXT, PVRTC or ETC reach typically a signal-to-noise ratio of between 28 to 30 dB for a compression factor of 1:6. This is low compared to normal image compression standards, but that is the price you have to pay for the much faster decoding. Many modern GPUs have hardware support for the decoding of these standards, thus accelerating it much further.

DXT was formerly known as S3TC or Savage3 Texture compression, and was the first texture compression standard ever. It is now mostly known as Direct X Texture compression (DXT). Due to it being an in-house development by S3, it wasn't presented in a formal publication at the time.

Both DXT and PVRTC are using basically the same technique: the texture will be divided in blocks with a size of 4x4, and each pixel in the block can have one of four different colors. This is basically a technique known as vector quantization, and has, in fact, been used for image compression since the 70s. In DXT, two of these colors are explicitly encoded for each block, while the other two are computed by linear interpolation between the two encoded colors. Note that the encoded colors can vary from block to block.

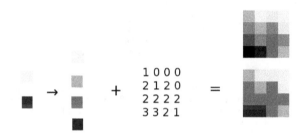

FIGURE 17. Decoding of a block with DXT: 2 colors are given (left), and two more are generated by interpolating between them (second to left). Each pixel is represented by a number which shows which color should be used (second to right), which together with the colors leads to the decoded block (right). The original block is shown above for comparison.

Both of these encoded colors use only 16 bits each, thus the 3 color channels can't each use the usual 8 bits. Instead, both the red and the blue channel are depicted by 5 bits each, while 6 bits are reserved for the green channel. The extra bit for green is not uncommon in 16-bit color since the human eye is more sensitive to green than to red or blue. Since we have four different colors which each pixel can have, each pixel needs 2 bits to select which color should be used for it. This means that altogether each block needs 64 bits. This corresponds to a compression factor of 1:6 and fits rather neatly with the requirement of random access.

PVRTC (PowerVR Texture Compression) was proposed by Fenney [95]. It goes one step further. Like DXT it encodes two different colors with 16 bits each for each block (using 5 bits for each of the color channels), but it treats them as downscaled versions of the original images. Before decoding, it takes the first colors of all blocks and upscales the resulting image by a factor of 4, which means to the original resolution of the texture. It does the same for the second colors of all blocks. Each pixel can then have the color on its position in either of the resulting two images, or one of two possible linear interpolations between them. Note that this is much more complex than DXT, and also reduces the random access significantly (since we now have to load the colors of neighboring blocks as well to be able to do the upscaling). Despite that, PVRTC does not reach a higher quality – it fares a little bit better with textures that contain smooth color changes, and slightly worse with those having hard changes. But in practice these differences hardly matter, and in average its quality is not better or worse than DXT. And since it reaches the same compression factor it is questionable if the higher complexity is really justified.

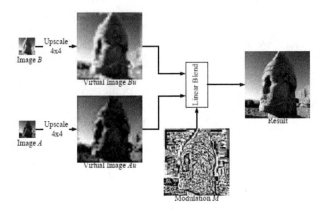

FIGURE 18. Decoding with PVRTC: the colors of all blocks (left) are upscaled (second to left). Together with the modulation map containing which of the colors should be used for each pixel (second to right) the image can be decoded (right). Image from Fenney [95].

ETC (Ericsson Texture Compression, also known as Packman) was proposed by Ström et. al. [96] It works a little bit different. It encodes only one color for each block, using 4 bits for each color channel. This color is then altered by 4 different modifiers, which are the same for each color channel, i.e. they only change the luminance. Each pixel in the block can then have one of the resulting four different colors. Altogether, there are 8 different sets of these modifications. Despite its limitations, ETC actually reaches a slightly higher quality than DXT or PVRTC, which is probably due to the fact that it is possible to do a full-search during encoding, i.e. trying every possible combination, and that it uses a smaller blocksize of only 2x4 pixels. Each block needs 32 bits, which means that it reaches the same 1:6 compression ratio as DXT or PVRTC. Its decoding complexity is slightly higher than DXT, its random access however a little better due to the smaller blocksize.

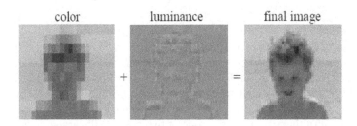

FIGURE 19. Decoding with ETC: each block is represented by a color (left), which is modified by a luminance factor (middle) to decode the image (right). Image from Ström et . al. [96]

Compressing textures with alpha components is more complicated. Both PVRTC and DXT have modes that include transparency and which reach the same compression factor as the normal RGB compression, however at the cost of a lower quality of the RGB color channels. DXT also offers different modes in which additional alpha maps are used.

It can be noted that the choice of texture compression isn't always a question of quality and performance but also one of ownership and patents. DXT is owned by S3, PVRTC by Imagination Technologies (producer of most embedded GPUs) and ETC by Ericsson.

3.8 Vulkan

A few years ago, AMD developed a new graphics API called Mantle, which was developed to get around some existing bottlenecks in the current graphics APIs. 2015, a successor was announced, called Vulkan, which was in development by the Khronos group, the maintainers of the OpenGL standard. In spring 2016, Vulkan was released. So, what is this? Is it the new OpenGL, a replacement for OpenGL?

I will here make some brief notes about why it exists, what it delivers and what it costs. Some of what I write is inspired by a recent thesis, which was presented during the fall 2016. [107]

The reason for Vulkan is to make it easier to take advantage of multi-core CPUs. CPUs are getting more and more cores, and although they are nowhere the parallelism of a GPU, wouldn't it be foolish to waste the power? The problem with the current APIs, like OpenGL, is that they don't support multithreading on the CPU. OpenGL works with global states, and even though OpenGL is less of a state machine than it used to be, the design is still largely based on states. The active texture, or VAO, or shader, these are all states, and the state changes must be notorously synchronized in order to allow any parallel threads. In practice, you want to issue all OpenGL commands from a single thread! The result is that in an OpenGL application, most cores will idle a lot.

Vulkan is designed to allow multithreading. Instead of sending sequential commands, like you do to OpenGL, you store commands into command buffers, which are then passed to a common command queue that Vulkan will handle. This is one central feature, but there are many other differences to OpenGL. In essence, Vulkan will give the programmer even more freedom than modern OpenGL (which is already much more openly programmable than older OpenGL).

The benefits of Vulkan is, as far as we can see today, extremely application dependent and will often be marginal. The reason is simply that it will only benefit significantly in an application that needs to be multi-threaded on the CPU. If the GPU is the bottleneck, there will be no difference.

Unfortunately, the cost in programming effort is, at this time, considerable. It is clear that Vulkan-using applications will build significant simplifying layers on top of Vulkan, even more than we need for OpenGL.

No, I will not present a concise example of Vulkan code, since it would eat a disturbing number of pages without really being enlightning.

One more thing: Portability. A major strength of OpenGL is its portability, running on all major operating systems and even on embedded systems. With its presence on the mobile market, it has a very strong position. One reason that Mantle became Vulkan must be the portability, to make it available for all manufacturers to port as they see fit. However, at this time Vulkan lacks some major supporters: Microsoft and Apple. Microsoft is updating DirectX, and Apple (a member of the Khronos group!) has released their own solution, Metal. However, there are third party solutions for these platforms so Vulkan can still be big on all platforms, On Apple, the library *Molten* makes a mapping between Vulkan and Metal.

Since Vulkan is still very new, my conclusions must be held modest. Vulkan does solve a problem for certain applications, and its increased programmability may prove powerful. Since it mainly allows more work to be put on CPUs, I would expect in to be the most important on hardware with strong CPUs but weak GPUs, but that is not much more than a hunch. We can not say more than that now, but we will keep out eyes open on the progress. The computer graphics subject is still changing!

4. Shadows

Now is the time to go deeper into a specific problem. An important problem which only got a brief mention in "Polygons Feel No Pain" was the problem of making objects cast shadows. It was no problem for ray-tracing and radiosity, but it is a harder problem in the real-time polygon rendering situation.

Let me start with a few definitions, illustrated in Figure 20:

The *receiver* is the surface on which the shadow is cast. The *occluder* is the shape that casts the surface by occluding a light source. An *attached shadow* is the shadow the occluder casts on its own back-side seen from the light source; the shadow that is generated by the Phong model. A *cast shadow* is any other shadow, where the occluder and receiver are different surfaces. A special case is *self-shadows*, which are shadows cast and received by different parts of the same shape.

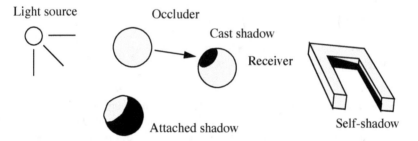

FIGURE 20. **Three different kinds of shadows**

In this chapter, I will describe the three most fundamental shadow algorithms: Planar shadows, shadow volumes and shadow mapping, plus outline how soft shadows can be generated.

Shadows are the most missing features in simple 3D animation. They are important for several reasons:

- They improve realism since we expect them to be there.

- They give information about the distance between objects.
- They also give information about the shape both the occluder (the object casting a shadow) and the receiver (the surface onto which the shadow is cast).

So, why is the important feature not automatic? Simply put, because it is harder to do than all the fixed pipeline functionality. There are also many ways to do it, with different behavior for each.

It is a fairly hard problem that has got good real-time solutions. Today, it is a necessity for good real-time graphics! It seems like rather new technology, but the fact is that all these methods build on results from the 1970s and 1980s.

You already know a few ways to create shadows:

- Ray-casting and ray-tracing
- Radiosity
- Light mapping based on either of these two

but none of these give us interactive, real-time, dynamic shadows. For dynamic shadows, there are three main categories:

- Planar shadows
- Shadow maps
- Shadow volumes

In the following sections, I will describe how all these three can be achieved.

4.1 Planar shadows

The simplest kind of shadows is shadows projected onto a flat surface. The trick is to project the object onto the surface, and draw it there.

The object is projected onto a surface by creating a projection matrix, which is postmultiplicated on the modelview. Just like we can project a 3D shape onto the viewing plane, we can project it onto any plane, and that what we do. After projecting it, the now flat object is rendered without texture. It is rendered in a single color, the desired color of the shadow (usually some shade of gray). This shade should be blended by multiplication, just like a light map.

In Figure 21, a torus is projected onto a surface. The light source is shown as a small, bright sphere. Note that the shadow is not black but blended onto the surface.

FIGURE 21. Planar shadow example

There are several problems involved in this method:

- Project the object onto the surface
- Mask the shadow by the plane using the stencil buffer
- Multi-pass drawing on the same surface with blending

4.1.1 Projecting the object onto a surface

Let us start with the projection. We want to draw the object once in its normal form, and once flattened onto the surface, using a projection depending on the light source.

The projection matrix can project along **Z**, like the ones from Volume 1:

$$
\begin{bmatrix} x_h \\ y_h \\ z_h \\ h \end{bmatrix} = \begin{bmatrix} f & 0 & 0 & 0 \\ 0 & f & 0 & 0 \\ 0 & 0 & -z_{vp} & z_{vp}z_{prp} \\ 0 & 0 & -1 & z_{prp} \end{bmatrix} \begin{bmatrix} x \\ y \\ z \\ 1 \end{bmatrix}
$$

Note that this projection is the one without normalized coordinates, written to make the **Z** value end up in the plane. That is exactly what we want in this case. But we can simplify it a bit. Since $f = z_{prp} - z_{vp}$, we may make the assumption that z_{vp} is zero (view plane goes through origin). Then we get

$$f = z_{prp}$$

and end up with

$$\begin{bmatrix} x_h \\ y_h \\ z_h \\ h \end{bmatrix} = \begin{bmatrix} f & 0 & 0 & 0 \\ 0 & f & 0 & 0 \\ 0 & 0 & 0 & 0 \\ 0 & 0 & -1 & f \end{bmatrix} \begin{bmatrix} x \\ y \\ z \\ 1 \end{bmatrix}$$

for a matrix that projects from distance f onto a plane through origin. Bracket this projection by rotations and translation to make it project onto the desired plane.

Assume that we want to make a procedure that takes the light source position as a point $\mathbf{l}$, and that the plane that we want to project onto is given by a point $\mathbf{p}$ in the plane and the normal vector $\mathbf{n}$. This is a straight-forward application of the technique used mainly for rotations in Volume 1.

The light source position is $\mathbf{l}$.

The focal distance is $f = (\mathbf{l}-\mathbf{p}) \cdot \mathbf{n}$.

The plane is given by the point $\mathbf{p}$ and the normal vector $\mathbf{n}$. The constant $d = -\mathbf{p} \cdot \mathbf{n}$.

The light source projected onto the plane is

$$\mathbf{l_p} = \mathbf{l} - \mathbf{n}(\mathbf{n} \cdot \mathbf{l} + d)$$

The variables are illustrated in Figure 22.

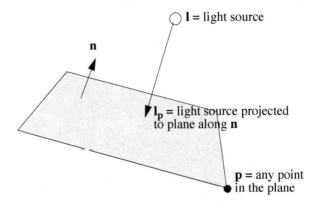

FIGURE 22. Building a projection for creating planar shadows

Then the sequence of transformations are:

- Translate the light source's projection on the plane to origin by $T(-l_p)$.

- Rotate the normal vector to be along the Z axis.

- Project with the matrix above.

- Rotate back.

- Translate back.

An implementation based on the VectorUtils3 library follows. It assumed an input of three vectors, l (light source position), n (normal vector of plane) and p (point in plane).

```
float d = -DotProduct(p, n);
float ndotlplusd = DotProduct(n, l) + d;
vec3 lp = VectorSub(l, ScalarMult(n, ndotlplusd)); // lp = l - n(n dot l + d)
mat4 toz = AxisToZ(n);
mat4 fromz = Transpose(toz);
float f = ndotlplusd; // Distance light source to plane = focal distance

mat4 shadowProjectionMatrix = CreateShadowProjectionMatrix(f);
mat4 sm = Mult(T(lp.x, lp.y, lp.z), Mult(fromz, Mult(shadowProjectionMatrix, Mult(toz,
T(-lp.x, -lp.y, -lp.z)))));
```

Thus, the "good old" rotation-around-arbitrary-axis approach from Volume 1 found itself another problem to solve!

4.1.2 Masking using the stencil buffer

Now, one more thing. You also need to use the stencil buffer, to limit drawing to the surface that you are drawing the shadow on. If you don't, then you will draw shadows outside the surface. This is a pretty straight-forward application of the stencil buffer.

- Erase the stencil buffer

- Draw the surface into the stencil buffer as well as standard drawing to the frame buffer and Z buffer.

- Create the projection, to project from light source to the plane.

- Draw the shadow onto the surface, using the stencil buffer as mask.

This must be repeated for all surfaces that should support the shadow.

- Finally, draw the object normally.

This must be repeated for all surfaces that should support the shadow.

So the floor is the receiver of the shadow, so let's start with making a floor:

```
GLfloat ground[] = {
                -25, 0,-25,
                -25, 0, 25,
                 25, 0, 25,
                 25, 0,-25
                };
```

```
GLfloat groundtex[] = {
                        -1,-1,
                        -1, 1,
                         1, 1,
                         1,-1
                      };
GLuint groundIndices[] = {0, 1, 2, 0, 2, 3};
```

The floor is uploaded to a VAO the usual way.

So we draw the floor in frame buffer, Z buffer as well as stencil buffer, like this:

```
// ** Ground in stencil and image
glEnable(GL_STENCIL_TEST);
glStencilFunc(GL_ALWAYS, 1, 0xFFFFFFFF);
glStencilOp(GL_KEEP, GL_KEEP, GL_REPLACE); // 1 if pass!

glBindTexture(GL_TEXTURE_2D, tex0);
// Upload any shader variables here
DrawModel(groundModel, texturedShaderId, "in_Position", NULL,
"in_Texcoord");
```

The first instructions specify that the value 1 should be written 1 in the stencil if the pixel is drawn. Then we draw the floor normally.

Then we draw the object with the projection transformation:

```
glDisable(GL_DEPTH_TEST); // We need this. Why?
glEnable(GL_STENCIL_TEST); // Try disabling this!
```
```
// Dumb stencil, gets problems with complex or multiple shapes
glStencilOp(GL_KEEP, GL_KEEP, GL_KEEP);

// Calculate the projected shadow
shadowmatrix(floorShadow, groundplane, lightPosition);
Transpose(floorShadow, ps); // By-column matrix to by-row
// Draw our model as shadow
Point3D axis = {0,1.0f,0};
rot = ArbRotate(axis, count * 0.1 * 20.0 * M_PI / 180.0);
rot = Mult(ps, rot);
// Make the shadow black
glUniform3fv(glGetUniformLocation(shader, "diffuseColor"), 1,
&black);
Draw_Model(rot);
```

The call "shadowmatrix" refers to the calculations in chapter 4.1.1 above.

Note that the object is drawn without neither lighting or texture, but with transparency. In the next step, we draw the same object normally, that is without the projection but with texture and lighting.

The object must either be drawn with the GL_LEQUAL Z-buffer test, or with the Z-buffer test turned off, so we don't get it rejected by the Z-buffer test. In this case, the Z-buffer is simply disabled.

There is one problem with planar shadows that I have not mentioned yet. Above, I used a single very simple shape, where every line from the light source through the object only intersects the object once (two surfaces). When you use a more complicated shape or multiple shapes, you get multiple intersections, and thereby multiple coverage. This will cause artifacts as shown in Figure 23.

FIGURE 23. Problems with multiple blending of the shadow using complex shapes

This can be solved rather easily by taking even more advantage of the stencil buffer.

```
glStencilFunc(GL_EQUAL, 1, 0xFFFFFFFF);
glStencilOp(GL_KEEP, GL_KEEP, GL_INCR); // 1 if pass, else keep
```

This makes the shadow only draw once for each pixel.

To summarize, planar shadows are easy to do with a projection matrix and using the stencil buffer for masking. On the negative side, they only support planar surfaces! This is awkward and slow for multiple surfaces, demanding that the stencil buffer is erased and redrawn for every surface!

Thus, they are too limited for advanced uses. We will now continue with shadow maps and shadow volumes, who give significantly better results!

4.2 Shadow maps

Shadow maps is a fairly advanced and increasingly popular shadowing algorithm. Compared to other methods, it some significant advantages; It demands practically no knowledge about the scene, and it handles self-shadowing automatically.

The basic algorithm, illustrated in Figure 24, works in two passes:

1) Render the scene from the light source. We only want the Z buffer from this rendering. The resulting Z buffer is our "shadow map", a 2D function showing the distance to the light source.

2) Draw the scene normally, but use the Z buffer as input data to decide what fragments are shadowed. Thus, the Z buffer is used as a projected texture, but not directly for drawing with!

The Z buffer becomes a texture with depth values. When it is projected over the scene, every fragment calculation is provided with a Z value. And then there are two cases:

- If the fragment (pixel) is lit, then the distance implied by the Z buffer is *equal* to the distance to the light source.

- If the fragment is shadowed, then the value implied by the Z buffer is *smaller* than the distance to the light source.

If we can test these conditions, then we know whether the pixel is shadowed! This can be done using a fragment shader or by advanced texture arithmetics. Clearly, a shader is preferable.

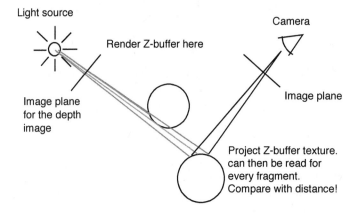

FIGURE 24. Shadow maps, principle

The first problem is how to render the depth image and then accessing it. You place the camera in the proper place (in the light source) and render. Then you can copy the Z buffer to a texture using

```
glCopyTexImage2D(GL_TEXTURE_2D, 0, GL_DEPTH_COMPONENT, 0,0, width,
height,0);
```

Once that is done, the Z-buffer values are in the texture, which a shader can read. This is the simplest way to get the Z-buffer. For higher performance but more complex code, you should consider using a framebuffer object (FBO) (see chapter 3.5). It is possible to create an FBO with Z-buffer only. See the code example below.

The next problem is to project the texture onto the scene, which was discussed in chapter 3.4.2. Figure 25 shows an implementation, and the code will follow.

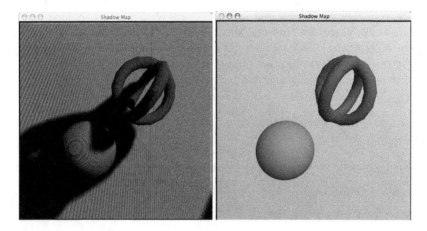

FIGURE 25. Example scene with and without shadows

We place the camera in the light source (Figure 26, left) and render the scene, generating the shadow map as the Z buffer (Figure 26, middle). Then we project the Z buffer over the scene as a texture (Figure 26, right).

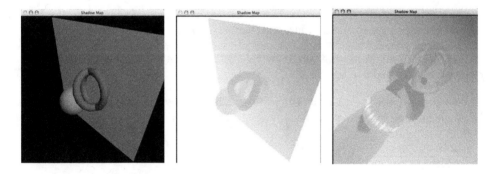

FIGURE 26. Rendering from the light source, image and Z buffer, and the Z buffer projected over the scene

Then we project the shadow map as a texture. If the corresponding distance match the distance to the light source, the point is lit.

The meaning of the projected image in the figure (rightmost image) may not be very obvious. Anyway, the dark areas in the middle and lower left of the image show areas where the distance and Z buffer mismatch badly, and that is also areas that should be shadowed.

4.2.1 Problems in shadow mapping

The algorithm has some weaknesses that must be overcome. The first one you will notice is that it can get random artifacts near edges. The problem is that it is hard to test for equal distance using floating-point numbers. Small roundoff errors will cause small differences. Thus, we must introduce some tolerance. If we have too little tolerance, almost everything will be shadowed. If we, on the other hand, overdo the tolerance and have too much, it will cause shadows to shrink. This is a minor problem and only a small offset will give good results.

A second problem is the resolution of the Z buffer. If the resolution is insufficient, you can get visible edge artifacts.

A third, fairly major problem, is that a shadow map only handles shadows in a limited part of the direction space. This is no problem when the camera faces along the light source, and for spotlights, but for omnidirectional light sources we need a set of shadow maps. The most popular solution is to use six shadow maps, a special kind of cube map.

4.2.2 Practice: A shader-based shadow mapping implementation

Below follows vital parts of the source-code to a fairly minimal implementation of shadow mapping, using shaders. The code is based on a tutorial by Fabien Sanglard [71], but rewritten, further optimized and generalized by myself.

Some parts of the program are skipped for space. You can find the original as well as my complete code on the Internet. (You are not supposed to type in long examples like this.)

Also note that some parts of the program (e.g. setTextureMatrix) dealing with projecting the texture are found in chapter 3.4.2.

As mentioned above, we need an FBO with depth buffer only. That can be created like the example on page 26, but with some differences. The following code will create such an FBO.

```
void generateShadowFBO()
{
    int shadowMapWidth = RENDER_WIDTH * SHADOW_MAP_RATIO;
    int shadowMapHeight = RENDER_HEIGHT * SHADOW_MAP_RATIO;

    GLenum FBOstatus;

    // Try to use a texture depth component
    glGenTextures(1, &depthTextureId);
    glBindTexture(GL_TEXTURE_2D, depthTextureId);

    // GL_LINEAR does not make sense for depth texture.
    glTexParameteri(GL_TEXTURE_2D, GL_TEXTURE_MIN_FILTER, GL_NEAREST);
    glTexParameteri(GL_TEXTURE_2D, GL_TEXTURE_MAG_FILTER, GL_NEAREST);

    // Clamp to avoid artefacts on the edges of the shadowmap
    glTexParameterf( GL_TEXTURE_2D, GL_TEXTURE_WRAP_S, GL_CLAMP );
    glTexParameterf( GL_TEXTURE_2D, GL_TEXTURE_WRAP_T, GL_CLAMP );
```

```
    glTexImage2D( GL_TEXTURE_2D, 0, GL_DEPTH_COMPONENT, shadowMapWidth,
shadowMapHeight, 0, GL_DEPTH_COMPONENT, GL_UNSIGNED_BYTE, 0);
    glBindTexture(GL_TEXTURE_2D, 0);

    // create a framebuffer object
    glGenFramebuffers(1, &fboId);
    glBindFramebuffer(GL_FRAMEBUFFER, fboId);

    // Instruct OpenGL that we won't bind a color texture to the FBO
    glDrawBuffer(GL_NONE);
    glReadBuffer(GL_NONE);

    // attach the texture to FBO depth attachment point
    glFramebufferTexture2D(GL_FRAMEBUFFER,
GL_DEPTH_ATTACHMENT,GL_TEXTURE_2D, depthTextureId, 0);

    // check FBO status
    FBOstatus = glCheckFramebufferStatus(GL_FRAMEBUFFER);
    if(FBOstatus != GL_FRAMEBUFFER_COMPLETE)
        printf("GL_FRAMEBUFFER_COMPLETE failed, CANNOT use FBO\n");

    // switch back to window-system-provided framebuffer
    glBindFramebuffer(GL_FRAMEBUFFER, 0);
}
```

Here follows the scene rendering code, first changing the positions of light sources etc. as desired, then rendering the scene from the light source, and finally rendering from the camera, using the Z-buffer as texture.

```
void renderScene(void)
{
    // Change light positions
    updatePositions();

//1. First step: Render from the light POV to a FBO, depth values only

    // Bind the depth FBO
    glBindFramebuffer(GL_FRAMEBUFFER,fboId);//Rendering offscreen

    //Using the fixed pipeline to render to the depthbuffer
    glUseProgram(0);

    // In the case we render the shadowmap to a higher resolution, the
viewport must be modified accordingly.
    glViewport(0,0,RENDER_WIDTH * SHADOW_MAP_RATIO,RENDER_HEIGHT*
SHADOW_MAP_RATIO);

    // Clear previous frame values
    glClear( GL_DEPTH_BUFFER_BIT);

    //Disable color rendering, we only want to write to the Z-Buffer
    glColorMask(GL_FALSE, GL_FALSE, GL_FALSE, GL_FALSE);

    // Setup the projection and modelview from the light source
    setupMatrices(p_light[0], p_light[1], p_light[2], l_light[0],
l_light[1], l_light[2]);

    // Cull front, render only backface, to avoid self-shadowing
```

```
    glCullFace(GL_FRONT);
    drawObjects();

    // Save modelview/projection matrice into the texture matrix
    // and add the scale and bias transformation
    setTextureMatrix();
```

Here starts the second pass, render to frame buffer, use shader, from the camera.

```
//2. Render from camera with the Z-buffer FBO

    glBindFramebuffer(GL_FRAMEBUFFER,0);
    glViewport(0,0,RENDER_WIDTH,RENDER_HEIGHT);

    //Enabling color write (previously disabled for z-buffer rendering)
    glColorMask(GL_TRUE, GL_TRUE, GL_TRUE, GL_TRUE);

    // Clear previous frame values
    glClear(GL_COLOR_BUFFER_BIT | GL_DEPTH_BUFFER_BIT);

    //Using the shadow shader
    glUseProgram(shadowShaderId);
    glUniform1i(shadowMapUniform,TEX_UNIT);
    glUniform1i(texunit,TEX_UNIT);
    glActiveTexture(GL_TEXTURE0 + TEX_UNIT);
    glBindTexture(GL_TEXTURE_2D,depthTextureId);

    // Setup the projection and modelview from the camera
    setupMatrices(p_cam[0],p_cam[1],p_cam[2],l_cam[0],l_cam[1],l_cam[2]);

    glCullFace(GL_BACK);
    drawObjects();

    glutSwapBuffers();
}
```

This is the heart of the main program, granted that we have the projected texture support described previously. Now we need a shader pair too. The vertex shader is the same as on page 19, but the fragment shader is expanded as follows:

```
#version 150

uniform sampler2D textureUnit;
in vec4 lightSourceCoord;
out vec4 out_Color;
uniform float shade;

void main()
{
    // Perform perspective division to get the actual texture position
    vec4 shadowCoordinateWdivide = lightSourceCoord / lightSourceCoord.w;

    // Offset to eliminate shadow acne and self-shadowing
    // The optimal value here will vary with different GPU's depending on
their Z buffer resolution.
    shadowCoordinateWdivide.z -= 0.002;

    // Look up the depth value
```

```
    float distanceFromLight = texture(textureUnit, shadowCoordinateWdi-
vide.st).x;
    distanceFromLight = (distanceFromLight-0.5) * 2.0;

    // Compare
    float shadow = 1.0; // 1.0 = no shadow

    if (lightSourceCoord.w > 0.0)
        if (distanceFromLight < shadowCoordinateWdivide.z) // shadow
            shadow = 0.5;
    out_Color = vec4(shadow * shade);
}
```

A few details should be pointed out, concerning the problems mentioned before:

Self-shadowing is a problem in shadow mapping. In theory, we should consider a surface lit if the distance in the Z-buffer is exactly the distance to the light source, but that is numerically unreasonable. So we can make the comparison with a slight tolerance. Moreover, there is a distance error that comes from the discrete samling of the depth buffer. The depth buffer samples do not exactly fit the image, and the misfit will cause an error. If we do the shadow map test with no offset at all, this will cause a moire-like pattern known as *shadow acne*.

There are three different kinds of areas to consider when handling this problem: Lit areas, self-shadowed areas and the border between a lit and self-shadowed area. The code above makes a few attempts to reduce the artifacts.

We can use culling to simplify the problem a bit. By culling front faces, lit surfaces are error free, and we only need to fine tune for self-shadowed areas.

The fine tuning for self-shadowed areas are in the fragment shader, the adjustment by 0.002 or 0.0005. Sadly, the value is not a trivial thing. If it is too small, the fix may not work on GPUs with low Z-buffer precision, but if it is large, you will get artifacts.

There is one more problem area left, the border between lit and self-shadowed areas. There is no simple solution for a good result there.

There are many ways to vary the concept. The example code given here is as straight-forward as possible, intentionally avoiding special-purpose calls and strange fixes. Feel free to try variations.

Finally, it should be noted that the artifacts mentioned are reduced by using more advanced shadow mapping, such as soft shadows by filtering. (See chapter 4.4). Another important method for improving the quality is *cascaded shadow maps*. This is an extension where multiple depth buffers are used at different distance. The basic principle is to cut the viewing frustum in multiple sections, rendering different shadow maps in different sections.

4.3 Shadow volumes

There is one more shadow algorithm that I want to cover, *shadow volumes*. This algorithm is an excellent example of how powerful the stencil buffer is, when its full power is used.

With shadow volumes, you project the edges of the shadowing object to be the edges of the shadowed volume. By using the stencil buffer, we can determine whether a fragment is inside or outside the volume.

Although this method is less popular than shadow mapping, it does have advantages. A significant advantage is that it avoids the resolution problems of the shadow buffer. This means that it is superior for generating hard shadows. It also supports omnidirectional lights and self-shadowing. However, and as models become more detailed, the generation of the shadow volume also becomes more cumbersome. Since it requires the shadow volume to be drawn over the scene, it also requires more extra passes per fragment.

The principle of shadow volumes is illustrated by Figure 27.

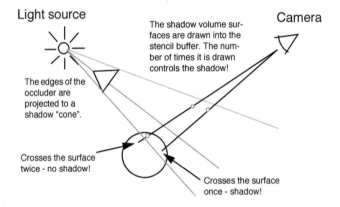

FIGURE 27. Shadow volumes

The algorithm works as follows:

- Create polygons that form the edges of the shadow volume
- Initialize the stencil buffer to 1 if the camera is inside the volume, otherwise 0.
- Draw all front sides of the volume in the stencil buffer, incrementing the stencil buffer value.
- Draw all back sides of the volume in the stencil buffer, decrementing the stencil buffer value.
- Draw the scene.
- Draw shadows in all pixels where the stencil buffer > 0

This algorithm is closely related to the non-zero winding number method (Figure 28), presented in Volume 1 as a method for determining whether a point is inside a 2D polygon. Shadow volumes is the same principle, applied to closed polyhedra in 3D. In both cases, we count up for one direction and down in the other.

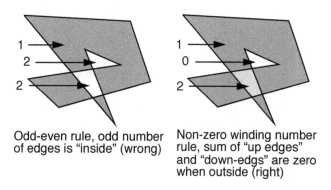

Odd-even rule, odd number of edges is "inside" (wrong)

Non-zero winding number rule, sum of "up edges" and "down-edgs" are zero when outside (right)

FIGURE 28. The non-zero winding number for 2D polygons

Let us look closer, in Figure 29, at how the stencil buffer is updated and how the decisions are made.

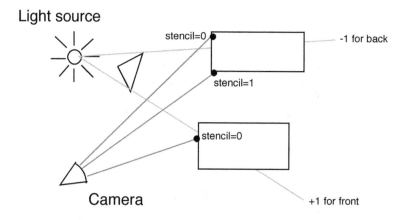

FIGURE 29. Different cases for rendering with shadow volumes

The stencil is initialized to zero before the volume is drawn to it. For the lowest of the three rays shown in the figure, the surface is not touched by the volume so it remains zero. For the middle one, the front side has incremented it to 1. The upper one, however, has both been incremented by the front side and then decremented by the back side, so the ray is found to pass through the shadowed area and ends up at a point that is lit.

As with most methods, there are variants. One such variant is shadow volume BSP trees, which is a method for dealing with many shadowing objects in a scene.

To summarize, shadow volumes have the following points in their favor:

- No resolution problems, high quality hard shadows.
- Low demands on the GPU, stencil buffer support is enough.
- Supports self-shadowing.
- Supports omnidirectional lights.

It also have some drawbacks:

- Calculation of the volume is complicated.
- Rendering requires multiple passes over the same areas.

Although the trend is in favor of shadow maps, the choice is not always trivial.

4.4 Soft shadows

All the methods above will create shadows with sharp edges. This is fine for point light sources, which in real life means small light sources on close distance, but realistic shadows are otherwise soft, with edges that are gradients from shadow to lit.

A great number of methods for solving this problem exists, with varying cost and precision. I will briefly outline a few here.

But first, we must make a few more definitions. Above, I have implicitly assumed that the light source is a point source. Real light sources are not infinitesimal, which is what makes shadow edges soft. The *umbra* is the fully shadowed area on a receiver, that is, a point in a receiver is in the umbra if no part of the light source can be seen from it. The *penumbra* is the soft edge, so a point is in the penumbra if some, but not all, of the light source can be seen from it. See Figure 30.

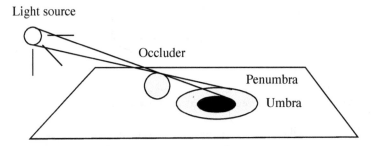

FIGURE 30. Umbra and penumbra

We also discern between the *inner* and *outer* penumbra. They are the parts of the shadow that are inside and outside the hard shadow. Thus, the hard shadow must be defined, i.e. as the shadow cast by a point light source in the center of the light source.

4.4.1 Accumulation buffer shadows

The simplest methods use the accumulation buffer, or an accumulation buffer replacement using a shader. Even this can be done in several ways. A costly but simple way is to move the light source and render the scene for each light source position, accumulating the results in the accumulation buffer. For best result, the weights should vary with the offset, to form a nice filter kernel.

This primitive method is remarkably capable. Since it moves the light source, it can model the shape and size to the light source to the precision we like, and the width of the penumbra will be larger with distance as it should.

The drawback is, obviously, that we must render a complete scene for each sample in the filter kernel, so we pay the full cost for the supersampling even in areas untouched by the penumbra (full light or full shadow). Other methods can optimize this to varying degrees.

A potential problem, that can be overcome, is that the accumulator buffer is not guaranteed to be supported in hardware on all GPUs. As long as the hardware supports FBOs and shaders (shader model 2 is sufficient), this is a minor problem since we can simulate the accumulator buffer with FBOs and a simple shader.

This method is mentioned in [17] as a method for smooth shadows using shadow volumes, but it is totally independent of the underlying method.

A variant of this method [17] is to render not the entire image but images of the shadows in the accumulator buffer, resulting in smooth shadow images that can then be rendered.

The only strong point with these methods from a computational point of view is that they are easy to adjust to the available processing power. However, it is all to likely that the number of frames that we can afford to accumulate is rather low, and then the quality is poor. We need many accumulated images to make a good shadow.

4.4.2 Percentage Closer Filtering (convolution)

Percentage Closer Filtering (PCF) is a simple soft shadow method for use with shadow maps. It is a supersampling method where several samples are taken for each fragment, and the result forms a filter kernel. This can be done in the fragment shader, accessing different texels in the shadow map when processing a single fragment.

This is done with a single "exposure" so only a single shadow map is used and a single light source position. The advantage is that the method is fairly fast and easy to implement, but the drawback is that the shadows are not very realistic. The shadow edges are blurred uniformly in all directions and will not vary with distance to the light source.

PCF can be optimized by detecting if the fragment is in the penumbra. This is done by taking the outermost samples of the filter kernel, 3 or 4 samples. If all samples are in shadow or all are lit, then we may conclude that the fragment is not in the penumbra and we can assign the result. This will not optimize as much as it seems, since the SIMD architecture

---

of the fragment processor will, blockwise, make all processors do the maximum processing for the most costly fragment in the block. Also, there is a risk for artifacts when using large filter kernels and complex geometry.

4.4.3 Smoothies and Soft Shadow Volumes

Smoothies [32] and Soft Shadow Volumes [33] are two similar methods for soft shadows on shadow volumes. Both methods calculate an extension to the edge of the shadow volume. Smoothies are explicitly "fake" even according to its inventors. It only produce the outer penumbra, and has other artifacts as well.

Soft Shadow Volumes are more precise. They work with a separate *visibility buffer*, where the scene is rendered in a first pass, including the extension to include the penumbra. In a second pass, penumbra visibility is calculated, with values from 0 to 1 including both the inner and outer penumbra. In a final third pass, the visibility values are used for rendering the appropriate shadow.

Both these methods are highly suitable for real-time rendering, allowing very respectable frame rates.

4.4.4 Single Sample Soft Shadows

Single Sample Soft Shadows is an algorithm for soft shadows when using shadow mapping. By working with a single shadow map, real-time performance is achieved. Before drawing the scene, the shadow map is processed, calculating distances between regions, which is then used for approximating the penumbra. Although the result is not entirely correct, it gives pretty convincing soft shadows, with penumbras that grow with distance.

4.5 Ambient occlusion

A dramatically different approach to approximating global illumination with soft shadows is *ambient occlusion*. This was first presented by Zhukov et. al. [92] as a method with lower computation demands than radiosity but better looks than the Phong model. In the simple three-component light model/Phong model (see part 1) there was a constant ambient level. Ambient occlusion makes a closer approximation of the ambient level, variable over the scene dependent on proximity to geometry, to occluding objects. See Figure 31 for an example.

FIGURE 31. The Stanford Bunny with ambient occlusion, from a thesis by Joel Jansson [97].

Essentially, ambient occlusion works with the assumption that the ambient level drops the more occluding objects there are nearby. This certainly isn't physically correct but can produce quite nice soft shadows, where concave corners will be darkened.

According to Zhukov et. al. [92], the amount of occlusion (obscurance) for a point P in a scene can be computed as follows. We integrate over a hemisphere with the points x. See Figure 32.

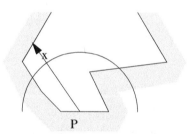

FIGURE 32. A hemisphere around a surface point P, aligned with the local normal vector. The distance to the closest surface from P through x is measured.

For each x, we find a distance along x-P to the closest surface. Then this distance is mapped with a function $\rho()$ (see Figure 33) which varies with distance up to a limit where it flattens out and gives to contribution to the obscurance.

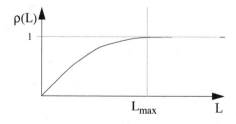

FIGURE 33. Obscurance falloff function $\rho(L)$, adapted from [REF]

Then the obscurance can be computed with the following formula:

$$w(P) = \frac{2}{\pi}\int_x \rho(L(P, x))\cos\alpha\, dx$$

What this tells us is that the obscurance is 0 (obscured) for surfaces at zero distance from P, while surfaces beyond L_{max} result in an obscurance of 1, which means unobscured, no effect on ambient light at all. The average obscurance for a point can then be used as ambient light level.

4.5.1 Object space ambient occlusion

Now the question is how we calculate this in an efficient and practical way. Object space ambient occlusion is the fundamental ambient occlusion algorithm. The principle is simple enough: Measure how much of the surrounding space that is filled with occluding objects and base a shading on that. The most basic and intuitive algorithm is to use ray-casting. For every point P, a number of rays are cast and the distance to the closest surface is measured.

Like other object space methods, this method easily gets into complexity problems with detailed geometry, but can be accelerated with octrees and similar methods. Also, it is possible to reduce the number of rays by applying a post-filtering step, to smooth the ambient light level.

4.5.2 Screen space ambient occlusion

Screen space ambient occlusion, abbreviated SSAO, is a popular method for getting a fast approximation for ambient occlusion in linear time. It was first proposed by Shanmugam et.al. [93] and got its name from Mittring [94].

SSAO is firmly based on the Z buffer. Instead of making measurements in the world, measurements are made in the Z buffer. Thus, a rendering is first done, generating both a texture of the scene (without AO effects but with other lighting) plus a Z buffer. This can be done with FBOs so that two different textures are produced that can then be input in a second rendering stage.

In the second stage, the Z buffer is sampled to calculate obscurance. We consider the Z buffer a height map for a terrain. This terrain is, however, only partial information. Any surface that isn't visible from the camera can not contribute to the obscurance.

Once you have an FBO that can provide the Z buffer as texture, most interesting things happen in the shaders.

The vertex shader is straight forward, just adapts positions to texture coordinate range.

```
#version 150
in vec3 in_Position;
```

```
out vec2 texCoord;
void main(void)
{
    gl_Position = vec4(in_Position, 1.0);
    texCoord = vec2(in_Position / 2.0 + vec3(0.5));
}
```

The next problem is to get the real depth from the depth texture. As was noted in Volume 1, the depth buffer should not store z values but rather a function of 1/z. How to do that follows from the "normalized coordinates" section in Volume 1. Moreover, the value we get is in the range of texels, 0 to 1, so the scale and bias adjustment appears again.

```
float readDepth( in vec2 coord )
{
    // These numbers must match the main program's perspective projection
    float zNear = 1.0;
    float zFar = 100.0;

    float z_from_depth_texture = texture(texture0, coord).x;
    float z_sb = 2.0 * z_from_depth_texture - 1.0; // scale and bias from
texture to normalized coords
    float z_world = 2.0 * zNear * zFar / (zFar + zNear - z_sb * (zFar -
zNear)); // Get back to real Z
    return z_world;
}
```

The "near" and "far" values from the viewing frustum must be correct for this to work. You may want to pass them as uniforms.

Now we can read correct depths anywhere in the image. The current fragment is the center of the operation, we will always need that.

```
    float depth = readDepth( texCoord );
```

From there, we will want to make offsets of one pixel to access neighbors.

```
    float dx = 1.0 / screenWidth;
    float dy = 1.0 / screenHeight;
```

Now that we know how to get the correct depth, we can outline the SSAO algorithm as follows:

for a number of neighbor samples in world coordinates do:

- project it back to screen space
- get the depth of the screen space coordinate
- find the difference between the sample and the current pixel
- then the AO contribution is diff/(1+diff^2)
- This is added to the total obscurance.

This is illustrated in Figure 34.

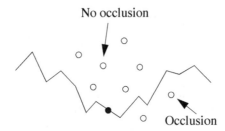

No occlusion

Occlusion

FIGURE 34. Screen space ambient occlusion. Samples in 3D space are tested against height given by Z buffer

This method has some problems with incorrect self occlusion for sloping surfaces. This can be corrected by taking the hemisphere model into account. In Figure 34 this is accounted for by all samples being located in the front of the normal in the center point.

In Figure 35, we see an example of ambient occlusion compared to SSAO by Shanmugam et. al. [93]

FIGURE 35. Ambient occlusion (left) and screen-space ambient occlusion (right). From [93].

4.5.3 A simplified SSAO approach

I will here demonstrate an SSAO approach that I consider more intuitive and quite a bit simpler, that will still generate something that looks somewhat like SSAO. My strategy is not necessary the perfect one but it removes the problem of working with world space samples, and also eliminates the problem with false occlusion from flat surfaces. It is rather an approximation of the original algorithm. The idea is to access two neighbors on either side, and compare the average height with the center in order to measure obscurance.

Essentially, we are looking for "valleys" in the Z buffer. Moreover, very big changes in Z should be ignored. A big change is usually not a sign of occlusion, but rather one object in front of another with open space between. Thus, we need a falloff or cutoff for bigger distance.

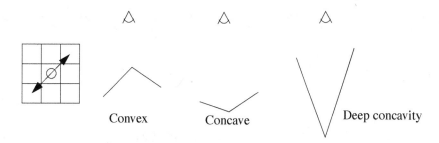

FIGURE 36. Detecting occlusion from depth variations.

In Figure 36, two pixels on either side of the center (left) are tested. If the average distance is lower than the center pixel, this signifies a convexity, that is no obscurance (second from left). If the average is higher (second from right) this is a concavity and therefore signifies obscurance. Also, as mentioned above, if the difference is large (far right) then the neighbors are likely to be at foreground objects and we should suppress such obscurance.

I solved this with a simple mapping function:

```
float myCompareDepths( in float d, in float d1, in float d2 )
{
    const float a = 5.0; // Difference that gives max occlusion

    float dav = (d1+d2)/2.0;
    float x = d - dav;
    float dao = max( 1.0/a/a*x*(2.0*a - x), 0.0);
// negative = no occlusion!
    return dao;
}
```

This defines a second degree polynomial function passing though zero at $x = 0$ and $x = 2a$, with a maximum of 1 at a. Note that it only gives a contribution within a certain range.

All in all, a number of samples are taken like this:

```
d1=readDepth( vec2(texCoord.x+dx,texCoord.y+dy)); // Diagonal
d2=readDepth( vec2(texCoord.x-dx,texCoord.y-dy));
ao2 += ao2Mod*myCompareDepths(depth, d1, d2);
```

The ao2mod value is a falloff over increasing distance from the center, and ao2 is the resulting occlusion.

Finally I must tune the result to a suitable level. For demonstration purposes, I chose to overdo the effect, hoping for a result that can be visible in print, but it is still more visible on screen.

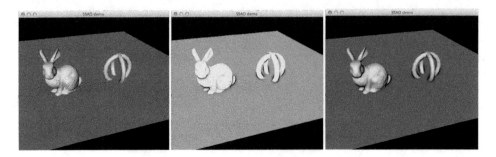

FIGURE 37. Screen Space Ambient Occlusion example

In Figure 37, we see the original scene (left) with diffuse light, SSAO only (middle) and the combined image (right). You should be able to see how the SSAO adds some shadows at the bottom of the models, and also adds a bit to the curvature of the bunny. The normal-based lighting tends to overshadow the SSAO, but I think the effect is still visible. Note that the upper edge of the objects gives no SSAO contribution since it is out of range for the mapping defined above, which is a highly desirable effect for a realistic SSAO.

Seriously, I came up with this approach when I wanted to include SSAO in the book, wanted a demo but found none that was simple enough. This approach may be a hack (it certainly needs some fine tuning to be "right") but I found it kind of interesting. No matter how you compute it, SSAO is an approximation, and this is one way to compute it.

4.5.4 Ambient self-occlusion and pre-computed ambient occlusion

For static scenes, ambient occlusion can be computed once and for all and re-used for any changes in the view. This was noted already by Zhukov et. al. [92].

A related, rarely discussed but not as rarely used ambient occlusion method is what I choose to call *ambient self-occlusion*. With that, I refer to the simplified object-space approach, where only the object itself is taken into account. This will give none of the global illumination qualities of full AO, but still give a respectable improvement.

For general objects, the occlusion can be calculated with the same ray-casting methods as mentioned in section 4.5.1 at page 56. For a rigid object, this can be pre-calculated once and for all, applied by light mapping, e.g. by vertex, combined with other light.

For low-polygon models, self-occlusion can easily be approximated in real time. A case in point is MineCraft-style geometry. Vertices are uniformly spaced in a grid, making the occlusion measurement a mere matter of counting neighbors. Even for arbitrarily shaped low-poly objects, similar measurements can be made for an insignificant computational cost.

4.5.5 Ambient Occlusion, conclusions

Ambient occlusion techniques is an easy way to add a better approximation of global illumination into your scenes. Combined with Phong shading and a shadow algorithm like shadow mapping, your scenes can have very realistic lighting without having to overdo it. Your first choice for ambient occlusion probably is some form of SSAO.

4.6 Shadows, conclusion

This is a brief overview of the soft shadow algorithms that I find the most interesting or significant. Other methods exist, like Layered Attenuation Maps and many others. See [17] for more information.

Shadows are perfectly realistic to include in modern games, to the extent that it is a necessity for any 3D game with any ambitions. Planar shadows are easy to do, but only works on flat surfaces. Shadow maps and shadow volumes work much better in general scenes, and each have important strengths and weaknesses. Soft shadows always cost more, and may require compromises.

5. Advanced shaders

Although we have already touched upon the subject of shaders, i.e. that shaders are typically used for the shadow mapping described in chapter 4.2, this is the chapter devoted to
shaders. Again, the term "advanced" is something relative. I have no intention of going
into the most complex and advanced shaders, but rather to cover some important problems
that are typically solved with shaders.

5.1 Multi-pass shaders

Simple shaders produce their output in one iteration, so geometry is rendered with some
interesting surface effect and that is it. More advanced shaders may need to use the output
from one iteration as input to another. This is solved by rendering to texture (see
chapter 3.5). The rules from that subject apply: glCopyTexSubImage2D works very well,
but framebuffer objects are faster.

This is typical for GPGPU applications (see chapter 6). Thus, a central operation in the
GPGPU program is to copy the entire (usually square) framebuffer to a texture either by

```
glCopyTexSubImage2D(GL_TEXTURE_2D, 0, 0, 0, 0, 0, n, m);
```

or the appropriate FBO code.

A common situation of multi-pass shaders is that they take full images as input, textures
filling the entire framebuffer. In such passes, rendering is very simple from a graphics
point of view. It is a single polygon over the entire frame buffer! Textures and frame buffer
often have the same size. So the geometry is often restricted to this:

```
GLfloat quadVertices[] = {
                    -1.0f, -1.0f, 0.0f,
                    -1.0f,  1.0f, 0.0f,
                     1.0f,  1.0f, 0.0f,
                     1.0f, -1.0f, 0.0f};
GLfloat quadTex[] = {
                     0.0f, 0.0f,
                     0.0f, 1.0f,
                     1.0f, 1.0f,
                     1.0f, 0.0f};
GLuint quadIndices[] = {0, 1, 2, 0, 2, 3};
```

Even this is more complicated than necessary. We can optimize this to a single triangle, covering the entire viewport, and at the same time give the renderer a chance to avoid artifacts at the crack between the two triangles. The triangle will be located like in Figure 38.

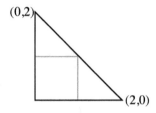

FIGURE 38. A triangle covering the entire viewport

In code, we can define this as follows:

```
GLfloat triangle[] = {
                 -1.0f, -1.0f, 0.0f,
                 -1.0f,  3.0f, 0.0f,
                  3.0f, -1.0f, 0.0f};
GLfloat triangeTexCoord[] = {
                  0.0f, 0.0f,
                  0.0f, 2.0f,
                  2.0f, 0.0f};
GLuint triIndices[] = {0, 1, 2};
```

Performance-wise the difference is irrelevant, and there may be a crack in the resulting quad depending on implementation. In both cases, what is actually drawn is a quad.

Naturally, we are not limited to rendering a single quad. We can play tricks when rendering too, but usually we simply want the entire input image mapped onto the output, and then this is the easiest way.

With FBOs, running several iterations of identical or similar operations is known as *ping-ponging*, as illustrated by Figure 39.

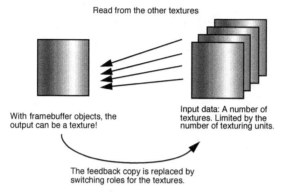

Read from the other textures

With framebuffer objects, the output can be a texture!

Input data: A number of textures. Limited by the number of texturing units.

The feedback copy is replaced by switching roles for the textures.

FIGURE 39. "Ping-ponging"

"Ping-ponging" is a name for multipass processing where we read from one (or more) tex-ture and write into another, and then swap the roles of the two for every pass. With FBOs, this can be made very efficient, with no time wasted on copying data between buffers.

You select a source with

```
glBindTexture(GL_TEXTURE_2D, tx1);
```

and the destination by

```
glBindFramebuffer(GL_FRAMEBUFFER, fb);
glFramebufferTexture2D(GL_FRAMEBUFFER,
    GL_COLOR_ATTACHMENT0, GL_TEXTURE_2D, tx2, 0);
```

When necessary, select shader with

```
glUseProgram(shaderProgramObject);
```

Render, repeat until finished.

An example of multipass shader is to do convolution, that is to apply a filter defined by a convolution kernel.

Convolution is a term commonly used in signal processing. Convolution is an integral between two functions (signals) that can be used to represent the impulse response of a fil-ter, and apply that filter on a signal. One of the two functions is reversed and shifted:

$$(f \otimes g)(t) = \int_{-\infty}^{\infty} f(\tau) \cdot g(t - \tau) d\tau$$

The name "convolution" refers to the reversal of one function[1]. In a digital domain, the convolution is replaced by a sum.

---

1. "faltning", "faltung"

$$(f \otimes g)(t) = \sum_{-\infty}^{\infty} f(\tau) \cdot g(t - \tau)$$

Image filters are nicely represented by two-dimensional digital convolution. A low-pass filter may look like in Figure 40.

1	4	6	4	1
4	16	24	16	4
6	24	36	24	6
4	16	24	16	4
1	4	6	4	1

/256

FIGURE 40. Low-pass convolution kernel, low-pass (blur) filter

Note the division by 256, to keep the level of the image after filtering.

When applying the filter kernel, there are two approaches for doing it. In either case we loop through all the pixels in the image. Either we use a *scatter* algorithm, where the center pixel is multiplied with each of the kernel valued and added to the appropriate neighbor (according to the kernel), or we use a *gather* algorithm, where we take each neighbor, multiply by the kernel value, and add to the center pixel. See Figure 41.

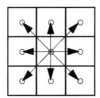 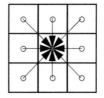

FIGURE 41. Scatter and gather algorithms for convolution

Gather corresponds to the usual formulation of convolution, as above, while scatter is *impulse summation*, where each input data is an "impulse" into the function.

When implementing an algorithm on the CPU, we can go either way. On the GPU, however, it is clear that the input values are a texture, which allows random access, and the output is one fragment at a time. Thus, on the GPU we should use a gather algorithm.

The kernel above is of course only one possible filter out of many, a medium-sized low-pass filter. With other weights, including negative ones, it is possible to define many other operations. For example, a gradient filter can look like in Figure 42.

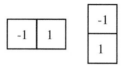

FIGURE 42. Gradient filters in the x and y direction

This particular filter in Figure 40 on page 66 has a special strength: It is *separable*. That means that it can be broken down to several smaller filters, that can be applied in sequence to produce the same result. This can be very important since running several small convolution kernels tends to be faster than the combined one.

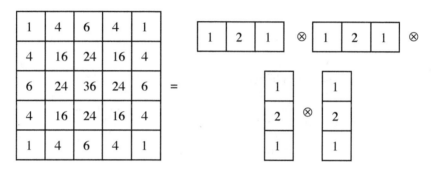

FIGURE 43. Separable filter kernels

In the example in Figure 43, we can see that while the kernel has 25 elements, the three separated kernels only consists of 12 elements together. This will shorten the shader program, reduce the number of texture accesses. It will also make the accesses more local, which can be an advantage since it gives fewer cache misses in the shader.

For more information on convolution of image data, see the image processing literature.

An alternative to separable filters, when working with low-pass filters, is to downsample the signal (texture). Then a simple 2x2 low-pass filter (separated into an 1x2 and a 2x1 kernel) can be used while doing repeated downsampling. By taking advantage of the built-in linear filtering, this is highly effective. Fahlén [18] reports that he downsampled down to 1/8 by 1/8, while further downsampling showed artifacts.

5.2 Floating-point data types and floating-point buffers

The framebuffer as well as textures are usually stored as 32 bits per pixel, with 8 bits each for red, green, blue and alpha, RGBA. Now, mathematical calculations will not be very precise with 8-bit integers. Thus, modern GPUs can work with floating-point numbers.

This is rumored to have been initiated by John Carmack (ID Software), probably for HDR effects! HDR (high dynamic range) really only refers to the extended range of the floating-point data types compared to 8-bit integers, but the first application you think of using it is most likely blooming effects. See chapter 5.3.

A GPU can support floating-point numbers with 16, 24 and 32 bits. Double precision (64 bits) has been unavailable up to very recent GPUs. With the 280GTX there is very limited 64-bit support, but it was still unavailable for the graphics pipeline at the time. Only at the pretty recent Fermi GPU, 64-bit support was given any priority, and there is a FP64 format in OpenGL 4.0.

So, the available formats are

FP32: s23.8

FP24: s16.7

FP16: s10.5

with FP64 as an upcoming possibility.

For HDR, 16 and 24 bits should work nicely, but for more demanding uses, the 32-bit format is by far the most interesting one!

When loading data to a floating-point buffer, we must specify other parameters than we are used to. It can look something like this:

```
glTexImage2D(GL_TEXTURE_2D,0, GL_RGBA32F,texSize,texSize,
            0,GL_RGBA, GL_FLOAT, data);
```

Note that the last parameter can be set to NULL if we wish to create an empty texture (for writing into). This is not clearly specified by the "red book".

5.3 High dynamic range

The floating-point buffers is a major step forward for GPUs. By not being limited to 8 bits integer values for each channel, but instead having 16 to 32 bits of floating-point, new applications were possible. Some will be discussed later, in section chapter 6. In this section, I will stick to the graphical effects known under the name *high dynamic range*.

The dynamic range is defined as the ratio between the largest and lowest measurable value of a signal. In the standard 24/32-bit color representation, we have only 8 bits per channel so the dynamic range is 256:1. In real world scenarios, the dynamic range can be as high as 100000:1. When rendering with high dynamic range, the pixel intensity is no longer clamped to the [0, 1] range. It will still have to be clamped before displaying, but we have the possibility to adjust the result in intelligent ways between the initial rendering and final display.

So we take advantage of HDR through a post-processing step. There are two major ways to do this: filtering and re-mapping the amplitudes (tone mapping).

5.3.1 Blooming/glow effects

Blooming is mainly a sensorial effect where brightly lit sensors will spread their higher value to surrounding areas. This takes place both in machine sensors and in the eyes. In the eyes, as well as in some analog machine sensors, the spread to nearby areas is mostly uniform. In many machine sensors the spread tends to follow the geometry of the sensor, as was the case with the sensor used for the Waco FLIR tapes [47]. For our purposes, *glow* is a synonym to blooming.

There is another, related effect, called *flare*. This is mainly caused by scattering in the lens. The flare consists of two effects, the *lenticular halo* and the *ciliary corona*. The ciliary corona manifests as lines, radial rays, while the lenticular halo shows as colored rings.

In his diploma thesis, Erik Häggmark discusses possibilities to simulate these effects as well as the theory [19]. Here, we will focus on the blooming effects.

For more widespread sources, James & O'Rorke describe how blooming can be implemented on the GPU. [50] Masaki Kawase describes blooming in a real project, including other effects like glare and depth of field, as well as separable filters. [54]

Since we perceive blooming when there are bright spots in the scene we are viewing, we use that information as an indication to how bright it is. Simulating blooming effects is thus a way to transfer such information to the viewer, even without the possibility to actually light the bright area over the limited maximum of a computer screen.

Take the simple case where you calculate brightness values with the Phong model. In highlights, you can easily get values over 1.0, and the simplest way to handle that is to truncate the value, limit it to 1.0.

The blooming simulation is a matter of using the areas with values over 1.0 in a better way. Instead of discarding the information, we can use it to create blooming. A blooming algorithm can work like this:

First, render the scene to an FBO (texture), as in Figure 44. Instead of truncating values above 1.0, these are the values we want.

FIGURE 44. A teapot with a big highlight that overflows

Subtract by 1.0 and truncate all values below 0.0. Thus, we have an image of the overflow, shown in Figure 45!

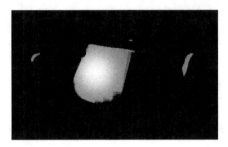

FIGURE 45. The overflow only

Filter the resulting overflow by an low-pass filter, like a Gauss kernel. This will spread out the blooming into surrounding areas. This filtering is typically applied as a separable filter kernel, as discussed in chapter 5.1. In Figure 46, we have used a very large filter.

FIGURE 46. Overflow after (in this case pretty over-done) filtering

The small overflows drowned in the filtering, but that is not surprising. Instead, the peak of the highlight dominates.

Finally, render the scene normally, but with the overflow image overlaid, added to the result in Figure 47.

FIGURE 47. Teapot with bloom added

This effect is not only for highlights on shiny objects. A lit window in the dark can benefit from blooming effects, as can many other bright parts of scenes with high dynamics. The effect is dramatic and should be used to its advantage.

5.3.2 Tone mapping

High dynamic range can also be used for *tone mapping*. This is a re-mapping of the dynamic range to make desired parts fit in the screen range, possibly with non-linear distortions that emphasize certain parts. This is somewhat similar to gamma correction, although the high range means that a part of the problem is to map in parts that would otherwise be truncated.

For more details about tone mapping, see Fahlén. [18]

5.4 Bump mapping with extensions

In Volume 1, we had a brief look at bump mapping, where surface detail was simulated by a bump function, which derivative was used for modulating the normal vector and thereby the shade calculated from the lighting. Alas, what you find there is a mere introduction.

In this section, we will have a closer look at bump mapping and its close relative normal mapping, and then go further, to more advanced variants like parallax mapping, where the perspective is corrected to give even more depth to the surface.

5.4.1 Basis vectors for texture coordinates; finding the tangent and bitangent

We need a few vectors to form the coordinate system that we need, a coordinate system for the texture space. The first of these is the unmodified normal vector of the surface, $\mathbf{n}$. We can assume that the normal vector is provided by the host program as usual, and if not we can simply use the cross product of two edges in the surface.

We need two more basis vectors, showing the direction in which the s and t texture coordinates vary. These will be located in the surface, tangents to the surface. That makes them the *tangent vector and bitangent vector*.

I will here refer to the tangent and bitangent as $\hat{s}$ and $\hat{t}$ (basis vectors for the texture coordinates s and t). There are infinite numbers of tangent vectors to a surface, so which ones should we use? Obviously we should use the ones that correspond to the variation of the texture coordinates!

In some situations, you can create $\hat{s}$ and $\hat{t}$ in an extremely simple way, simply by taking the cross product between the normal vector and anything, like this:

$$\hat{s} = \frac{\hat{x} \times \hat{n}}{|\hat{x} \times \hat{n}|}$$

$$\hat{t} = \hat{n} \times \hat{s}$$

This is clearly cheating, we don't care at all about the variation of the texture coordinates. The result may be horrible, but there are also cases where this works perfectly. A typical case where it works is when the bump map is just noise, with no structures.

However, for the general case we want a better method. That will be our next step.

5.4.2 Calculating the tangent and bitangent by matrix inverse

A much better method is to calculate the tangent and bitangent by some rather straight forward calculus, known as *Lengyel's Method* [99]. Let us consider a single triangle and the coordinate systems around it, in Figure 48.

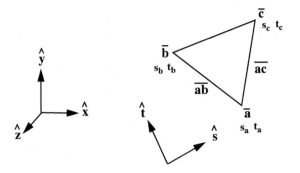

FIGURE 48. A triangle with texture coordinates and the texture coordinate basis vectors

Now we can express the edges **ab** and **ac** like this:

$$\mathbf{ab} = \mathbf{b} - \mathbf{a} = (s_b - s_a)\hat{s} + (t_b - t_a)\hat{t} = ds_1\hat{s} + dt_1\hat{t}$$

$$\mathbf{ac} = \mathbf{c} - \mathbf{a} = (s_c - s_a)\hat{s} + (t_c - t_a)\hat{t} = ds_2\hat{s} + dt_2\hat{t}$$

In Figure 49, we see how this works for the edge **ab**.

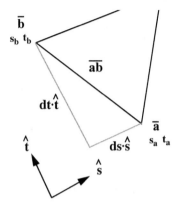

FIGURE 49. The edge ab expressed as components along s and t

We will now split the vectors to their components. Then the expressions above become as follows:

$$
\begin{bmatrix} ab_x \\ ab_y \\ ab_z \end{bmatrix} = \begin{bmatrix} s_x \\ s_y \\ s_z \end{bmatrix} ds_1 + \begin{bmatrix} t_x \\ t_y \\ t_z \end{bmatrix} dt_1
$$

$$
\begin{bmatrix} ac_x \\ ac_y \\ ac_z \end{bmatrix} = \begin{bmatrix} s_x \\ s_y \\ s_z \end{bmatrix} ds_2 + \begin{bmatrix} t_x \\ t_y \\ t_z \end{bmatrix} dt_2
$$

We can rewrite this as a single expression in matrix form:

$$
\begin{bmatrix} ab_x & ac_x \\ ab_y & ac_y \\ ab_z & ac_z \end{bmatrix} = \begin{bmatrix} s_x & t_x \\ s_y & t_y \\ s_z & t_z \end{bmatrix} \begin{bmatrix} ds_1 & ds_2 \\ dt_1 & dt_2 \end{bmatrix}
$$

Now the solution should be rather obvious: We are looking for the st matrix, and we can isolate that by multiplying both sides by the inverse of the 2x2 matrix!

$$\begin{bmatrix} ab_x & ac_x \\ ab_y & ac_y \\ ab_z & ac_z \end{bmatrix} \begin{bmatrix} ds_1 & ds_2 \\ dt_1 & dt_2 \end{bmatrix}^{-1} = \begin{bmatrix} s_x & t_x \\ s_y & t_y \\ s_z & t_z \end{bmatrix} \begin{bmatrix} ds_1 & ds_2 \\ dt_1 & dt_2 \end{bmatrix} \begin{bmatrix} ds_1 & ds_2 \\ dt_1 & dt_2 \end{bmatrix}^{-1}$$

Now we get our solution!

$$\begin{bmatrix} s_x & t_x \\ s_y & t_y \\ s_z & t_z \end{bmatrix} = \begin{bmatrix} ab_x & ac_x \\ ab_y & ac_y \\ ab_z & ac_z \end{bmatrix} \begin{bmatrix} ds_1 & ds_2 \\ dt_1 & dt_2 \end{bmatrix}^{-1} = \begin{bmatrix} ab_x & ac_x \\ ab_y & ac_y \\ ab_z & ac_z \end{bmatrix} \begin{bmatrix} dt_2 & -ds_2 \\ -dt_1 & ds_1 \end{bmatrix} \frac{1}{ds_1 dt_2 - dt_1 ds_2}$$

In C code, this will become (taken from my working demo):

```
float ds1 = sb - sa;
float ds2 = sc - sa;
float dt1 = tb - ta;
float dt2 = tc - ta;
vec3 s, t;
float r = 1/(ds1 * dt2 - dt1 * ds2);
s = ScalarMult(VectorSub(ScalarMult(ab, dt2), ScalarMult(ac, dt1)), r);
t = ScalarMult(VectorSub(ScalarMult(ac, ds1), ScalarMult(ab, ds2)), r);
```

or with C++ operator overloading:

```
float ds1 = sb - sa;
float ds2 = sc - sa;
float dt1 = tb - ta;
float dt2 = tc - ta;
vec3 s, t;
float r = 1/(ds1 * dt2 - dt1 * ds2);
s = (ab * dt2 - ac * dt1) * r;
t = (ac * ds1 - ab * ds2) * r;
```

This gives us the $\hat{s}$ and $\hat{t}$ vectors for one particular triangle. What we should do now is to calculate them for each *vertex* instead. This is most conveniently done by finding all polygons where the vertex is a member, and take the $\hat{s}$ and $\hat{t}$ for each of these polygons, sum together and normalize. Then the $\hat{s}$ and $\hat{t}$ coordinate system will vary smoothly over the surface.

I find this solution quite elegant, and it does produce good results. That is, with some care in the implementation. You must check for special cases, in particular "bad" triangles where the texture coordinates don't vary at all (making the determinant one over zero) or where an edge has zero length.

Advanced shaders

5.4.3 Approximative method for calculating the tangent and bitangent

I would like to present one more way to calculate $\hat{s}$ and $\hat{t}$. This method is not as exact as the previous one (at least I don't have any proof for its precision) but the results are quite good.

The approach is to let each edge of a triangle contribute to the vectors, based on the direction of the edge and the variation of the s and t coordinates along the edge. Let us only consider $\hat{s}$. For an edge **a** to **b**, **ab**, there will be the s coordinates s_a and s_b. Then that edge will add a contribution s_{ab} as follows:

$$ s_{ab} = \frac{ab}{|ab|}(s_b - s_a) $$

How can this work? Because all vertices will add to $\hat{s}$, while their t components will cancel each other out (approximately). See Figure 50.

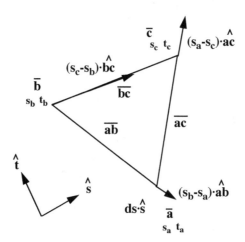

FIGURE 50. Each edge gives a contribution to an estimate of the s basis vector.

What Figure 50 tries to tell you is that, given the $\hat{s}$ in the figure (which is what we want) the s variation is large along **bc**, and therefore it will give a large contribution. If the s difference is negative, the edge will contribute in its negative direction, which is the case for both **ab** and **ac**. We can see significant contributions in the $\hat{t}$ direction, but they will go both ways and cancel out.

In my opinion, this method is more intuitive and may help you understand how this works. However, I would prefer the matrix inverse method since it gives an exact result.

In Figure 51 (right), you can see the Utah teapot rendered with the bump map (left image) using the method above to calculate basis vectors.

Note that $\hat{s}$ och $\hat{t}$ are assumed to be calculated in model coordinates. Thus, they must be transformed to view coordinates, again using gl_NormalMatrix. I will here denote the transformed, view coordinate vectors as $\mathbf{p_s}$ and $\mathbf{p_t}$.

$$\mathbf{p_s} = \text{gl\_NormalMatrix} * \hat{s}$$

$$\mathbf{p_t} = \text{gl\_NormalMatrix} * \hat{t}$$

5.4.4 Conversion between coordinate systems

There are no less than three coordinate systems that we must keep track of in bump mapping. Geometry is specified in *model coordinates*. We transform that to *view coordinates* to put it in the same space as light directions and viewing directions. But we also have *texture coordinates* and *tangent coordinates* (which we may here assume are the same thing).

Texture coordinates is a 3-dimensional space defined by $\mathbf{p_s}$, $\mathbf{p_t}$ and $\mathbf{n}$. We will find that there are cases where we will prefer to work directly in texture coordinates.

The transformation from model coordinates to view coordinates are, as mentioned above, done using gl_NormalMatrix. The transformation from view coordinates to texture coordinates are slightly less obvious. It is done using a rotation matrix built from $\mathbf{p_s}$, $\mathbf{p_t}$ and $\mathbf{n}$:

$$M_{vt} = \begin{bmatrix} \mathbf{p_s} \\ \mathbf{p_t} \\ \mathbf{n} \end{bmatrix} = \begin{bmatrix} p_{sx} & p_{sy} & p_{sz} \\ p_{tx} & p_{ty} & p_{tz} \\ n_x & n_y & n_z \end{bmatrix}$$

The matrix is trivially extended to 4x4 as needed.

Now, a few comments about the terminology. $\mathbf{p_s}$ is usually (correctly) called the *tangent vector* and is called **t** in many text, despite the obvious confusion with the t coordinate, which is along $\mathbf{p_t}$. $\mathbf{p_t}$ is often called the *binormal* (with the symbol b), which is clearly incorrect since it is rather the *bitangent*. The term binormal is most likely from a text about local coordinate systems along 1-dimensional functions, where the term is perfectly appropriate. For a surface, however, we should say bitangent. I choose to avoid the symbols t and b, using the symbols $\mathbf{p_s}$ and $\mathbf{p_t}$ instead (originally from [65] although with the names $\mathbf{p_u}$ och $\mathbf{p_v}$).

The texture coordinates, texture space, is also called *tangent space*. We may discern between the concepts *tangent space* and *texture space*, by letting tangent space be an orthonormal base while texture space has the tangent and bitangent strictly aligned with the texture directions. I choose not to consider the difference further, and rather consider the orthonormal base to be an approximation of the strict texture space. See further Dietrich in [38]. The difference is in the direction of $\mathbf{p_t}$.

Finally, a few words about the meaning and names of the textures involved. By the term *bump map,* I refer to an image that holds height values. It could just as well be called height map, but since it is used for lighting and not geometry, I think it is reasonable to use different terms. A *normal map* is a pregenerated texture with normal vectors see below). It is sometimes called bump map, so we have some possible sources of confusion.

5.4.5 Modifying the normal vector

When we are working in view coordinates with the vectors $\mathbf{p_s}, \mathbf{p_t}, \mathbf{n}$, we can calculate the modified normal vector as

$$b_s = db/ds$$

$$b_t = db/dt$$

$$\mathbf{n'} = \mathbf{n} + b_s \cdot \mathbf{p_s} + b_t \cdot \mathbf{p_t}$$

This is the formula that was introduced in Volume 1. However, we can also consider a slightly modified definition:

$$\mathbf{n'} = \mathbf{n} - b_s \cdot \mathbf{p_s} - b_t \cdot \mathbf{p_t}$$

This is identical except for the signs. This is a pure question of definitions, namely whether the bump map height represents bumps that are out from the surface or into it. The first one is into the surface, which is arguably better since it will cause less visible artifacts than one that extends from the surface. The latter, however, is somewhat more intuitive.

This definition requires that $\mathbf{p_s}, \mathbf{p_t}, \mathbf{n}$ are orthogonal. If they are not, or not close enough to get away with it, the formula should rather be

$$\mathbf{n'} = \mathbf{n} + b_s \cdot (\mathbf{p_t} \times \mathbf{n}) + b_t \cdot (\mathbf{n} \times \mathbf{p_s})$$

After the modification, $\mathbf{n'}$ also needs to be normalized.

The calculation of b_s and b_t are done with a simple subtraction between two neighbor texels in the bump map:

$$b_s = b[s+1, t] - b[s, t]$$

$$b_t = b[s, t+1] - b[s, t]$$

This concludes bump mapping in view coordinates. But it is also possible to do this calculation in texture coordinates! Before normalization, the modified normal then becomes

---

$$\begin{bmatrix} b_s \\ b_t \\ 1 \end{bmatrix}$$

or (depending on the definition of the bump map direction)

$$\begin{bmatrix} -b_s \\ -b_t \\ 1 \end{bmatrix}$$

Both approaches, working in view of surface coordinates, produce the same result, as in Figure 51. The texture coordinate solution looks wonderfully simple, but we still need to transform light and viewing direction from view coordinates to texture coordinates. This makes the simplification a bit less exciting, but it will gain importance when using normal mapping, which is our next subject.

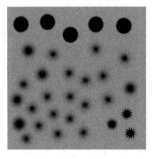 

FIGURE 51. A bump map and the Utah Teapot rendered using this bump map and using the texture coordinate basis vectors derived from chapter 5.4.3.

5.4.6 Normal mapping

Normal mapping is a simple precalculation of bump mapping. In practical implementations, this is the dominating method today, Thus, we should not skip it as a triviality, but instead look at its details.

The whole point with normal mapping is that we precalculate the normal vector, in texture coordinates. Above, we found that it can be calculated as

$$\begin{bmatrix} -b_s \\ -b_t \\ 1 \end{bmatrix}$$

Advanced shaders

(or, again depending on definition, without the negations). This is calculated straight from the bump map image data, as

$$-b_s = b[s, t] - b[s+1, t]$$

$$-b_t = b[s, t] - b[s, t+1]$$

$$1$$

It is then normalized, which means that each component is within the interval [-1..1]. It should then be placed into a texture. To store it in a texture, we need to scale and bias the data, since textures can only hold the interval [0..1]:

$$R = (x+1)/2 \qquad G = (y+1)/2 \qquad B = (z+1)/2$$

After this transformation, we store the data in the red, green and blue channels of an image. This procedure creates a normal map from a bump map as shown in Figure 52 (images from an example found on the web, source unknown).

FIGURE 52. A bump map commonly used in demos (left), and its normal map (right).

In Figure 51 (middle), you can see a normal map combined with the bump map. That makes the result somewhat hard to watch but the combined data can be useful.

When rendering, the normal vectors are recovered by

$$x = 2R-1 \qquad y = 2G-1 \qquad z = 2B-1$$

which gives us the normal vector in texture coordinates as $\mathbf{n}^t = (x, y, z)$.

The light direction is transformed to texture coordinates

$$L_t = M_{vt} \cdot L$$

and likewise for the viewing direction. Thereby, we have normal vector, light direction and viewing direction all in the same coordinate system, which is sufficient to make lighting calculation as desired.

Thus, normal mapping requires some extra calculations, but also save on two important points: We save the normalization of the modified normal vector, and we reduce the texture accesses by 50%.

5.4.7 Extensions to bump mapping

The drawback of bump mapping and normal mapping is that the bumps only change the normal vector and thereby the shade, but not the positions.

There are a number of algorithms that improve this situation, to make a displacement of the texture with respect to the height and perspective. They include

- Parallax mapping
- Relief mapping
- By-pixel displacement mapping
- By-vertex displacement mapping

Out of these, parallax mapping and by-pixel displacement mapping seems like good choices for real-time use. The following presentation will be illustrated by screen shots from a course project by Jonas Lindmark [43], who implemented all methods in a very nice demo. To begin with, he demonstrated the flatness of plain texture mapping and bump/normal mapping as in the screen shots in Figure 53.

FIGURE 53. Plain texture and bump/normal mapping from Lindmark's demo. [43]

Whether bump mapping really is that bad can be argued, but the flatness is quite noticeable in a moving scene.

5.4.8 Parallax mapping

Parallax mapping is a rough approximation of the offset needed for a proper displacement of the texture, invented by Kaneko et. al. [42]. It reads the height of the bump map at the default location, and then calculates an offset from that value, thus making a single step over the surface. See Figure 54.

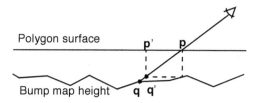

FIGURE 54. Parallax mapping.

The point **p** is where the view vector hits the polygon surface. This is known from the geometry. The bump map height shows the height that the surface should appear to have. Thus, we want to use information (texture and normal vector) from the point **q**, where the view vector intersects the bump map height.

In parallax mapping, the bump function is assumed to vary slowly. Then, we can make a simple step ahead from **p** using the view vector, which brings us to **q'**, our approximation of **q**. What we do in practice is to move from **p** to **p'**, just calculating the step length. (See below for the exact calculation.)

For a slowly varying bump map, this will work very well. However, the approximation gets worse the more the bump map varies. The Figure 55 shows three cases with significant errors, making over- and underestimations, and worst of all (right) passing through a bump in the bump map.

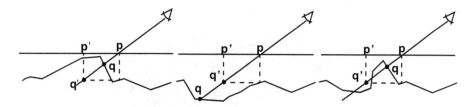

FIGURE 55. Parallax mapping problems. Left: A case where the approximation overshoots the target. Middle: A case where it undershoots. Right: A case where it passes through a bump.

Implementing parallax mapping is a matter of, again, keeping track of the coordinate systems properly. We can get the view direction in viewing coordinates as the vertex position. Using a varying variable, we interpolate it by fragment. We call the interpolated version v_v, that is, the viewing direction in view coordinates.

The viewing direction is then transformed to texture coordinates using the M_{vt} matrix.

$$\mathbf{v} = M_{vt} \cdot \mathbf{v_v}$$

This vector is split into the xy-components (really st) in the surface, $\mathbf{v_{xy}}$, and its z-component (along $\mathbf{n}$) which is denoted v_z.

If we started in the original texture coordinates $\mathbf{t_0} = (s, t)$, we can now calculate a modified position as

$$\mathbf{t_n} = \mathbf{t_0} \pm b(s, t) \cdot \mathbf{v_{xy}} / v_z$$

We use addition or subtraction depending on whether the bump map is defined out from or into the surface.

The closer to the surface we are, the bigger the offset will be, and since the method is such a rough approximation, the errors will be much worse in steep angles. This problem can be reduced by *offset limiting*, which simply removes the denominator:

$$\mathbf{t_n} = \mathbf{t_0} \pm b(i, j) \cdot \mathbf{v_{xy}}$$

This will make the bump map seem "flatter" in steep angles, the perspective effect will not increase as expected. This seems like a bad thing at first glance, but since this is the problem where the errors are the most disturbing, we reduce a problem at the cost of lost depth.

In practice, we will want to combine the parallax mapping with normal mapping, so we can reduce texture lookups just like in the "flat" normal mapping. The obvious solution is to provide the bump map separately, but the customary solution is to include the bump map height as part of the normal map. In the normal map, R, G and B are used for the normal vector, but the alpha channel is unused. Thus, it is stored as the alpha channel of the normal map. This requires that the normal map is stored in a format that supports an alpha channel. One such format is the Targa (TGA) format.

FIGURE 56. Parallax mapping, the simplest method for improving bump mapping.

Advanced shaders

Lindmark's implementation is shown in Figure 56. Again, the method assumes that the bump map varies so slowly that the height value will be close enough to the value at the actual intersection. It should only be used with low frequency bump maps. Still, as can be seen in the screen shot above, the result is fairly convincing and errors are not very disturbing. In particular, the errors are smooth. We do not get any grainy artifacts but an overall erroneous displacement.

The problems are worst in steep angles, where the big offsets will cause big errors since the demand of a slowly varying bump map becomes even higher. Even a low frequency bump map will cause significant errors and small bumps can cause occlusions. In Figure 57, the errors are quite noticeable, but have been reduced by offset limiting.

FIGURE 57. Parallax mapping works poorly in steep angles.

5.4.9 Relief mapping

A more exact but slower method is *relief mapping*, described by Policarpo [40]. The method performs a search along a line, taking a number of steps from the starting point until a height is found that is larger than what the ray hits, thus hitting the ground at or before that point. From there, a binary search follows to find the point of intersection between the two last tested points. See Figure 58.

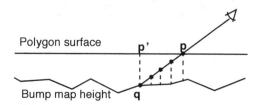

FIGURE 58. Relief mapping works from the intersection and samples until the intersection is found.

As long as the step length is small enough not to miss any fine details, this method will perform well, but the smaller details the bump map has, the smaller the steps must be or we will shoot through narrow protrusions. This problem is illustrated by Figure 59.

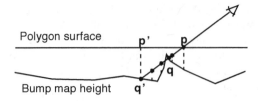

FIGURE 59. Problem case for relief mapping: A narrow protrusion is missed by the sampling.

Essentially, the step size needs to be adjusted depending on significant higher frequencies in the bump map. Being able to do that is a big improvement from parallax mapping, but balancing errors with performance is not trivial. All in all, I would consider this method an intermediate development step between the previous and next methods, and not really something I would use in practice. However, Policarpo has more recently presented refinements where the steps are replaced by *cone step mapping*. [41]

Figure 60 shows a screen shot from Lindmark's demo, where some errors are visible, caused by randomly missing and hitting certain details. Lindmark does, however, use a similar but somewhat simpler algorithm than Policarpo's, "Parallax occlusion mapping". The errors are similar to those of Zink [44] so it seems they use the same algorithm.

FIGURE 60. Parallax occlusion mapping (simplified Relief mapping).

The errors are even more apparent in the following screen shot:

FIGURE 61. The errors in Parallax occlusion mapping, magnified

5.4.10 Per-pixel displacement mapping

Donnelly [39] suggested a method that overcomes the problems of both these methods, *Per-pixel displacement mapping with distance functions*. The fixed step length in relief mapping is replaced by a step length that is determined from a distance function over the surface. The distance function is a discrete array of distance values, usually referred to as a *distance map* or *distance transform*. Such a distance map can be an array of scalars or an array of vectors, and the distances can be Euclidean or approximations thereof. [45][46]

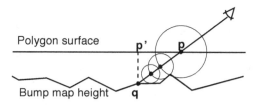

FIGURE 62. Per-pixel displacement mapping uses the distance map to take steps with the distance to the closest surface (circles).

Donnelly uses a 3-dimensional distance map, stored as a 3D texture. The resulting algorithm is pretty straight-forward. The principle is shown in Figure 62. The drawback is that the distance map takes much VRAM, and it also needs to be precalculated by the CPU since the distance transformation used is sequential. This problem is alleviated somewhat by making the height dimension limited; we do not need high resolution in height, only enough to find more efficient step lengths.

With older GPUs such as the FX and 6000 series, the number of iterations run was needed to be fixed, which limited the usability somewhat. As shown in Figure 63, the result is excellent.

FIGURE 63. Per-pixel displacement mapping. (The errors to the left are from the relief mapping part.)

Finally, a few words about per-vertex displacement mapping. This kind of methods is the oldest kind of displacement mapping, and not really related to bump mapping. They were used as early as 1984 [49] for non-real-time purposes. In per-vertex displacement mapping, vertices are displaced by some displacement function. Just like in other off-line methods, like radiosity, the geometry was subdivided into more vertices and polygons, so a complex function (bump map) describing the surface would result in very complex geometry, which is exactly what bump mapping and its successors are used to avoid. I prefer to strictly discern between methods that avoid adding geometry, and those who do.

5.5 Recursive temporal filtering

Let us go back to filtering, with a simple but useful case. We have discusses filtering within an image, spatial filtering, but let us not forget temporal filtering, filtering along the time axis, that is between successive images.

Temporal filters need to be *causal*, that is, they only extend backwards in time, not into the future. They come in two major variants, either weighting together a limited number of images, which needs to work with many frames in the same iteration, or *recursive*. The recursive temporal filter is the easiest one to implement since it only needs a single buffer of old data. See Figure 64.

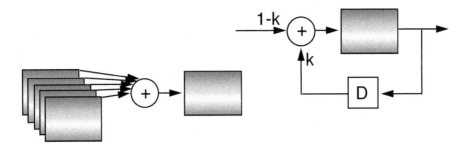

FIGURE 64. Temporal filters, using a stack of past images (left) or recursive (right)

I will only discuss the recursive variant in more detail. It can be implemented either using FBOs or copying to texture. In this case, we don't win much by the FBO, since the same data must reach the screen anyway, so I chose texture copying for this example.

The implementation works like this:

• Render the scene as usual, using a shader that uses the RTF buffer as texture input. Note, however, that the scene must render geometry in all pixels (e.g. using a skybox), not leaving parts as background.

• Copy the result to the RTF buffer

On the CPU, this is simple enough.

```
glActiveTexture ( GL_TEXTURE1 );
glBindTexture (GL_TEXTURE_2D, rtftex);
```

Render scene. Make the RTF buffer active again so we can copy to it.

```
glBindTexture(GL_TEXTURE_2D, rtftex);
glCopyTexSubImage2D(GL_TEXTURE_2D, 0, 0, 0, 0, 0, 512, 512);
```

The vertex shader needs to access the RTF buffer on the same locations as we are drawing to. This is easily done once we have projected the fragment to screen coordinates:

```
out vec2 screenCoord;

screenCoord = vec2(gl_Position) / gl_Position.w / 2.0 + vec2(0.5);
```

Finally, the fragment shader should blend its result with the RTF buffer.

```
outColor = texture(tex, texCoord) * (1.0-k) + texture(rtftex, screen-
Coord) * k;
```

This last stage can also be performed by the frame buffer blending, but then we need to blend using only a quad, so we don't blend multiple times.

What happens is that we first multiply the current contents of the RTF buffer by k (say 0.95), fading it out a bit. The new image is blended in by (1-k) (say 0.05). Finally, we read out the contents to the frame buffer to be the next iteration of the RTF buffer. The result may look like in Figure 65.

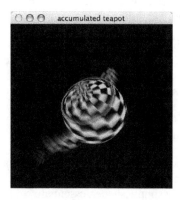

FIGURE 65. A rotating, textured teapot with motion blur using recursive temporal filtering

Doesn't this sound pretty hilarious to render a frame and only blend it in by 5%? This is purely a factor of frame rate and appearance. When running in 60 fps, the movement speed used gives a pleasant motion blur. With other speeds and frame rates you can vary the fading parameters from anywhere between 0.5 and 1.

This particular effect is useful for "whoosh" effects, game transitions like speed boosts.

5.6 Processing particle systems by multi-pass shaders

As mentioned in Volume 1, particle systems are highly useful for many effects, including rain, snow, explosions etc. In Volume 1 it was noted that large particle systems are best made using billboards. We stand by that claim here, but let us take it a few steps further.

Simple, small particle systems are easily modelled as an array of instances of some model (i.e. billboard), controlled by the CPU. However, when making a large system, we want to do the updates on the GPU as far as possible. We can do that by using textures and multi-pass shaders (FBOs), as described by Latta [103].

We will now propose the following model:

For a particle system, each particle will need some data. A bare minimum should be

- position (vec3)
- velocity (vec3)

Instead of storing this in some array, we propose to store that in *textures*. These textures should be *floating-point buffers*, just like we used for high dynamic range, otherwise the precision will be insufficient. Since every texel may hold four values, we can store position and velocity as RGB in two texels and still have two scalars left for other data. If this is not enough for your needs, add more textures for additional data.

Let us decide to store these in two separate textures, positionTex1 and velocityTex1. (They could also be in the same texture, alternating positions and velocity. Nothing stops you from doing that but your shaders will be unnecessarily complex.) We also need a second copy of each, positionTex2 and velocityTex2, so we can perform ping-ponging between them.

Our particle system algorithm will now be as follows:

1) Render positionTex1 to positionTex2, using velocityTex1 as additional input, using a shader that reads position and velocity from the input textures to create new positions in the output. This will be a very simple shader, essentially adding the velocity times a time step to the position.

2) Render velocityTex1 to velocityTex2 using another shader that somehow decides how the velocity should be updated. It may need to take the position texture as input. In the simplest case, this may just add gravity. In more elaborate cases you may want information about the surrounding geometry or handling collisions between neighbor particles, which will lead to much more challenging situations.

3) Use the position textures to draw the particle system!

On every other turn, switch the "1" and the "2" above!

This process is illustrated by Figure 66.

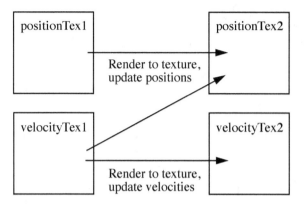

FIGURE 66. Updating particle systems by rendering to textures

One notable case with dependent particles is *cloth simulation*. For such a simulation, we may choose to let each particle only be affected by its closest neighbors, typically modelled as springs (section 12.3 at page 192).

Finally, the particle system is rendered using the position texture as input. This must be read by the vertex shader, which provides the position of the particle. In the case of separate particles, drawn as billboards, I would strongly suggest the use of *instancing* (see Volume 1), so you draw the entire particle system with one single call and then look up positions using the instance number.

An important aspect of particle systems is transparency. You will usually want to use transparency when using billboards. As described in Volume 1, this requires sorting to avoid conflicts with the Z buffer (depth buffer). Under some circumstances, you can set the Z buffer to read only, and then draw all particles on top of each other in any order. This will, however, depend on how the billboards are designed. For very simple looking billboards it may work, but in other cases you really want to sort your particles by distance.

A complete sorting is a costly process. It would be possible to sort on the CPU by transferring the data back and forth, but that would give very bad performance. We absolutely need to perform the sorting on the GPU!

QuickSort is data dependent and not feasible using shaders in the rendering process. You can use it using compute shaders/CUDA/OpenCL (see chapter 6) but even then it is complex and you need to interface between the systems. A more popular sorting algorithm on GPUs is Bitonic Merge Sort. However, do not forget what the problem is! What we have is data that has not changed much since the previous frame. That means that it is already partially sorted! That means that much simpler sorting algorithms can be used with much higher performance. I would suggest the following, which is essentially a parallel version of Bubble Sort:

Render the data (positions and velocities) to new textures. When rendering, each output will select between two possible inputs, the textels own position and one neighbor.

Depending on whether the position is "odd" or "even", the one with higher or lower distance to the camera is chosen. This is done with different steps so that data can travel multiple steps over time. See Figure 67.

This process may be repeated a couple of times per frame. However, we do *not* try to do a complete sort every frame! The data will be sorted within a few frames, so we can safely do an incomplete sorting with very little visible artifacts.

It is notable that the most vital area for sorting are *near the camera*, so you may optimize the process by doing a more ambitious sorting (more iterations) in that area only.

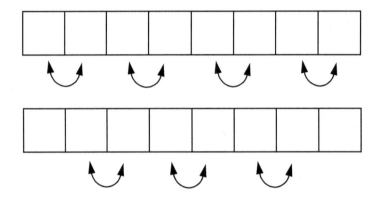

FIGURE 67. Local sorting on the GPU, swapping neighbors pairwise

Thus, in short, you manage your large particle system by

- storing particle data in floating-point textures
- binding the textures to FBOs
- updating by rendering, using ping-poinging
- sorting
- drawing using instancing

Beyond this, we have a few outstanding issues. How can you handle collisions with the rest of the scene? How can you make the particles dependent of each other? The problem quickly grows, but I will give some pointers and suggestions how to proceed.

Collisions with the rest of the scene may be easier than you think! My recommendation would be to render the scene to a Z buffer from some suitable direction. Actually, the viewing direction may not be too bad, and that Z buffer already exists. Another option is to render from above, which would be good for e.g. water falling down, and then you can render the scene without perspective to make calculations easier. Then you use that Z buffer for tests with the particle locations! See Figure 68. Another case where particle-scene collisions are not hard to resolve is when the collisions can be made against a regularly sampled terrain, where you can easily find the terrain height below each particle.

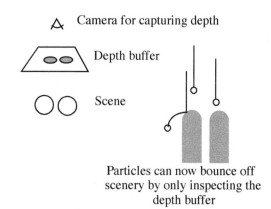

Camera for capturing depth

Depth buffer

Scene

Particles can now bounce off
scenery by only inspecting the
depth buffer

FIGURE 68. Collision detecting for particles using the depth buffer

The last case, making particles depend on each other, may be the hardest. If your data is
sorted for drawing, you can take advantage of this to reduce your search for neighbors, but
that will only reduce one dimension which may be too little. Then you will to use some
kind of grid with separate lists for each part of space, like a regular grid or an octree. For
pure collision detection, you will work within cells and their closest neighbors. If you
want to model things like gravity, things get more compicated since the particles will
affect each other at a distance, but this can still be simplified. At large distance, you will
only need to know how many particles there are in a certain cell, not their exact positions,
and theat their influence as one large particle.

Finally, it should be mentioned that there are many other options for solving this problem.
You may replace the textures with pure vertex lists, updated using transform feedback
(which allows you to save transformed data to use as input on a later iteration), and you
may use pure GPU computing solutions as mentioned above.

5.7 Geometry shaders

With OpenGL 3, the rendering pipeline was extended with the option of customizing the
primitive assembly stage with geometry shaders, shaders that can not only modify locations like the vertex shader can, but also add and remove geometry.

A geometry shader can take one out of four different inputs (see Figure 69):

A line segment (two vertices).

A line segment with adjacency (four vertices).

A triangle (three vertices).

A triangle with adjacency (six vertices).

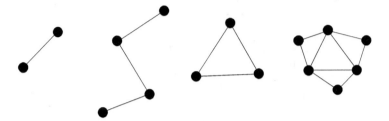

FIGURE 69. Geometry shader primitives

The "adjacency" concept, to bundle a primitive with some adjacent vertices, is probably new to anyone who haven't used geometry shaders before. A primitive has to be uploaded with adjacency information in order for the geometry shader to get the information; OpenGL can not find adjacency for you. With straight triangles, however, you can upload your geometry as usual, but then possibilities are limited.

As a first example, here is a pass-through shader for vertices only:

```
#version 150

layout(triangles) in;
layout(triangle_strip, max_vertices = 3) out;

void main()
{
   for(int i = 0; i < gl_in.length(); i++)
   {
      gl_Position = gl_in[i].gl_Position;
      EmitVertex();
   }
   EndPrimitive();
}
```

This will work straight out of the box and you don't have to do much more than load one more shader into your shader program. As most minimal examples, it shows some potential, but also lacks some information that makes you wonder "How do I do that?" We can see that we take triangles as input (gl_in[i].gl_Position), and we can emit vertices (gl_Position and EmitVertex) - not necessarily the same ones, same locations or same number. We may take decisions like removing some primitives altogether, split the primitive into more (up to a point) and emit totally different geometry.

The next step towards a useful geometry shader is to include additional information, like normal vectors and texture coordinates. That gives us a new pass-through shader that looks like this:

```
#version 150

layout(triangles) in;
layout(triangle_strip, max_vertices = 3) out;

in vec2 texCoord[3];    //[3] because this makes a triangle
in vec3 exNormal[3];
```

```
out vec2 texCoordG;
out vec3 exNormalG;

void main()
{
  for(int i = 0; i < gl_in.length(); i++)
  {
    gl_Position = gl_in[i].gl_Position;
    texCoordG = texCoord[i];
    exNormalG = exNormal[i];
    EmitVertex();
  }
  EndPrimitive();
}
```

It is still a simple pass-though, but note that every vertex emit from the shader now passes on the additional information too. This time, we can no longer just pop it in into existing code and hope it will work, since the normal vectors and texture coordinates must change name in the geometry shader. Thus, my vertex shader emits "texCoord" and "exNormal" as "out" variables, while the fragment shader must, for this example, input "texCoordG" and "exNormalG".

So let us take one more example, this time something that changes something. The following shader will move all vertices a bit to the middle, creating cracks between all polygons.

```
#version 150

layout(triangles) in;
layout(triangle_strip, max_vertices = 3) out;

in vec2 texCoord[3];     //[3] because this makes a triangle
in vec3 exNormal[3];
out vec2 texCoordG;
out vec3 exNormalG;

void main()
{
  vec4 middleOfTriangle = vec4(0.0);

  for(int i = 0; i < gl_in.length(); i++)
  {
    middleOfTriangle += gl_in[i].gl_Position;
  }
  middleOfTriangle /= gl_in.length();

  for(int i = 0; i < gl_in.length(); i++)
  {
    gl_Position = (gl_in[i].gl_Position + middleOfTriangle) / 2.0;
    texCoordG = texCoord[i];
    exNormalG = exNormal[i];
    EmitVertex();
  }
  EndPrimitive();
}
```

The result can look like Figure 70, for the Utah Teapot:

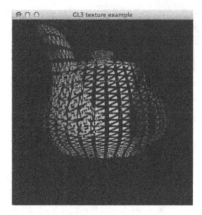

FIGURE 70. Utah Teapot with a "breakup" geometry shader

This particular shader is not particularly useful beyond being a simple example of geometry shader. You can do much more interesting things. Now that we have a normal vector with every vertex, we can add geometry, like fur (add geometry following the normal vector), and you may add more information for other effects.

5.8 Tessellation shaders

Geometry shaders are useful for many things, for example generating hair and fur and (to some extent) evaluating splines, but they are unsuitable for generating large amount of geometry from each primitive. This problem was reduced by introducing *invocations*, making geometry shaders faster.. But there was also yet another kind of geometry generating stage added in OpenGL 4, *tessellation shaders*.

Just like vertex and fragment shaders work together in pairs, tesselation shaders also come in pairs, the *tesselation control shader* and the *tesselation evaluation shader*. These are executed between the vertex and geometry shaders.

The input to the tesselation shaders is an arbitrary number of vertices. The connectivity between these are undefined, it is up to you. The output, however, consists of a number of triangles arranged as a triangle or quad. This means that you can easily define a Bézier patch using 16 vertices, something that is awkward to do with geometry shaders.

The job of the tesselation control shader is to specify the detail level of the geometry that is being created. This is done once per edge of your output triangle or quad, and once for the interior. See Figure 71, where the outer detail level for one of the edges has been specified to 3, causing that edge to be split the desired number of times. Note that the other edges may have different detail! The inner detail is the number of layers the surface is split to. This is only specified once for the whole primitive.

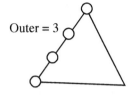 

Inner = 3

FIGURE 71. The meaning of outer and inner detail level specified by the tesselation control shader

Then an intermediate, non-programmable stage creates the desired geometry and passes it to the tesselation evaluation stage. In that stage, you calculate the actual positions of the generated vertices, possibly by using splines.

I will continue using a single triangle as example, but now with working code and screen shots. The main program does not change too much, except that it loads more shaders than usual. Here is the tesselation control shader:

```
#version 410 core

layout(vertices = 3) out;
in vec3 vPosition[]; // From vertex shader
out vec3 tcPosition[]; // Output of TC

uniform int TessLevelInner; // Sent from main program
uniform int TessLevelOuter;

void main()
{
    tcPosition[gl_InvocationID] = vPosition[gl_InvocationID]; // Pass
through the vertex at hand
    gl_TessLevelInner[0] = TessLevelInner; // Decide tesselation level
    gl_TessLevelOuter[0] = TessLevelOuter;
    gl_TessLevelOuter[1] = TessLevelOuter;
    gl_TessLevelOuter[2] = TessLevelOuter;
}
```

In this demo, I determine the detail level by a uniform. Real programs rather do that by other means, like the distance from an edge to the camera.

Here follows the evaluation shader:

```
#version 410 core

//layout(triangles, equal_spacing, cw) in;
layout(triangles) in;
in vec3 tcPosition[]; // Original patch vertices

void main()
{
    vec3 p0 = gl_TessCoord.x * tcPosition[0]; // Barycentric!
    vec3 p1 = gl_TessCoord.y * tcPosition[1];
    vec3 p2 = gl_TessCoord.z * tcPosition[2];
```

```
    gl_Position = vec4(p0 + p1 + p2, 1); // Sum with weights from the
barycentric coords any way we like

// Apply vertex transformation here if we want
}
```

As commented in the code, it is notable that you get the barycentric coordinates for the vertex rather than some index. From these coordinates, we may calculate the actual position that we want the vertex to have. For this demo, I do it as pass-through I can.

Let us now look as the resulting tesselation, in Figure 72.

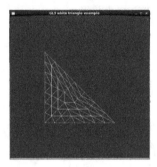

FIGURE 72. A tesselated triangle

So, given a single triangle I could split that up in a number of triangles. If you look at the result, it seems like I have something like detail level 7 on each edge and 4 inner layers. Now, let us see what happens if I play around with the detail level, see Figure 73.

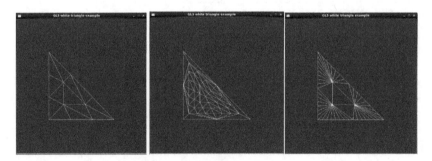

FIGURE 73. A tesselated triangle with varying detail. Left: Low detail on both outer and inner. Middle: Low outer, high inner. Right: High outer, low inner.

What is missing here is clearly to do some nice deformation, following some shape, but also additional data that we may pass through the shader pipeline.

And there is one more thing to consider. Doesn't it cost computations to make this tesselation for every frame? Yes it does, and therefore OpenGL has a feature that lets you create geometry this way and then save it to reuse multiple times! This feature is called *trans-*

form feedback. It allows reuse of online generated/tesselated geometry as well as multi-pass processing of geometry.

So, to repeat:

• Tesselation control determines how many steps of tesselation that you want, how dense output.

• Tesselation evaluation is called for each generated vertex, with unique coordinates from which the position is calculated.

It is very important to notice that, and why, the outer detail is specified for each *edge*. This solves the problem with "gaps" that you can get in level-of-detail implementations when the detail level varies over a model. Here, the edge bordering two neighbor patches should have the same detail, while other edges of those patches may have other detail.

Finally, I want to mention that even if tesselation shaders were new in OpenGL 4 and requires pretty recent hardware, tesselation in OpenGL is *not* new. It existed even in early OpenGL versions, under the name "evaluators". So did we get any real progress or just a repackaging? I say we did. The big advantage here, as with many other features, is *programmability*! We didn't just get the tesselation back in a new form, we got new possibilities to do creative things.

5.9 Other graphics algorithms

There are many other graphics-related shader programming problems, for example volumetric light scattering (God rays) and many others. You are encouraged to explore those topics yourself, possibly as course projects. But we have more in the following chapters.

6. General purpose computations on graphics hardware

An interesting use of graphics co-processors with shader programmability is to use them for general computations that do not necessarily have anything to do with graphics. Concerning games, this implies that the GPU can be used for problems in physics and AI.

This trend has spawned its own name, GPGPU (General Purpose Graphics Processing Unit programming) and its own home page, gpgpu.org. The term GPGPU is, however, being replaced by the more descriptive GPU Computing.

Why should we do non-graphics computations on the GPU when we can do it on the CPU? CPUs have vector co-processors built in, and they get faster, right? A strong argument for GPGPU is that GPUs have shown very large performance improvements while the improvement of CPUs have slowed down considerably.

Examples to applications of GPU programming include:

- Image processing
- Image analysis
- Equation system solving
- Wavelet transforms
- Fourier transforms
- Cosine transforms
- Level sets
- Video coding

There are several technologies for GPU computing, and I will cover three here. One is using shaders, which was the first and therefore "classic" approach. Another, very famous technology is CUDA from NVidia. Finally, there is OpenCL, a technology similar to CUDA but cross-platform.

6.1 GPU computing using shaders

Let us start with general computing with shaders. This may be the "old" way, but let me stress that it is not a bad path. It is mature, your programs will work on just about any reasonably modern hardware, no extra software installations are needed, and the performance is actually very good. I would recommend you to consider this for "real products", image-related ones in particular.

The memory model for GPGPU programming is very different from conventional processing. There is no stack, heap or pointers. It should rather be considered a stream processor, where there is data input and output, and processing kernels that can operate on the stream. No data can be saved other than to the output. It is possible to read from common memory (textures) but not to read and write the same texture.

This model is highly suitable for efficient processing with many parallel kernels, and that is exactly what we have. The processors in the GPU are very simple, but very powerful at the fairly limited things they can do.

In older GPUs, the vertex processors were MIMD processors, while the fragment processors were SIMD. On more recent GPUs, the NVidia 8000 series and up, the architecture is unified so all processors are the same, a kind of "groupwise SIMD".

The GPGPU model can be summarized as follows:

- We have an array of input data. This is put in a texture (or several).
- We produce an array of output data. This arrives in the frame buffer.
- This is produced by a computing kernel, which is a shader.
- The computation is done by one or several rendering passes.
- When we need several passes, the output is rerouted/copied to the input data of the next pass.

6.1.1 Input and output

You load your input data from CPU/RAM to GPU/VRAM using glTexImage2D or similar calls (glTexImage1D etc.).

If our input data is a one-dimensional array of floating-point values, they will end up distributed over the four channels of the texture if you use glTexImage2D the standard way. It is, however, possible to upload into a monochrome texture.

```
array = [a, b, c, d, e, f, g, h…]
textur = [a,b,c,d], [e,f,g,h], …
```

So we load data just as usual:

```
image = readppm("maskros512.ppm", &n, &m);
...
// Load image to texture
glGenTextures(1, &tx1);
glBindTexture(GL_TEXTURE_2D, tx1);
glPixelStorei(GL_UNPACK_ALIGNMENT,1);
glEnable(GL_TEXTURE_2D);
glTexImage2D(GL_TEXTURE_2D,0,3,n,m,0,GL_RGB,GL_UNSIGNED_BYTE, image);
glTexParameterf(GL_TEXTURE_2D,GL_TEXTURE_MAG_FILTER,GL_NEAREST);
glTexParameterf(GL_TEXTURE_2D,GL_TEXTURE_MIN_FILTER,GL_NEAREST);
```

Getting the data out afterwards is not harder. It is copied to CPU/RAM from GPU/VRAM using glReadPixels();

```
// Avoid dithering that might damage data
glDisable(GL_DITHER);
// Read the pixels to the buffer
glReadPixels(0, 0, n, m, GL_RGB, GL_UNSIGNED_BYTE, image);
// Pass it to output
writeppm("rpout.ppm", n, m, image);
```

This operation was a very expensive step in the days of AGP cards, where readout had very low priority, but this is not a lot better with PCI Express cards.

6.1.2 The computation kernel = the shader

The shaders are read and compiled to one or several program objects. A GPGPU application may have several shaders loaded.

Activate the desired shader as needed using glUseProgram[1]();

```
uniform sampler2D texUnit;
void main(void)
{
    vec4 texVal = texture2D(texUnit, gl_TexCoord[0].xy);"

    gl_FragColor = sqrt(texVal);
}
```

Since this is not about rendering fragments in polygons but processing arrays of data, it is more interesting than usual to work with the coordinates of the fragment.

The shader can, for example, look as follows. This particular shader comes from a demo that I believe was an introductory example at GPGPU.org. This is a Laplacian filter for detecting high frequencies, shown in Figure 74. Edges will give a high response, but even more so will local maxima and noise.

---

1. glUseProgramObjectARB for older SDKs

-1	-1	-1
-1	8	-1
-1	-1	-1

FIGURE 74. A simple 3x3 Laplacian filter for detecting high frequencies

If this filter had been properly normalized, it should divide the result by 8, but that would make the resulting signal too low to view.

```
uniform sampler2D texUnit;
void main(void)
{
   const float offset = 1.0 / 512.0;"
   vec2 texCoord = gl_TexCoord[0].xy;"
   vec4 c  = texture(texUnit, texCoord);"
   vec4 bl = texture(texUnit, texCoord + vec2(-offset, -offset));"
   vec4 l  = texture(texUnit, texCoord + vec2(-offset, 0.0));"
   vec4 tl = texture(texUnit, texCoord + vec2(-offset, offset));"
   vec4 t  = texture(texUnit, texCoord + vec2(0.0, offset));"
   vec4 ur = texture(texUnit, texCoord + vec2( offset, offset));"
   vec4 r  = texture(texUnit, texCoord + vec2( offset, 0.0));"
   vec4 br = texture(texUnit, texCoord + vec2( offset, offset));"
   vec4 b  = texture(texUnit, texCoord + vec2(0.0, -offset));"
   gl_FragColor = -8.0 * (c + -0.125 * (bl + l + tl + t + ur + r + br + b));
}
```

See Figure 75 below for an example of the effect of this filter.

6.1.3 Computation = rendering

In the typical GPGPU situation, rendering is done just like in other multipass shader rendering as detailed in section 5.1 at page 63; a single polygon over the entire frame buffer! Textures and frame buffer often have the same size.

Texture   Frame buffer

FIGURE 75. Typical GPGPU situation, processing an entire texture to the frame buffer

The geometry is, again, a single polygon. It can be convenient to set up the camera so that we can render in pixel-based (m by n) coordinates like this:

```
GLfloat quadVertices[] = {
                    0.0f,  0.0f,  0.0f,
                    0.0f,     n,  0.0f,
                       m,     n,  0.0f,
                       m,  0.0f,  0.0f};
GLfloat quadTex[] = {
                    0.0f,  0.0f,
                    0.0f,  1.0f,
                    1.0f,  1.0f,
                    1.0f,  0.0f};
GLuint quadIndices[] = {0, 1, 2, 0, 2, 3};
```

Thus, we can keep the geometry matched to the image size at all times, so we don't have to think in normalized coordinates as often. For our purposes here, that can make sense.

6.1.4 Feedback

In section chapter 5.1, I described how shaders can work in several passes, by using the output from one iteration as input to the next. This kind of feedback is ever-present in GPGPU applications. The bandwidth over the bus to the CPU is limited, so the more that can be done before passing back the data to the CPU, the more efficient will the processing be.

The example we have already seen is running separable filter kernels. Other obvious examples include FFT, but many other problems are solved by multipass shaders.

6.1.5 Interpolation

Texture lookup in the GPU supports linear interpolation, which makes a difference whenever the texture is accessed with coordinates that do not exactly match a texel (GL_LINEAR). While this usually is a matter of filtering to reduce resampling errors, it can sometimes be exploited for accelerating some computations.

A simple example is convolution. Convolution is a simple problem, which can be done without shaders, e.g. using the accumulation buffer. With shaders, the trivial solution works like this:

```
put the data (image, signal) in a texture
for every output sample
    for every element in the convolution kernel
        read from the texture
        multiply by the convolution kernel value for the position
        add to the result
    write result to the output (pixel)
```

This can be optimized by separable convolution kernels, as mentioned in [50]. However, we can sometimes optimize further due to the linear interpolation.

Example: Take two neighbor samples, (c_x, c_y) and (c_x, c_y+1), with convolution kernel coefficients a and b, respectively. Then their contribution to the convolution is

$$r = r + a \cdot t[c_x, c_y] + b \cdot t[c_x, c_y+1]$$

where $t[x, y]$ is the texture lookup. If a and b have the same sign (both positive or both negative), it can be rewritten to

$$r = r + (a+b) \cdot t[c_x, c_y+b/(a+b)]$$

Thus, we access two texels with a single call, which may give us significant speedups in some situations.

6.1.6 Data packing

On older GPUs, the subject of data packing was important, since the hardware was designed to work with groups of four values (RGBA). On modern GPUs, the architecture is more flexible, and the simplest data packing is to upload data into a grayscale buffer. However, other arrangements can be interesting since a texture can not be wider than 8k items. Thus, even though we can avoid the packing into four channels, we may need to pack 1D data into a 2D or 3D texture. Pettersson [20] discusses the packing problem in more detail.

6.1.7 Sorting

Now, over to problems that are common in GPGPU applications. Sorting is one such problem. Sequential sorting algorithms like QuickSort do not work on the parallel architecture. An algorithm that is suitable is *bitonic merge sort*.

The principle for parallel bitonic merge sort is that you can sort parts of the data set separately (typically split in half), and then merge the results. Figure 76 illustrates the process:

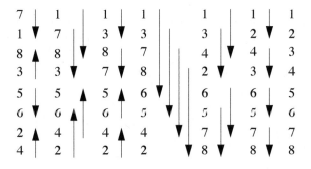

FIGURE 76. Bitonic merge sort

Although the computational complexity of this algorithm can not compete with Quick-Sort, it scales linearly with the number of processors so it is very fast.

6.1.8 Reduction, find maximum

Another common kind of problems is reduction problems. That is problems where we want to extract some limited data from a large data set. A simple case is to find the maximum value. In a sequential program, this is a straight-forward problem, a linear search over the data. In a parallel architecture, however, things look different. The problem is still simple, so it is a nice example of how a problem changes from one architecture to another.

The maximum search on the GPU is performed like this:

We use a resolution pyramid, a set of textures where the smallest is a single pixel and each level is 2x2 bigger. Thus, the textures are 1x1, 2x2, 4x4, 8x8... just like in mip-mapping.

Start at the highest resolution. For each iteration, the shader gets four values from the source texture, takes the maximum and stores that into the smaller destination texture. For an nxn texture, the process takes log(n) iterations, each iteration faster than the previous.

Minimum and mean calculation are equally simple. There are, of course, other reduction problems, like the median, that are less straight-forward.

6.1.9 Conditional execution, "if" statements

The SIMD model gives them both advantage and disadvantage. The biggest disadvantage is the inability to branch. Still, GLSL supports "if" statements! That is by evaluating both branches! What this is all about is that the language emulate functionality that the processors really don't have!

Since both branches of an "if" statement need to be executed as long as any processors get different result, the cost of an "if" statement can be big. There is little point in optimizing away processing by making "if" statements.

Another way to handle conditional execution is *early Z-cull*. [30] Early Z-cull, EZC, performs a depth test before the rasterization unit, and only if it makes the test, the fragment is processed in the fragment processor. This totally avoids the "if" statement in the shader. Instead, the argument to the "if" statement is rendered to the Z buffer as a separate step, writing values like +1 or -1 to the buffer depending on the result. In a second rendering pass, the data is drawn in a Z value between the two values.

6.2 CUDA

Since GLSL and other shading languages are not designed for general computations, other languages have been designed for GPGPU use. Two early examples are *Brook for GPUs* and *Sh*. The strongest player in this field today is probably CUDA.

CUDA (NVIDIA CUDA™) is a GPU processing language designed by NVidia. It is (for better or worse) based on C. CUDA is officially an acronym for "Compute Unified Device Architecture". It will run on any NVidia board with a G80 or better architecture, which means the 8000 series and up, starting with the 8400 board.

With CUDA, important features of the GPU are made accessible. For example, there is a local memory shared by groups of processors (e.g. 16 processors), usually called *shared memory* in CUDA terminology. Using CUDA, this memory can be accessed, and used for local intermediate results. Thus, the rule that only the output image is saved between runs is relaxed.

Also, the destination is not locked to a single fragment the way it is in a shader. This makes scatter algorithms somewhat possible. However, gather is still more efficient.

Still, many of the old GPGPU rules still apply. The interpolation trick, for example, remains. The GPU and GPGPU world does change rapidly, but all rules don't go away in every move.

6.2.1 Hello CUDA

Most CUDA tutorials start with some simple example that is often dubbed "Hello World", although that is usually an ignorant statement since the examples usually do not output "Hello World!" as their result. This is understandable, since it is not entirely obvious how to make an example of parallel computing which has the sole purpose of producing the string "Hello world!". However, not without pride, I can present you with exactly that: A program that is short, simple, does perform parallel processing on the GPU using CUDA, and the result is indeed "Hello World!"!

So, here it is, the *real* "Hello world" for CUDA:

```
// This is the REAL "hello world" for CUDA!
// It takes the string "Hello ", prints it, then passes it to CUDA
// with an array of offsets. Then the offsets are added in parallel
// to produce the string "World!"
// By Ingemar Ragnemalm 2010

// nvcc hello-world.cu -L /usr/local/cuda/lib -lcudart -o hello-world

#include <stdio.h>

const int N = 16;
const int blocksize = 16;

__global__
void hello(char *a, int *b)
{
    a[threadIdx.x] += b[threadIdx.x];
}

int main()
{
    char a[N] = "Hello \0\0\0\0\0\0";
    int b[N] = {15, 10, 6, 0, -11, 1, 0, 0, 0, 0, 0, 0, 0, 0, 0, 0};
```

```
    char *ad;
    int *bd;
    const int csize = N*sizeof(char);
    const int isize = N*sizeof(int);

    printf("%s", a);

    cudaMalloc( (void**)&ad, csize );
    cudaMalloc( (void**)&bd, isize );
    cudaMemcpy( ad, a, csize, cudaMemcpyHostToDevice );
    cudaMemcpy( bd, b, isize, cudaMemcpyHostToDevice );

    dim3 dimBlock( blocksize, 1 );
    dim3 dimGrid( 1, 1 );
    hello<<<dimGrid, dimBlock>>>(ad, bd);
    cudaMemcpy( a, ad, csize, cudaMemcpyDeviceToHost );
    cudaFree( ad );
    cudaFree( bd );

    printf("%s\n", a);
    return EXIT_SUCCESS;
}
```

I hope the source itself explains what it is doing; it takes a string and an array of offsets to produce "World!" from "Hello ". But a few more clarifications are called for.

What you see here is, in one and the same file, both CPU and GPU code. This integration is very elegant. The amount of code to compile and launch the GPU kernel is extremely small.

The __global__ code is the kernel, executed on the GPU, in parallel. Note the threadIdx.x. That is the thread identifier, which must be used to calculate where in the data to operate. "Real" CUDA programs use both thread and block identifiers.

We allocate memory on the GPU from the CPU, using cudaMalloc. We can then upload and download data with cudaMemcpy, using the arguments cudaMemcpyDeviceToHost or cudaMemcpyHostToDevice to denote the copying direction. Finally, we can dispose of GPU memory using cudaFree.

One of the most challenging issues when you start with CUDA is the concepts of grid, block and thread. The grid is the whole computing, which is split into a number of blocks, which each contains a number of threads. This division scheme describes how the computing is distributed over the GPU.

The weird statement

```
hello<<<dimGrid, dimBlock>>>(ad, bd);
```

is the actual execution of the kernel.

6.2.2 Threads, blocks, warps and grid

A number of concepts are introduced to describe how computing is distributed over the hardware. This is important since the scope of shared memory depends on the blocks.

When running a kernel, it runs on one *grid*. A grid can be divided into a number of *blocks*. On every block, a number of *treads* run. This is illustrated in Figure 77.

The concept of a *warp* describes how many threads are actually active at a time. This concept is actually of less importance for your programming at the moment. Let us focus on the threads, blocks and the grid. But there is one detail that you need to know: *All* your threads are not executed in parallel! They are executed a bunch at a time. So you can *not* design with total parallelism in mind, where all threads execute the same instructions at the same time. You can get racing problems in your code, and then you must synchronize yourself. (See below.)

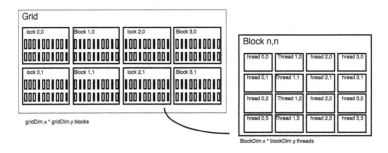

FIGURE 77. Distributing computing over threads and blocks

As exemplified in the Hello World! example, we must use the thread and block indices when computing in order to know what data a particular thread should access. Here is a somewhat more complete example (for 1-dimensional data):

```
// Kernel that executes on the CUDA device
__global__ void square_array(float *a, int N)
{
    int idx = blockIdx.x * blockDim.x + threadIdx.x;
    if (idx<N) a[idx] = a[idx] * a[idx];
}
```

In this simple example, we calculate the square of each item. Note that one argument, N, tells the size of the array, so any thread with an index outside the array will not do any useful work, and it shouldn't.

6.2.3 More about the architecture

Since we get closer to the architecture when using CUDA and similar GPU computing solutions, we need to discuss a few more details.

The GPU was originally built around the graphics pipeline. Shaders were executed in specific parts, one for vertex processors and another with fragment processors. With the G80 architecture (see section 6.6 at page 114) the GPU was transformed to a more general parallel processing architecture, with a few special parts remaining of the pipeline.

The shaders, of any kind, were now executed in an array of generic processors. This array is built in a number of groups, called *Streaming Multiprocessors* (SMs), each containing a number of *Stream Processors* (SPs). The latter is what is usually called "cores" in GPU specifications, although the number of "cores" is a highly debatable number.

An SM is really a vector processor which can operate on a number of elements at once. You usually don't think of the hardware that way though. You should rather consider each thread to be an (almost) independent executing process. It has its own identification number with which you can decide what data it should operate on.

This is where the blocks and threads above fits. The SMs correspond to a block in CUDA, and the SPs to threads. That is, you can have many more blocks than SMs and more threads than SPs, since they will be queued until all are executed, but one block will, when running, execute on a specific SM and a thread on a specific SP.

The queuing of blocks and threads is a main feature of the hardware. You not only can but *should* have more threads than SPs in an SM, and more blocks than SMs. This lets you keep the hardware occupied. A major feature is to have threads running while other threads wait for memory access.

6.2.4 Memory access in CUDA

One of the major problems with parallel processing in general and GPU computing in particular is memory access. We are used to having large amounts of primary memory available, with huge caches that hide memory latency. With CUDA, this works differently. Pre-Fermi hardware had very little caching capability. Fermi changes that somewhat, but we will focus on pre-Fermi here.

Global memory, that is the VRAM of the GPU, is very expensive to access. We are actually talking about *hundreds* of clock cycles! To hide this, we use many parallel threads, so whenever a thread is waiting for memory access, another thread kicks in and starts working. This is how the GPU achieves performance in general, it is not limited to CUDA, but with CUDA the problem becomes more visible.

Another, equally important issue, is to take advantage of local memory. The local memory is a small memory bank connected to a group of processors. Its latency is far lower than the global memory. We should use that as a kind of "manual cache".

This gives us a modified computing model:

- Upload data to global GPU memory
- For a number of parts, do:

- Upload partial data to shared memory
- Process partial data
- Write partial data to global memory
- Download result to host

For any algorithm that will access the same data several times, this can make a big difference. However, this also leads to the next problem - synchronization.

As soon as you do something where one part of a computation depends on a result from another thread, you must synchronize! This is done in the kernel with

```
__syncthreads()
```

Thus, your code may work like this:

- Read to shared memory
- __syncthreads()
- Process shared memory
- __synchthreads()
- Write result to global memory

There is one more major issue with memory access: coalescing. Memory latency does not only depend on what kind of memory we use, but also in which order. If you read an array linearly, one item at a time in order, the access will be faster than unordered access. The difference can be as big as 10 times! In the next section, we will look at an example of memory coalescing.

6.2.5 Matrix transpose example

Let us take an example: Matrix transpose. This involves no computations, it is a pure reorganization problem, so the entire computation consists of memory accesses.

A naive implementation may look like this:

```
__global__ void transpose_naive(float *odata, float* idata, int width,
int height)
{
    unsigned int xIndex = blockDim.x * blockIdx.x + threadIdx.x;
    unsigned int yIndex = blockDim.y * blockIdx.y + threadIdx.y;

    if (xIndex < width && yIndex < height)
    {
        unsigned int index_in  = xIndex + width * yIndex;
        unsigned int index_out = yIndex + height * xIndex;
        odata[index_out] = idata[index_in];
    }
}
```

Perfectly sensible, isn't it? Can't be done differently? Oh yes it can. Consider the memory access pattern. You read column by column and write row by row. This gives a memory access pattern like in Figure 78:

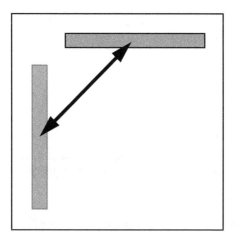

FIGURE 78. Matrix transpose gives coalescing problems due to order of access

And this is bad! Either when reading or writing we access the expensive global memory non-coalesced! This will cost performance.

And there is another way, namely to use shared memory. Then you can read a small block at a time, flip it when in shared memory, and then write the entire block to the output, as in Figure 79. It takes more operations and more code, but you will come out a winner since all the global accesses are optimized.

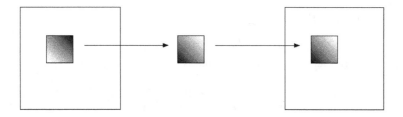

FIGURE 79. Matrix transpose, coalescing solution

To use shared memory, we declare a block of memory as __shared__. It must be small enough to fit in the shared memory, which is typically around 16k.

So here is the better version:

```
__global__ void transpose(float *odata, float *idata, int width, int
height)
{
    __shared__ float block[BLOCK_DIM][BLOCK_DIM+1];
```

```
    // read the matrix tile into shared memory
    unsigned int xIndex = blockIdx.x * BLOCK_DIM + threadIdx.x;
    unsigned int yIndex = blockIdx.y * BLOCK_DIM + threadIdx.y;
    if((xIndex < width) && (yIndex < height))
    {
        unsigned int index_in = yIndex * width + xIndex;
        block[threadIdx.y][threadIdx.x] = idata[index_in];
    }

    __syncthreads();

    // write the transposed matrix tile to global memory
    xIndex = blockIdx.y * BLOCK_DIM + threadIdx.x;
    yIndex = blockIdx.x * BLOCK_DIM + threadIdx.y;
    if((xIndex < height) && (yIndex < width))
    {
        unsigned int index_out = yIndex * height + xIndex;
        odata[index_out] = block[threadIdx.x][threadIdx.y];
    }
}
```

The result is bigger, more complex code, but it is much faster!

There are a few rules of thumb to follow when doing coalesced memory accesses:

- The data block should start on a multiple of 64
- It should be accessed in order (by thread number)
- It is allowed to have threads skipping their item
- Data should be in blocks of 4, 8 or 16 bytes

Not too hard? Well, I wouldn't say that. You will need to find your bottlenecks and make them fit the rules. That is not always easy.

6.2.6 Other issues with CUDA

I hope this brief text will get you started on CUDA, but we do not have space here to make a full coverage. Just let me give you the pointers to the most important issues.

There are several kinds of memory to access, not only global and shared memory but also constant memory and, most importantly, *texture memory*. The interesting thing with texture memory is that it comes with a read-only cache. This can make it very fast if the data patterns are suitable (i.e. with many local accesses). We also get texture filtering in hardware, that is linear interpolation, and texture memory is especially good for handling 4 floats at a time (float4).

You can bind data to a texture unit with cudaBindTextureToArray(). However, the experience by myself as well as others is that texture memory is a troublemaker in CUDA, where much of the elegance is lost. Your mileage may vary, but I would advise you to work by example, in this case more than ever.

Finally, let me mention debugging. Debugging is a hard problem on GPUs. Various solutions are being worked on, new debugging tools have been announced. However, CUDA has had one debugging tool from the start, CUDA emulation mode.

When using the emulation mode, CUDA programs are compiled to CPU only versions, using the compiler switch

```
--device-emulation
```

This lets you run CUDA (slowly) on the CPU, which means that you can at least emulate it on non-NVidia hardware, and you can use standard debugging tricks, like printf().

6.3 OpenCL

A related effort is OpenCL, which has the advantage that it runs on different architectures. OpenCL was released in 2009. It does not have the integration of CUDA. Your OpenCL main program rather looks somewhat like a GLSL program, loading kernels from text files, compiles and runs. An advantage of this approach is that you do not need any special compiler for the host program, but you can compile it with GCC (if you write in C), and OpenCL can easily be used from any language. Personally, I have successfully used it from FPC.

The kernel language is very similar to what CUDA uses. However, there are a few differences in terminology, so expect a little confusion at first.

6.4 Compute shaders

The concept of *compute shaders* was first introduced in Microsoft DirectX. More recently, OpenGL has incorporated the concept in order to get a GPU computing solution more tightly coupled to graphics than CUDA and OpenCL.

6.5 Performance and bottlenecks

Above, I have outlined the principles and major problems with GPGPU applications. Now, with the complexity that it implies, with complex sets of shaders or kernels running parallel programs with poor debugging possibilities, and overhead for moving data to and from the GPU, is this really worthwhile? Why can this be an advantage?

- The parallelism of the GPU is clearly the major argument for it.
- The GPU works natively with floating-point.
- The mass-market target brings the price down.
- The processors in a GPU are more specialized than a CPU and therefore simpler, so more processors can fit on a single chip.
- The programming tools give the flexibility needed to solve non-graphics problems even on shaders, and even more so with CUDA and OpenCL.

The GPU as a number-crunching unit has the following performance:

The NVidia 6800 Ultra, which I would not consider extremely old, has 6 vertex processors and 16 fragment processors. This implies a very respectable 35 GFLOPS, which is comparable with a Cray X1. The newer NVidia 280GTX has 240 shader processors (unified), and performs as much as 933 GFLOPS, while the even more recent NVidia 480GTX does 1345 GFLOPS.

There are some important bottlenecks to consider:

- The GPU works best with algorithms that are inherently parallel. It is not possible to use the result of neighbor pixels from the same iteration in shaders. This is possible when using CUDA or OpenCL.

- The data bus was, for a long time, an important bottleneck! The processing in the GPU can sometimes take less time than the readout of the result. This was a big problem with AGP cards. With PCI Express, this has improved a lot. In well optimized cases, with large amounts of data at a time, it is possible for the newest boards to output 5 Gb/s, which should be enough for most practical purposes, since the CPU won't be able to handle it anyway.

- The numerical precision is not on par with CPUs! Only single-precision floating-point, and not fulfilling the IEEE 754 standard (1 bit worse). Cuda can do it better but it costs performance.

So does it pay? The CPU speed increase has been declining, but multi-core CPUs are common and the number of cores are increasing. Can the GPU really challenge a 8-core CPU? It seems it can, at least for some applications, and in many cases it does much more than that. Back in 2005, Erik Pettersson made his master thesis on image processing on the GPU [20]. Even at that time, the difference was impressive. A speed increase of over 18 times was reported comparing a high-end GPU of the time (7800GTX) to a high-end CPU (P4), and with mobile GPUs the difference was still as big as 8 times! Today, it is not hard to find algorithms that run 100 times faster than the CPU, and even algorithms that do not fit the GPU all that well can still often outperform the CPU!

What this is all about is the transition to parallel computing for high-performance computing. GPU computing is a central part in that process.

6.6 GPU history

Finally, let me look back down the history of GPUs, not only for nostalgic reasons.

The stone age of GPUs starts at the 70's. Highly specialized graphics hardware was designed, often as pure research projects. In Linköping, the PICAP series was built, mostly used for image processing. It was the base of several spin-off companies and was followed by several other image-related hardware projects (GOP, LAPP).

In the 80's, some 3D games were showing up on personal computers, running mostly in software or with the limited hardware support that could be used. The first steps towards consumer-level GPUs were taken with hardware sprites.

In the 90's, software rendering for 3D games was a hot topic up to 1995, with games like Wolfenstein 3D and Doom, typically running in 320x240 pixels. The 3D engines were limited, typically only allowing vertical and horizontal surfaces, not arbitrary slopes.

In 1991, there were 2D accelerator boards for graphics professionals, accelerating 2D operations. 3D accelerators appeared as a separate line of products, and dedicated graphics work stations, especially from SGI, were outstanding in the early 90's.

Shader programs appeared already in Pixar's Renderman in 1988. This was purely for off-line rendering, like Toy Story. The language used was *Renderman shading language*, a language with some similarities to C. There were as much as 6 different types of shaders in the system: Light source shader, Volume shader, Transformation shader, Surface shader, Displacement shader and Imager shader.

The big revolution came in 1996, with the 3dfx Voodoo 1. This board was the first 3D acceleration board for the consumer market. It had the following specifications:

- 50 MHz
- 4-6 Mb VRAM
- cost about 3000 Swedish crowns

The board had no VGA controller and no support for 2D graphics. It was plugged in between the 2D graphics board and the screen by special cables, so it could assume control over the screen when needed.

It had a single texture unit, so there was no multi texturing support. Despite the clumsy installation and in our view horrible performance, it was a major revolution at the time, a quantum leap in price/performance for 3D graphics. Blocky, limited graphics in 320x240 was replaced by interpolated graphics with many limitations removed, running in 640x480 or more! This makes it the start of the GPU era, the most significant GPU release ever.

The very first game that supported the Voodoo 1 was the unscrupulous Indiana Jones rip-off Tomb Raider. This may be one of the reasons why the series became so popular and long running. Among other important games with Voodoo 1 support was Quake 1.

The period 1996-2000 gave us faster GPUs, higher fill rate but also more and more features. 3dfx Voodoo 2 had two texturing units. In 1999, the first GeForce board introduced transformations and lighting calculations in hardware, lowering the CPU burden and thereby allowing higher polygon counts.

A surprising event was the decline of 3dfx. The company did some miscalculations, and ran into conflicts with partner manufacturers, while NVidia came to dominate the market more and more. Finally, 3dfx went out of business, selling the remains to NVidia.

2001 gave us the second major revolution, the GPU with shader program support. GeForce 3 was the first, and ATI soon followed with Radeon 8500. From there, the shader support improved rapidly.

The first generation, 2001, had vertex shaders with 128 instructions, and no flow control. The fragment shaders were limited to as little as 8-14 instructions! Already the next year, 2002, came the second generation in ATI 9000 and GeForce FX. The vertex shader now allowed 256 instructions, and fragment shaders the more respectable 96-512 instructions.

The third generation came 2004, with NVidia 6000/7000 and ATI X. The shader sizes were now 512 instruction or more in both vertex and fragment shaders, and there were also dynamic flow control and prediction in both.

The fourth generation came 2006 with the NVidia 8000/9000 series, introducing a unified architecture that runs vertex and fragment shaders in the same processors. New boards and processors still arrive in a high pace. After some time with relatively slow pace, we recently have seen Geforce GTX280, 260, Radeon HD4870 and 4850 providing a step up in performance. They are still similar to the 8000 series.

In 2010, the fifth generation arrived, the Fermi architecture, that is the GeForce 400 series. High precision floating-point capability is boosted, and single-precision computing power now peaks at 1345 GFLOPS.

2012 gave us the Kepler architecture, the NVidia 600 series followed by the 700 series, and the special high-end board Titan. Kepler was mainly an effort my NVidia to take back the lead in gaming performance, so the GPU computing performance is essentially unchanged from Fermi, despite a huge increase in number of cores (to a level similar to what AMD has had for some time).

It has been said that the performance of GPUs are increasing by "double Moore", double in 9 month rather than 18! This has been somewhat less consistent recent years, but the performance race between NVidia and ATI/AMD is fierce. The number of computing cores (stream processors) in the GPUs is an interesting measure from G80 and onwards. The original G80 could have as many as 128 cores, excellent for its time.

While NVidia was focusing on general computing performance with the Fermi series, AMD could take the lead in graphics performance. AMD's 6000 series had as much as 1500 cores in 2010, and the newer 7000 series has over 2000. NVidia has been catching up in 2012, with the Kepler series (600 series) with as much as 1500 cores on a chip.

Note, however, that the number of cores is somewhat misleading. The 512 cores in the 400-500 series from NVidia is not really as much that the 1500 in the 600 series. It is a question of how you count them. We have things like pipelining to take into account.

More recently, NVidia has followed the Kepler series with Maxwell (900 series) and Pascal (1000 series) and the Titan boards (as well as corresponding professional boards), while AMDs current boards are the Rx 400 series. For graphics and gaming purposes, benchmarks currently indicate NVidia to be in the lead. However, the leadership varies.

When bitcoin mining on GPUs was hot, the AMD R9 was in great demand as the primary choice.

It is clear that the astonishing raw performance improvements slowed down around 2005, but the development has not stopped. A modern dual-core CPU (3 GHz dual-core Pentium 4 Extreme Edition) performs around 25 GFLOPS, so the CPUs have much to catch up.

For desktop systems, I would say that any GPU older than the G80 is of no practical interest. Over that, it becomes a question of performance and new features. However, with the arrival of Vulkan, we have one new limit to consider. NVidia supports Vulkan from Kepler and up, AMD from 700 series, fully from R9. Intel, finally, has full support from the Skylake CPUs. This will be increasingly important when CPUs get more and more cores.

But all computers are not stationary, dedicated gaming machines! The stationary computer market is declining, while portable computers have grown more popular. It seems as if low-cost portable computers is a bigger market, and the GPUs in them are notoriously less powerful. And if that is not enough, we must also consider various pocket-size devices like cellular phones.

So the conclusion from the history is that we still need to look backwards sometimes. When the most powerful hardware is available, we can do all that we wish, but all too often we do not have that hardware and must fall back on simpler, older solutions.

6.7 Future

Now that I have just covered history, I must note that new history is being written around us. OpenGL 3.0, released in 2008, signalled that OpenGL will change more rapidly than before, moving along the same lines as OpenGL ES (OpenGL for embedded systems). OpenGL 4 emphasizes this even more. The fixed pipeline, burdened with many special fixes, is being phased out. As I noted in the section about multi-texturing, there are advanced methods there that I claimed was not very interesting since you can use shaders instead. The ARB seems to agree. Shaders is the future of computer graphics.

On the more scary side, all that old code with fixed pipeline stuff and no shaders has to be rewritten to stay current, and the learning curve is getting steeper. 3.0 does not break the old code, but OpenGL 3.2 and beyond has a strict "core" profile where many old calls are removed, accessible only through a "compatibility mode". Note, however, that it is not very hard to write a simple layer of glue code re-implementing the most vital parts of the fixed pipeline, so most old code will not break as badly as it may seem.

Another important news in 2009 is the release of OpenCL (mentioned above, page 113), the cross-hardware competitor to CUDA. In 2012, WebGL and WebCL are new, interesting additions, providing web interfaces to high-performance graphics and computing.

So in case anyone doubted it, computer graphics keeps moving. Things are still changing pretty fast.

7. Other graphics topics

This is a catch-all chapter for graphics topics that did not fit elsewhere. The topics of text rendering will be covered, and I will also spend some time on hair and clouds. Most topics here are only covered briefly.

7.1 Clouds

Rendering clouds is a trivial thing on the most basic level, clouds seen from the ground. They are usually part of a skybox/skydome texture, or, if we want them to move over the sky, billboards with pictures of clouds. The fixed sky is a bit dull, but billboards are all we need for most ground-based games and animations.

There are, however, a few features that we need more sophisticated models to fulfill. They include the following:

- Clouds that change over time, change form, break up.
- Clouds that have different shape when viewed from different directions.
- Clouds that correctly reflect and transmit light.
- Clouds that you can fly through while still looking realistic.

Clearly, the needs are highest for flight simulators with high realism. There are several approaches to get a higher realism:

A particle system, where each particle is rendered as a billboard. The billboards are highly transparent. The number of billboards can be fairly low.

Metaballs are more ambitious, a point-based approach where each point contributes to a density function, typically by a function like $y = r^{-2}$. This kind of methods are similar to the point-based methods for deformable objects (chapter 12.8) but then used for extracting an isosurface at a treshold value. For the cloud rendering case, we rather want a smoother transition. A ray-tracer may work directly with the density field, while real-time methods should consider intermediate representations, like storing the density function in a volumetric texture.

A noise function, as suggested in Volume 1, can give good results. In Volume 1, I suggested that a noise function with a frequency spectrum of f^{-1} is a good start. Perlin [21] did the classic work in this field. Thus, colored noise functions are often called *Perlin noise*.

Out of these two, the point-based method has the important advantage that it is easier to control the dynamics of the cloud. Both can be rendered using a volumetric texture, but we can also save memory and rendering time by working with sets of billboards or sets of textured ellipsoids.

Simulating a realistic light in clouds is a field of its own. Some general facts can be used for rough approximations. Clouds should be darker on the bottom side than the top. This can be the only basis for lightning, but it clearly ignores the position of the sun and will be highly incorrect at mornings and evenings.

Most work on more realistic cloud lighting is for off-line rendering. An exception is the work of Harris [22].

There are models for lighting of clouds that are based on the scattering of light in the water drops. The model can be based on a single reflection, or multiple, where the latter is the most exact. Harris [22] uses a multiple scattering model called "multiple forward scattering" based on the assumption that most of the light goes forward, skipping the backwards component.

John Nilsson [23] did his diploma thesis on cloud rendering and implemented a cloud rendering algorithm for commercial flight simulator use. He designed his clouds using sets of ellipsoids, sampled a set of random points over these ellipsoids, and rendered using a billboard-based approach with level-of-detail. His algorithm is illustrated by Figure 80.

FIGURE 80. Cloud generation using ellipsoids for the overall shape and random particles for distributing billboards for rendering.

In the figure, the final cloud has no lighting applied. Nilsson also applied lighting similar to Harris [22], taking both light source position and viewer position into account.

Modern GPUs have made the border between on-line and off-line fuzzy, and this applies to cloud rendering as well. In 2010, the project "Cloudy" in the TSBK03 course [75], investigated volume cloud rendering, and found that real-time performance was possible if

Other graphics topics

the size of the volume was kept under a suitable limit, in their case 64x64x64, while higher resolutions still requires off-line rendering times. An example from the project is shown in Figure 81.

FIGURE 81. The "bunny cloud" example from the Cloudy project [75]

7.2 Vegetation

In Volume 1, fractals and other procedural methods were used to get a groundwork for generating vegetation, trees in particular. I will continue the discussion here, based on the overview of the problem made by Emil Jansson [31] in his diploma thesis. I will mainly talk about trees, but the discussion applies to most kind of plants.

We discern between *mechanistic* and *descriptive* models [52].

A mechanistic model simulates the growth of the tree, and is therefore suitable for systems where the vegetation should change over time. The models can be based on biology and thus be very realistic. The growth of the tree can be affected by outer forces.

The photograph in Figure 82 is a real-life example of the effect of outer forces on trees. The right tree has grown naturally, while the left has been a "work of art" by being covered by a net. The work of art was called "under the influence" and was one of the best works of art ever at Linköping University. Not that there is much competition... but that is another discussion.

I will not make any claims whether the mechanistic models can handle this kind of deformation or not, but a mechanistic model has the possibility, while a descriptive model would need two completely different parameter sets, despite that they are two trees of the same kind.

FIGURE 82. Two real trees at Linköping University

A descriptive model focuses only on describing the appearance of the tree, with no basis in how it came to look that way. They are intuitive to use and suitable for most real-time purposes. The fractal-based method in Volume 1 was a descriptive method.

Another cathegorization is *local-to-global* and *global-to-local* modeling. A local-to-global model is specified explicitly part by part, and then assembled to a whole. The global-to-local method works from a set of parameters and generates the tree from them.

Finally, trees can be generated using recursive or non-recursive methods. Fractal-based methods are highly recursive and self-similar. The self-similarity is, however, not always an advantage and can limit the freedom and possibilities to control the look of the tree as desired. It is obvious that the local-to-global/global-to-local and recursive/non-recursive cathegorizations are pretty dependent. Local-to-global methods are typically non-recursive while global-to-local methods are by nature nice to implement recursively.

Weber & Penn [51] describes a descriptive method for generating trees, based on a parameter set that they made an effort to keep small. The need for a small parameter sets becomes obvious when you want to populate large worlds using only the parameters in the world data. That allows great variety while keeping the data size down.

Level-of-detail methods are important when rendering plants, since a detailed tree needs an enormous amounts of polygons. The level of detail are controlled by two methods, geometrical simplification and instancing. Geometrical simplification is often used by replacing parts of the tree by billboards. Instancing simplifies by reusing parts, which reduces the amount of data to store the tree. The simplest instancing is to use the same leaf for all leaves in a tree. The two methods are not exclusive but can be used in combination.

Jansson [31] created a full-featured system with both instancing and billboarding, partially based on Weber & Penn's work. Close-up, the tree is rendered at full detail, with a polygon for every leaf. At higher distance, larger and larger parts of the tree are rendered using bill-

Other graphics topics

boards, until the whole tree is a billboard, and even several trees on a billboard. See Figure 83 for a screenshot from this work.

FIGURE 83. Computer generated tree by Emil Jansson. From [31].

Another issue when rendering plants is to *animate* them. Making a tree wave with the wind may seem like a simple problem, but the many parts makes it awkward. We may choose to make every branch a rotational joint, but this would be incorrect since the whole branch bends in a real tree. It would be more realistic to deform the tree using deformable object methods.

7.3 Hair, fur and grass

Rendering realistic hair used to be one of the impossible dreams in computer graphics, especially in real-time animation. It should be noted that grass, although strictly being vegetation, is animated in the same way as hair and fur. It shares the same problem; the shape is not a problem while the numbers is, while other vegetation have complex geometry.

In old 3D games, there was an old-style way of doing hair, and that is giving the character hilarious "caps" of low-polygon meshes, which gives them a manga/anime look. But today, that style is no longer needed. Instead, we can render the hair with high realism.

For off-line graphics, the movie Monster's Inc. was one of the significant breakthroughs, with the fluffy hair of the main character, Sullivan. Doing the same thing in real-time, with a result like Figure 84, is also possible today. This is a good example of how the massive improvement of performance makes the impossible doable.

There are several methods that can be used today, including methods based on volume textures and parallax mapping. It is not strictly impossible to model each separate hair or strain of grass as polygons. That can be done with geometry shaders (see chapter 5.7). Another approach that is often used is to use sets of billboards with hair texture. [6] The possibility to reuse the same texture over and over is big since the detail is so self-similar.

FIGURE 84. Rendered hair or fur

When rendering hair and fur, Heise [6] suggests that you should use two kinds of fur polygons. On the skin of the furry object, you put several layers of shell polygons, with transparent textures of the fur. The multiple layers give it depth. Then you add polygons sticking out from the body, called *fins*, as in Figure 85.

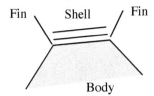

FIGURE 85. Principle for fur rendering, with multiple shell polygons on the body and fins sticking out.

Designing the textures may be a problem, but it is mainly a question of drawing straws in a more or less random pattern, and including proper noise.

7.4 Water

Modeling and rendering water is yet another challenge which I want to introduce briefly.

The task of modeling water can be done in several different ways, like:

- Array of volume elements.
- Array of surface elements (a simplification of the former).
- Particle system.
- Harmonic functions modeling wave patterns.

The most exact models are made using mathematical models, i.e. Navier-Stokes equations, which are about physics simulation, not graphics. See chapter 12. These equations have been successfully applied for creating very realistic fluids, using arrays of volume elements.

Rendering water is another matter. Two problems have to be solved, extracting the surface and rendering.

Extracting the surface is trivial for the harmonic function models, but the others will need a surface extraction algorithm. I recommend the *marching cubes* algorithm [73], which suits fluids very well. For the volume elements approach, it can be applied directly. For a particle system, you need to divide space into a grid, counting the number of particles in each cell. Another approach for particles is to map a density function onto each particle, using the summed density as a function from which to find a treshold.

Here we are moving into a broader field, that of volume graphics, graphics based on volumentric data. This is the subject for chapter 7.5.

7.5 Volume graphics

A relatively new trend in computer graphics is to work with volumetric data rather than surfaces [98]. The support for 3D textures as well as the rising performance of GPUs have made it managable to work with these much larger amounts of data in real time.

Volumetric data can, as mentioned in many places in this book, be created from particle systems, or be a simulation of continuous data such as fluids, but it may also be created by conversion from surface representations such as a mesh.

The conversion of a scene into a volumetric representation has many applications, often based on the fact that a volumetric representation is much easier to navigate than a mesh-based one. Remember that we often accelerate collision detection by splitting the scene into cells. Here we take it further, into more detail.

Global illumination is a lot easier in a grid. Similarily, ambient occlusion is downright easy in this domain. The problem of following a ray in ray-casting and ray-tracing is simplified to a simple scanning similar to a line drawing algorithm. A particularly interesting method in this area is *voxel cone tracing*, where illumination data is accessed at varying resolution/filtering using 3D textures and the built-in mip-mapping. [108] Other applications include processing of faulty mesh objects [101] and detecting suitable boundary shapes for collision detection [99].

7.5.1 Voxelization, creating volumetric data from surfaces

When creating a voxel representation from a mesh, it may, as always, be important to remember what the application is. What do we really need? Do we want a volume where every voxel inside the model is filled (*solid voxelization*), or do we rather want a thin layer of filled voxels along the surface (*surface voxelization*)? This will affect the choice of algorithm.

An obvious but slow way to voxelize a (filled) volume is to check each potential voxel with inside-outside tests, similar to the 2D ones from Volume 1. This requires much calculations for computing intersections with all polygons.

A popular approach is to render each polygon into the 3D data, much in the same way that a polygon is rendered to screen. It is possible to use the polygon rendering system in the GPU, which obviously is good for performance. [104] Actually, it is rather an extension to the standard polygon rendering, where you convert the pixel found to a voxel and write the voxel with using the imageStore() functionality.

Since this is performed by the ordinary polygon rendering algorithm, using this for surface voxelization comes natural. This rendering is performed like this: We must select a face of the volume on which the polygon will seem to be drawn. It is not really drawn there, but at the proper depth into the volume.

A problem with approach this is that the polygon rendering algorithm is made for finding all pixels that needs covering from a specific direction, not creating a continuous surface in 3D. Thus, there may be gaps in the surface. In order to overcome this problem, the polygons must be rendered from the side corresponding to the *largest component in the normal vector of the polygon*. See Figure 86.

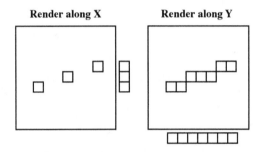

FIGURE 86. 2D illustration of the problem of rendering polygons based on the surfaces of the volume

In the figure, we render a line of voxels in the box by rendering the line shown at the border. If this is done along the X axis (left), the line will need very few pixels, and the result will be broken up in the box (volume). However, along Y (right), we are rendering along the main axis of the line (polygon) and therefore we will render voxels without gaps. This is in perfect analogy with the line drawing algorithms in Volume 1.

Figure 86 is, obviously, just illustrating the principle mapped to 2D. In 3D we can illustrate it like in Figure 87 (adapted from [104] which does it much better).

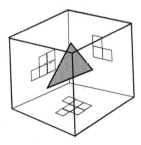

FIGURE 87. Rendering a polygon from different sides of the volume.

Even this may not be sufficient. In order to avoid further errors, so called *conservative rasterization* may be used, which means that any voxel touched by any part of a primitive should be considered filled. On recent NVidia GPUs (Maxwell and up) this has built-in support.

Does this sound complicated? Another approach is to use the depth buffer [102]. For convex objects, this is very easy, especially if we want the volume to be filled rather than finding edge voxels. For non-convex shapes, the method is not guaranteed to give a perfect result, but on the other hand, the errors will often be in areas where they can't be seen anyway.

The simplest approach to voxelization by depth buffer is to render the model twice, once with back-face culling and once with front-face culling, producing depth buffers giving the depth of both sides of the model. It should be obvious that this rendering must be made with parallel projection, unless we desire to sample the volume non-uniformly.

We can trivially expand this to rendering along all three basis axes, generating multiple depth buffers which will be able to represent concavities in the model from most directions.

After producing the depth buffers, the contents of these buffers are used to produce the voxelization. Here it makes sense to return to imageStore, rendering a quad over the entire side of the volume, and filling any voxels inside all depth buffers. The disadvantage with this compared to the polygon based approach above is that it is only suited for solid voxelization, while attempts to use this for surface voxelization on non-convex shapes will cause gaps.

Now, if we have an existing voxelization, the question is how to store it. Storing volume data can be very expensive, so there are many methods for optimizing it, like octrees. The "sparse voxel octree" (which essentially simply means an octree) will give a highly optimized storage, but to the expense of highly data dependent computing with irregular memory access patterns. Therefore, it may be better to choose less optimized storage strategies. For example, simple range encoding can be very efficient.

7.5.2 Extracting surfaces from volumetric data with Marching Cubes

The marching cubes algorithm (and its little brother in 2D, marching squares) extracts surfaces from sampled data by scanning through the data, placing surfaces anywhere the data passes a given treshold. This algorithm is particularly popular in visualization of volumetric data, such as tomography scans, but it is just as useful for rendering fluids.

The marching cubes algorithm is a bit hard to clarify in limited space, but the marching squares is a lot easier. An example is given in Figure 88, where each data point is given as the corners in a grid, and the extracted surface is made by calculating suitable intersections in this grid using a treshold of 2.5.

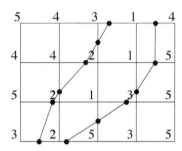

FIGURE 88. Marching squares (2D version of marching cubes) applied to some data with a treshold of 2.5. The black spots indicate the calculated treshold position.

From the calculated intersections, surfaces are constructed, working on one cube/square at a time. In 2D, you have only four edges to consider, with 0, 2 or 4 intersections, making the construction fairly straight-forward. In 3D, the construction is more complicated, with 12 edges to consider, so you can build a binary pattern from which a configuration can be found in a lookup table, telling exactly which points should be connected to surfaces.

Fluids is just one application of marching cubes. Figure 89 shows marching cubes being used in an augmented reality project from 2010 by Frida Schlaug, editing 3D shapes by operating in thin air, affecting the density of a volume grid [74].

FIGURE 89. Marching cubes used in an augmented reality project (picture from [74])

Note that marching cubes is a well established algorithm, so it is easy to find sample implementations, if you don't want to make your own. Making your own is always a good thing, but that depends on whether you want an experience or a tool.

Finally, we have the problem of rendering. Water is transparent as well as reflective, so a good water rendering should handle reflections, transparency and, hardest of all, refraction. Realistic refraction requires the scene behind the surface (e.g. ocean floor) to be pre-rendered to a texture so it can be accessed from your shader. If you also need to handle scene changes under the water (fish, submarines) you need to do multi-pass rendering, preferably using FBOs. The same goes for reflections, of course.

Other graphics topics

In chapter 12, we will have a look at some models for deformable shapes that can be suitable for water modeling.

7.6 Shading and BRDF

Now, let us switch to the topic of light models and shading. From Volume 1, you should be familiar with the Phong model:

$$\text{color} = k_a \cdot I_a + \Sigma \left(k_d \cdot I_i \cdot (N \cdot L) + k_s \cdot I_i \cdot (R \cdot V)^n \right)$$

as well as the half-vector variant, the Blinn-Phong model.

This is the simple default model that the fixed pipeline in OpenGL uses, per vertex, with Gouraud shading between vertices. It is easy to use but the result is only half-decent. With a shader program, you can improve it by using Phong shading. Static lighting can also be improved by light mapping. So far, no news. The result is not physically based, and can not represent all materials. See Figure 90 for a few radically different reflection types.

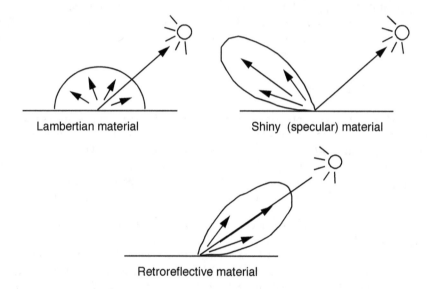

Lambertian material   Shiny (specular) material

Retroreflective material

FIGURE 90. Examples of materials with different reflectiveness

But you can also improve the situation by using more advanced lighting models. A *bi-directional reflectance distribution function* (BRDF for short) is a function that maps incoming light to outgoing.

$$\text{BRDF}(\Theta_i, \phi_i, \Theta_o, \phi_o)$$

The four parameters describe incoming and outgoing direction by two angles each. It can also be expressed as a function of two vectors, in- and outgoing.

$$\text{BRDF}(\mathbf{L}, \mathbf{V})$$

Thus, given any viewing direction $\mathbf{V}$ and a light vector $\mathbf{L}$ the function returns a lighting value.

We do not state any specific function that the BRDF should be. The BRDF can be assigned any function of the parameters. This means that we have much freedom in describing the light exchange. While simple models like Phong and Blinn-Phong can only describe a limited set of materials, a BRDF can describe materials with very different behavior. One such kind of material is retroreflective materials, which is what you see in e.g. road signs.

A more typical material that needs a BRDF for properly describing it is brushed metal.

Finding the BRDF for a specific material is a matter of using a surface model. Such models include the Microfacets model, the Oren-Nayar model, the Cook-Torrance model and the Ashikhmin model. See Astle [6] for more information and code snippets.

Depending on what model you use, you may be able to use an analytical function for the BRDF, but if that is not possible, then the BRDF can also be defined by an array sampling the function, stored in a texture. If we can reduce the degrees of freedom somewhat from the original four, we can reduce the size of such a texture. Another approach to simplify the problem is to separate the function into two.

7.7 Deferred shading

Deferred shading [6] is an optimization method for shading calculations. It was introduces as by Deering as early as 1988 but has not been practical for real-time use until more recently. The traditional *forward shading* performs all lighting calculations as the geometry passes through the graphics pipeline. This results in much unnecessary shading calculations for surfaces that are not visible. With deferred shading, the rendering of the geometry and the shading are done in separate steps.

The trick is that the geometry is rendered to an intermediate buffer, the G-buffer (geometric buffer). The G-buffer holds pixelwise information about the position (x, y, z), normal vector (x, y, z), material and more. Astle [6] uses three channels (RGBA values per pixel) while Fahlén [18] uses four. Since the G-buffer needs more than a single RGBA, it needs to be several image buffers, which make the multiple render targets feature highly desirable, or we will need to run several passes. Floating-point textures are also needed, and, obviously, programmable shaders.

The algorithm for rendering is, roughly, like this (adapted from [18]):

```
for each object
    render to the G-buffer
for each light
    for each pixel in the framebuffer
        accumulate framebuffer value from light and G-buffer
image space post-processing
```

Other graphics topics

The post processing may include effects like blooming and tone mapping (see chapter 5.3).

- The method has some advantages, including
- Each triangle is rendered only once
- Each pixel is shaded only once
- Post-processing effects are easy to integrate.
- Works with any shading technique.

but there are also drawbacks:

- Transparency is difficult.
- All lighting calculations must be done per pixel.
- High hardware requirements.

In scenes with massive overdraw, deferred shading could help, but I don't consider it the most important technique today. The effect is usually not major and there are other ways to deal with performance. For a deeper treatment of the method, see [6].

7.8 3D displays for games

This section was written with Jens Ogniewski, partially based on a research paper [88] and an internal presentation [87].

3D displays create the illusion of three-dimensional images with strong impression of depth by offering each eye of the beholder a different view of the scene. Unfortunately, from a computer graphics point of view, it is not quite as simple as rendering the same scene from two different viewpoints. In this section I will give a brief overview of common pitfalls and discuss how to use 3D displays. Some of the advice will seem to be limiting, but than again this is often the case for usability guidelines. Keep in mind that you can bend (or even break) them a little, as long as you know what you are doing. By adhering to only a few points, you should be able to use a 3D display correctly, which can heighten the atmosphere and the immersion of the user immensely. Note, however, that every game will profit differently, some might not even gain anything at all.

Not much research has been done on using 3D displays for gaming. They are much better understood by the video community, and most of the results we find there can be applied to computer games as well. Most of this section is based on these works.

The following text deals with the following topics:

We discuss important 3D display techniques. This is mainly stereoscopical techniques, but also motion parallax. The stereoscopical techniques include

- Anaglyph 3D
- Shutter-based systems

- Polarization-based systems
- Autostereoscopic systems

We also discuss motion parallax as an interesting alternative.

Then we discuss problems with 3D display, including:

- Crosstalk
- Eye strain
- The wander off problem

Then we conclude with a discussion on design considerations and performance.

7.8.1 Stereoscopy systems

Nearly all current 3D displays are using *stereoscopy*. Stereoscopy is the ability of seeing three-dimensional based on the differences in perception between the left and the right eye. This is accomplished by presenting each eye a different view of the scene. They vary only in the way these images are delivered to the correct eye. Glasses-based systems use optical filters (shutter or polarization based) for that purpose, while glasses-free (so called autostereoscopic) systems rely on lenses or lenticules.

The simplest form of glasses-based 3D is *anaglyph 3D*, using *anaglyphical glasses*, the infamous red-green glasses used in early 3D TV experiments and also many printed stereoscopic images. Two different images are presented on the same surface, in different colors, and the color filters in the glasses separate the two images. This technique is very old, first presented around 1853 [90].

Shutter-based systems are the most commonly used 3D displays in home electronics. They use glasses which contain transistors that can switch between being either completely transparent and completely opaque. They will be transparent for one eye if the screen shows an image that is meant for this eye, while they are opaque for the other one. By swiftly switching between images for each eye it is barely noticeable that only one eye sees an image at any point in time. This method is nothing new, already in the 80:s you could buy a set of glasses to be used with the Sega Master System, though the number of available games were limited.

Polarization-based systems uses polarized light to separate the different images. You probably know that light can be considered as a sinus curve. The question is: if the light ray is moving along the x-axis, and oscillating in y direction, how does it moves in z-direction? The answer in this special case is: not at all. If you look at this ray *from the front* it will appear like a line on the y axis. But it hasn't got to be that way. It could equally oscillate around the z-axis and look like a line on the z-axis instead, as well as everything in between. This angle between the y- and z-axis is called the polarization of the light. There are filters available that let only light pass that is polarized in a certain way, and these can be used to construct a 3D display. This has the disadvantage that some light may pass to the wrong eye, especially if the observer tilts her/his head. Therefore, so called *circular polarization* is used nowadays (see Figure 91).

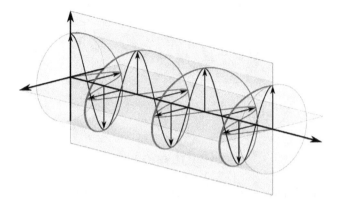

FIGURE 91. Polarized light: polarized around the x-plane, around the z-plane, and circular polarization. (Wikimedia Commons)

The light is given a spin so that it changes its polarization over time. Note that there are two possible ways how this change can go: clockwise (from +y to +z) or counterclockwise (from +y to minus z), so we can use one for the right eye image and the other one for the left eye image. In fact, this is the technique that modern 3D cinemas have been using for years, going as far back as to the first color 3D movies in 1952.

Shutter-glasses can be more easily adopted to existing home-electronics systems (since they only require a high framerate), and in fact many of the current displays on the market already support 3D by this method, especially the more expensive ones. Polarization-based systems are a little bit more complicated, since the polarization filter has to be built into the display, which also reduces the resolution of the display by half (one half for each eye). However, polarized glasses are much cheaper, since shutter-glasses need a built-in electronic to synchronize with the screen (to be able to set the glasses transparent/opaque in accordance with the image on the screen). Shutter-glasses also need battery supply for these electronics, they are heavier and they can be susceptible to flicker.

Finally, *autostereoscopic displays* don't use glasses at all, but lenses or lenticules to direct the light of some pixels in one, the rest in another direction (see Figure 92). The observer has to remain on a certain position for this to work. There are techniques to get around this, though none have made a huge impact in the mass market yet.

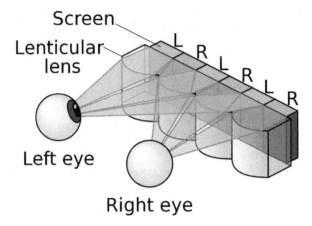

FIGURE 92. Autostereoscopic display using lenses or lenticules (Wikimedia Commons)

The brute force method to give the viewer more freedom is to have more than two channels, more than two images side by side. Commercial systems exist that use 5 channels. This does give more freedom, for the cost of lost horizontal spatial resolution.

When using lenses, the viewer can get much of the emitted light with good efficiency. A simpler but less efficient method is to use barriers, as shown in Figure 93.

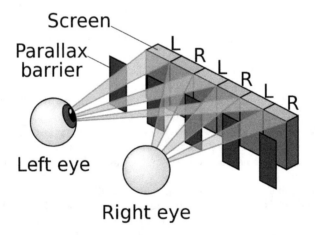

FIGURE 93. Autostereoscopic system using barriers (Wikimedia Commons)

Autostereoscopic 3D is one of the most common and long-lived 3D systems in existence, in the form of 3D still images, like 3D post cards. These cards are made with a simple raster surface with two or more channels. Apart from the 3D effect, they are sometimes used for simple, short animations, using the channels as animation frames.

7.8.2 Motion parallax

A totally different method of producing an impression of 3D is *motion parallax*. This is related to "parallax scroll" which was an example of depth cues for pseudo-3D animation in Volume 1. Instead of stereo this uses motion as major depth cue, taking the viewer's position into account. This gives the possibility to observe the object from different viewpoints, based on the position of the beholder. You can watch demonstrations of this technology on-line, by Johnny Chung Lee [85].

In order to implement motion parallax effects in your games you need some kind of *user tracking*, to know where the viewer is located. This can be done by a webcam and some image processing, or devices such as the Microsoft Kinect. This problem simplifies for hand-held devices, where we can use the up direction delivered by a gyroscope or accelerometer. Some hand-held games do indeed exploit motion parallax with good results. However, the technique has the drawback that it is only usable for single-viewer systems.

A study on motion parallax effects, based on using a webcam with user tracking using the OpenCV library was done in our group in 2010 by Yen Tran [89]. As expected, a strong 3D impression resulted even without 3D glasses or similar stereoscopic technology. A related study was made by Jonas Andersson Hultgren in 2011 [91], applying motion parallax to a driving simulator. In both cases, the user will experience improved realism though the ability to "look around corners", moving the head sideways to get a different view.

It is notable that motion parallax can be used in conjunction with stereoscopic 3D.

7.8.3 3D display limitations and problems

Since all 3D displays only direct part of the light to each eye, their brightness is reduced compared to a similar 2D display. Also, the light separation is not 100%, so each eye may see part of the light which is intended for the other one. This is called *crosstalk* or *ghosting*. Guardbands are introduced to minimize these artifacts, e.g. the glasses of a shutter-based system will be opaque for both eyes while it switches between the images. Similar techniques exists for the other 3D display techniques as well. These guardbands minimize the brightness further, and in fact this trade-off (brightness vs. crosstalk) is one of the most important decisions when designing a 3D display.

It should be pointed out that a low percentage of the populace (less than 10) isn't able to see stereoscopic at all, although it is possible for most of them to learn it.

The last, and biggest problem with 3D displays is, however, *eye strain*.

Eye strain means that there is too much stress on the human visual system. It expresses itself in different symptoms, from which headache is the most common. It should be pointed out that 3D displays are not the only ones subjected to it. Every display can cause it to some degree. E.g. tube-based screens can induce it by their flickering. 3D displays, however, are especially prone to eye-strain, since they cause objects to appear at places at which they are not, and thus deliver conflicting signals to the human visual system. More scientifically, the *vergence distance* (where the objects seems to be according to the differences between the images of each eye) and the *accommodation distance* (where the objects really are) are not the same. The accommodation distance is based on physical properties like focal length, and it is in fact the same principal if focusing with a photo camera. If watching a 3D display you might notice that the image is either a little bit blurry (meaning your eyes are trying to focus according to the vergence distance) or that you get double images (in case your eyes are focusing more based on the accomodation distance). See Figure 94.

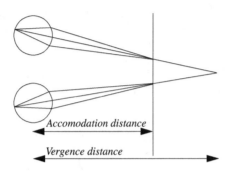

FIGURE 94. Vergence distance versus accommodation distance

The main goal for the game designer regarding 3D displays is then to try to reduce the eye-strain as much as possible. A possibility to do this is to keep the scene as simple as possible, meaning using as few objects as possible and limiting the number and speed of motions were possible, especially the ones in depth.

Luckily, there are other measures as well, which increase the experience and limit the eye strain at the same time. Stereoscopy is only one of the so called depth cues that allows the human visual system to place objects in space. Others include occlusion, distance blur and shadows (among others) and have been exploited by artists for literally centuries to add depth to their paintings. It is important that all these cues work together correctly. As well as they can maximize user-comfort and heighten the immersion if they match, can depth cues not only limit the experience, but also inevitably lead to eye-strain, if they are contradicting. A classic example in this regard, which unfortunately can be seen all to often in current computer graphics, are objects more far away which occlude other objects which are closer to the observer. This happens mainly due to hub-elements, like the current score or lives etc. which are blended with the scene after rendering it at a certain, constant depth.

Another important question is whether objects should be placed behind or in front of the screen. While objects in front are more eye-catching, they are, unfortunately, more stressing for the human visual system. They also suffer from artifacts which I call the *wander off problem*; If objects placed in front of the screen they can be truncated by the screen's border. This looks very strange and unnatural. Therefore, you should take care to avoid these situations. I would advise objects to be placed behind the screen in most cases, and save in front objects for certain shock events, like a trench penetrating the windshield after a car crash. This will also help these rare events to stand out more, delivering a more intense experience to the user when it really counts.

7.8.4 Design discussion

A last thing you should think about is whether your graphical techniques will work in 3D or not. Basically all effects that fake a 3D impression are questionable and result in compromised quality. Billboards, for example, will look like a picture of the object in question, but not like the object itself. A list of popular techniques and if they work or not (and how it might be possible to make them work) has been made available by NVidia [86]. Also, be aware that artifacts may be more annoying in 3D than they are in 2D. Aliasing, for example, can become quite a problem, especially if it is different for each eye. But since this mainly occurs with objects far away from the observer you can often solve it by introducing distance blur (which is also a depth cue). For that, you need to render the whole scene twice, which seems to be a little bit costly. But if you are using any other after-effects (like a HDR-bloom) you might be able to combine them with the distance blur into the same pass. Polarization-based as well as autostereoscopic 3D displays need to blend the two pictures for the eyes on the screen anyway, so you might be able to introduce the distance blur in that step.

As you can see, designing a game for a 3D display has its own challenges, and there are even more details than I mentioned here. If you want to know more, take a look at a short seminar I did last year [87], which is a good starting point, especially since it provides you with many useful references. But to give you a short summarized guideline:

Make sure that all depths and depth cues, especially stereoscopy and occlusion, are consistent and natural.

7.9 Other topics

The field of computer graphics is vast and well researched. There are many other topics where we could go deeper.

One such area is photon mapping, an algorithm related to ray-tracing. In photon mapping, rays are traced both from camera and light sources. However, this is a typical off-line method that I currently consider of fairly little interest for game programming. For movie making, things are different.

Yet another subject, which we touched upon above, is augmented reality. This concept is a mix of computer graphics and computer vision, where artificial objects are inserted into real videos. Games have been produced based on augmented reality, e.g. using smartphones.

Other topics, more interesting for games, are advanced level-of-detail methods and automatic generation of content, subjects that were introduced in Volume 1. They are well worth going deeper into.

8. Rigid body animation

Realistic movement and realistic collisions are increasingly important in games. We are not happy with dull, repetitive keyframe animation or over-simplified, nonrealistic movement. We want animation based on the laws of physics, physically based animation.

This chapter is about game physics with rigid bodies. I will intentionally be rather brief on the basic physics. Most of the physics involved is too basic to deserve a detailed treatment here. In case you need to brush up your high school physics, by all means look it up in other sources. A great free source is the SIGGRAPH course notes by Baraff et al. [9] It is significantly better than most "game physics" textbooks, so start there. Among available text books, Parent [8] is a good choice. But seriously, download Baraff's manuscript and use that as a complement to this text. This text is a summary, Baraff's text is the real thing.

Now, let us look at the problem of rigid body animation. There are several aspects of this problem. I choose to approach the problem from the gaming/animation side. There is a lot of knowledge in physics, but I will deliberately only consider the theory that is most needed. So let us take some cases that we want to handle, and see what we can do about them.

First of all, let me mention a few different cases that are of interest, and give an overview of the problem.

Cases:

- Movement and collisions of small objects. This is nicely handled by particle systems.

- Movement and collisions of convex rigid bodies. This requires some more tools.

- Movement and collisions of deformable bodies. This is a totally different case, which requires totally different methods. Some of them - but not all - consist of particle systems where the particles no longer move independently. This case will be covered by a later chapter.

There are a number of subproblems:

The first problem is to model the shape, not only its shape but its position, speed, rotation... There will be some new data needed here. A part of this problem is to update the data for each frame, to take a step forward in time.

The second problem is to actually detect a collision. This was treated in Volume 1, and most of what was said there still holds: Work with simplified bounding shapes, go down on detailed meshes when needed. Subdivide space to make the tests faster. We will add some new methods for doing the narrow phase.

The third problem is to handle the collision. This is where things get interesting. There are many options and surprisingly many pitfalls.

Let us consider each subproblem for two cases: *point masses* (particles) with spherical shape and a simple *rigid body*, an arbitrary polyhedron.

8.1 Case 1: Animation of point masses

Since this was covered pretty well in Volume 1, this is mostly a repetition.

8.1.1 Data representation

For objects modeled by point masses, we may represent the object with position, speed and mass, allowing no rotation or setting it explicitly.

All the information about the particle can be represented by a simple data structure:

```
X(t) translation
v(t) speed
f force accumulator
m mass
```

So in order to run an iteration, you sum all forces that affect the particle (gravity, friction...), calculate acceleration as $a = f/m$, update the speed from the acceleration ($v(t+\Delta) = v(t) + \Delta \cdot a$) and the position from the speed ($X(t+\Delta) = X(t) + \Delta \cdot v(t+\Delta)$). This is Euler integration, which is generally OK for independent particles. The more they interact, the better integration you will need. See chapter 10 for better integration methods.

8.1.2 Collision detection of point masses

For spheres, it is just a matter of distance. Finding the point of impact is reasonably simple. The spheres can be separated at the shortest possible distance. This is simple and works well as long as speeds are not too high. An alternative is to calculate the point of impact from their speeds.

8.1.3 Collision response

As described in Volume 1, making particles collide in realistic ways is not too hard. First of all, you might want to separate the objects, since you may get repeated collisions if you don't. Second, you need to calculate the new speed.

For equal mass, it is a matter of splitting the speed vectors in normal and tangent components, and exchange the normal components between the objects. For the more general case, you preserve momentum (m·v) and calculate the result from that.

Many of the possible problems that may occur here are similar to what happens in the full rigid body case, so I leave it for now. All in all, point masses are really simple to work with. But what if we want an object that can rotate, so an off-center hit will make it rotate, as well as if it slides over a floor? This will turn out to be a whole lot harder.

8.2 Case 2: Animation of rigid bodies

With rigid bodies, we add one feature: rotation. This is, of course, a very big step. Rigid body dynamics can fill entire courses. We do not have the room for a full treatment here. This will rather be an overview.

8.2.1 Data representation

In order to support rotation, we must add rotation parameters to the state. In the simplest case, a shape that is totally rotation symmetric, the rotation and rotation speed will do. In order to handle other shapes, we also need to model the moment of inertia[1] of the shape.

Most other sources start this problem by going through all the components, and then putting it together at the end. I will take the opposite approach. Let us start with the result and then look at the parts. The question is: what do you have to do to implement a simulation?

I will mostly follow the model of Baraff [9].

The total state vector is:

```
X(t) translation (vector)
R(t) rotation (matrix)
P(t) linear momentum = ∫ r dm (vector)
L(t) angular momentum² = ∫ r x v dm
```

The shape needs a set of constant parameters:

```
m: the mass
J: Inertia matrix
Center of mass
```

---

1. Tröghetsmoment

2. Rörelsemängdsmoment

The center of mass may be given implicitly by placing the model properly centered on it, so the center of mass is at the origin of the model coordinates. In that case, no extra data is needed for the center of mass.

The speed and rotational speed are implicit from the momentum and angular momentum, so we do not need to include them as separate variables.

In order to update the state, we need the first derivatives:

```
v(t)          speed
w*(t)·R(t)    angular speed multiplied by rotation
F(t)          linear force
T(t)          torque
```

Given the first derivatives, it is possible to integrate the state vector to a new state. Alas, I have not given formulas for computing the first derivatives.

8.2.2 Calculation of the first derivatives

The next question is how we calculate each of the parameters in the first derivative. Once we have all first derivatives, we can update the system by stepping in that direction.

The speed is the easiest part, it is calculated from the momentum and mass as the momentum over the mass:

$$v(t) = P \cdot \frac{1}{m}$$

The linear force $F(t)$ is simply accumulated from external forces. How to calculate them is a matter that we will have to return to later.

The Torque[1] $T(t)$ is similar: For each external force f, you take the cross product between the force vector and a vector r from the center of mass to the point of impact. The cross product is the torque.

$$T = r \times f$$

Just a note about applying forces. Should we really apply the force both as a full linear force and a rotational one? Isn't the force split into different effects, so some of the energy is spent on rotation and some on translation?

Consider a force f acting on a point at radius r from the center of mass, as in Figure 95. You can assign three help forces, one f at the center of mass and the other two f/2 at radius r at opposite direction. These three help forces cancel each other and change nothing.

---

1. Vridmoment

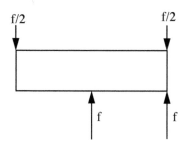

FIGURE 95. A force (bottom right) with help forces (top and lower middle)

The two forces on the right can be summed together and we get the result in Figure 96:

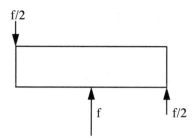

FIGURE 96. Resulting forces with translational and rotational effects separated.

It is pretty obvious from the figure that we have a force f that acts directly on the center of mass to cause translation, and forces of $2 \cdot f/2 = f$ that only cause rotation.

This double effect of a single force is also discussed by Baraff [9] in his section 5.5, "Force vs. Torque Puzzle".

In the figure above, the force is perpendicular to the surface. When this is not the case, a first step should be to consider friction. Then you need to split the force into a tangent and a perpendicular part, and change the tangent part depending on friction. This splitting of forces was also discussed in Volume 1.

Let us continue with the first derivatives. The rotation speed is the biggest problem. The rotation speed (denoted ω) as such is simply a 3-component vector, where the direction shows the rotation axis and the length speed. However, its dependency of forces and torque is somewhat complex since it depends on the current rotation of the shape. It can be calculated this way:

The rotational (angular) momentum $\mathbf{L}$ and the rotational speed has the following relation:

$$\mathbf{L} = \mathbf{J} \cdot \omega$$

where J is the moment of inertia[1]. In 2D these are scalars, but in 3D $\mathbf{L}$ and ω are vectors while J is a matrix. Thus:

$$\omega = J^{-1} \cdot L$$

Since it is a 3x3 matrix, inverting it should not be a problem.

The moment of inertia, J, is the relation between torque and resulting rotation, how much it "resists rotation" to put it in simple words. Let us wait yet some time with its definition and calculation, and return to it below (after the summary box). For now, it is a 3x3 matrix that is given by the geometry of the object (and its mass, density, density variation...).

However, J above is the inertia matrix[1] for that specific rotation of the body. This will be different for every possible rotation. In order to get J and its inverse, we start with the moment of inertia matrix calculated for the shape in its non-rotated position, model coordinates or "body space" as Baraff calls it. Let us call it J_{body}.

We invert it to J_{body}^{-1}. But in order to calculate the rotation speed, we must also rotate it to match the current orientation of the object in world coordinates. This is done by

$$J^{-1} = R \cdot J_{body}^{-1} \cdot R^T$$

Thus, we need to keep J_{body}^{-1} with the shape, and calculate J^{-1} and from that ω. Fine. That leaves the weird last step:

$$dR = \omega^*(t) \cdot R(t)$$

Not only did we need the rotation speed, we also need to form a matrix from it, w^*. Given a vector $\omega = \omega_x, \omega_y, \omega_z$, it looks like this:

$$\omega^* = \begin{bmatrix} 0 & -\omega_z & \omega_y \\ \omega_z & 0 & -\omega_x \\ -\omega_y & \omega_x & 0 \end{bmatrix}$$

This is an antisymmetric matrix that really is the cross product rewritten to a matrix:

$$\begin{bmatrix} 0 & -\omega_z & \omega_y \\ \omega_z & 0 & -\omega_x \\ -\omega_y & \omega_x & 0 \end{bmatrix} \begin{bmatrix} x \\ y \\ z \end{bmatrix} = \begin{bmatrix} -y\omega_z + z\omega_y \\ x\omega_z - z\omega_x \\ -x\omega_y + y\omega_x \end{bmatrix} = \begin{bmatrix} \omega_x \\ \omega_y \\ \omega_z \end{bmatrix} \times \begin{bmatrix} x \\ y \\ z \end{bmatrix}$$

Now we have most components in place and I can make a summary in Figure 97:

---

1. The moment of inertia is often denoted I, when it is scalar, but as a matrix this conflicts with the identity matrix I.

1. Tröghetsmatris

```
State  d/dt                    Calculations:
x      v                       F = sum all forces
R      dR                      v = P·1/m
P      F                       T = RxF
L      T
                               Calculation of dR:
Constants:                     J⁻¹ = R·J⁻¹model·Rᵀ
J⁻¹model
m                              ω = J⁻¹ · L
                               ω* = CrossMatrix(ω)
Temporary:                     dR = ω*·R
v
ω
```

FIGURE 97. Summary of rigid body motion

Now there is just one big hole in this presentation: The moment of inertia.

For a point mass rotating around a specific axis at distance r, the moment of inertia is a scalar $J = m \cdot r^2$. For a set of particles we can sum them together. When this is generalized to 3D, we get the following matrix [9]:

$$J = \sum_i \begin{bmatrix} m_i(r_{iy}^2 + r_{iz}^2) & -m_i r_{ix} r_{iy} & -m_i r_{ix} r_{iz} \\ -m_i r_{ix} r_{iy} & m_i(r_{ix}^2 + r_{iz}^2) & -m_i r_{iy} r_{iz} \\ -m_i r_{ix} r_{iz} & -m_i r_{iy} r_{iz} & m_i(r_{ix}^2 + r_{iy}^2) \end{bmatrix}$$

It is, of course, possible to express this as an integral. If it is easiest to calculate by an integral or a sum is up to the implementation. A sampling of a body will give a perfectly usable inertia matrix, while the integral, of course, will be more exact.

It is possible to simplify this matrix to only include the diagonal components, to *diagonalize* it, if its default position is aligned with its principal axes. This principal axes are found as the eigenvectors of the inertia matrix. [28] For simple bodies like a rectangular box, its principal axes are parallel to its edges, so the inertia matrix of an AABB is a diagonal matrix!

So calculating the inertia matrix is not impossible in any way. Do you still feel like making simplifications? As long as your object is not extremely asymmetrical, you can assume that the inertia matrix is a diagonal matrix, and if it is compact, you can assume that the components along the diagonal are similar. As a more general simplification, you can calculate the moment of inertia by a straight sum of the vertices, each with an equal part of the mass, and you can put a big mass at the center if you want to make it behave less like a thin shell.

That was quite a few symbols, and some non-standard operations, but the number of pages to describe it is pretty small. The same holds for a straight-forward implementation.

8.2.3 Implementation

I will now outline the algorithm as such. It will be somewhat similar to the code snippets by Baraff [9].

I assume that you have bunch of linear algebra functions:

- Dot product
- Cross product
- Matrix multiplication
- Inverse of 3x3 matrix
- Transpose a 3x3 matrix

We need one less obvious utility function:

- CrossMatrix, creates the matrix for cross product from the speed vector, as given above.

A data structure is needed for the shape and its state:

```
RigidBody = record
    // Constant
    mass: GLfloat;
    J, Ji: Matrix3D; // inertia matrix + inverse

    // State
    x: Point3D;
    R: Matrix3D;
    P: Point3D; // linear momentum
    L: Point3D; // angular momentum

    // Accumulated quantities
    F: Point3D; // accumulated force
    T: Point3D; // accumulated torque

    // Temporary variables
    Jiloc: Matrix3D; // Inverse, local coord
    v: Point3D; // speed, calc from P
    omega: Point3D; // rotation, calc from L
end;
```

I use instances of this structure, named rb (rigid body) below.

Initialization:

Set the constant parts, including calculating and inverting the inertia matrix. Set the state to the desired initial value.

Run an iteration like this:

Rigid body animation

- Zero accumulated quantities (F and T).

- Calculate speed (v) and inertia matrix (Jinv):
```
rb.v := rb.P * (1/rb.mass); // P/mass;
Rt := Transpose(rb.R);
rb.Jiloc := rb.R * rb.Ji * Rt; // R * Ji * Rt
rb.omega := rb.Jiloc * rb.L; // Jiloc * L
```

- Apply forces, accumulating F and T. We must have a resulting position for the impact of the total force.
```
rb.F := rb.F + F;
rb.t := rb.t + localImpact x F;
```

- Calculate the first derivative of the rotation. I calculate it times the time step since that is what we need later anyway.
```
Rd := CrossMatrix( rb.omega * deltaT ) * rb.R);
```

- Update: Using the first derivative, simple Euler integration is performed by, for each component, adding the derivative times the time step.
```
rb.x := rb.x + deltaT * rb.v;
rb.R := MatrixAdd(rb.R, Rd, deltaT);
rb.P := rb.P + deltaT * rb.F;
rb.L := rb.L + deltaT * rb.T;
```

Finally, we must make sure R stays orthonormal!

```
OrthoNormalizeMatrix(rb.R);
```

I deliberately chose to make a simple Euler step, which makes my implementation a lot shorter and simpler than others. Baraff packs the entire state into a vector, sends it to an integrator, and unpacks. This is not a bad thing, but I left it out to add as a separate feature, which is the subject of the next section.

8.2.4 Integration of rotation

This additive approach is just fine for all components but one: The rotation. Linearly adding a fraction of the derivative of a matrix to the matrix in order to find new states, does that really have any meaning at all? Sure, the infinitesimal step is correct, but since the function is inherently non-linear, it will obviously go wrong very fast. A very first, minimal thing to do about this is to make an othonormalization step after each iteration.

What Baraff suggests is to make a single, dumb vector out of the entire state and integrate the best you can, and put back. It is made a vector in order to be sent to an integrator that will have no knowledge of the meaning of each part, and thereby be general and easy to replace.

What we have now is a physics simulator that actually works. As long as the speeds as well as the step lengths are small, it will behave pretty well even with Euler integration. I can apply a force and the object will translate and rotate. With better integrators (Baraff suggests fourth-order Runge-Kutta) it will be more stable and allow higher speeds.

But using better integration methods is only a part of the solution. Since we give the simulation the very strange task of integrating matrices, which is somewhat like interpolating between them, as a way to do rotation, we should ask if the representation is truly suitable.

The standard answer is "use quaternions", and that is not a bad idea. A quaternion is an entity that consists of four numbers. When used to represent rotation, three of its components actually form the rotation axis. Just knowing that is enough to realize that quaternions are not magical at all. We will return to them in a later chapter.

There is one more answer. How about representing the rotation by a vector, just like the rotation speed? This is, surprisingly, an option that is ignored by most literature. (Not, however, by Parent [8].) You can fully represent a 3D rotation by not four but three number, a simple three-component vector, by making the magnitude the amount of rotation.

In both cases, it becomes easier to apply the rotation by a change of rotation instead of corrupting a rotation matrix.

8.3 Collision detection

In Volume 1, I covered the following collision detection methods:

- Spheres are tested using their radius.
- Polyhedra-polyhedra collisions are tested based on the Separating Axis Theorem (SAT).
- Mixed situations, spheres to polyhedra, is done with a modified approach.
- Spatial subdivision (hierarchical groupings, BSP, quadtrees) are used for limiting the number of tests.
- Simplified bounding shapes are used to simplify the tests (the broad phase-narrow phase method).

The weakest part here is the polyhedra-polyhedra collisions. The basic SAT-based intersection tests will detect a collision of convex polyhedra, but it will not do it very efficiently, and it will not report a well-chosen point of impact. Every vertex in each shape is tested against every plane in the other, both ways, and the same is done for edges, which is even more expensive.

We can see some possibilities to optimize this. One is hinted in Volume one: If you remember which plane that was the separating plane the last time, it may be the right one in the next frame as well. Such information can accelerate the process significantly.

We may do further optimizations, e.g. by testing those vertices and surfaces that are closest to the center of the other. We can consider adding some information to our models. Polyhedra are typically built from triangles, referring to vertices by indices. A simple improvement of the representation of a polyhedra is to add information to each vertex, referring to each triangle it is used by. Then we can iterate over the surface searching locally for the point we are looking for. This is indeed what is done in some algorithms.

In the following, I will discuss two specific methods:

- Intersection volume calculation.

- Closest point calculation with the GJK algorithm.

8.3.1 Intersection volume calculation

A very straight-forward collision detection is to calculate the intersection volume. This may sound complicated, but it is not necessarily more demanding than the SAT-based algorithm from Volume 1.

In order to calculate the intersection volume, all vertices of one polyhedra A are tested against the faces of another polyhedra B. We do that one face at a time. Each face defines a plane, splitting 3D space in two halves, the "inside half-plane" and "outside half-plane".

Using this information, all parts of A that are in the "outside half-plane" are cut away. Faces with all vertices outside are discarded, and those with some vertices outside are split. See Figure 98.

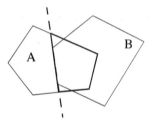

FIGURE 98. Intersection calculation. The polygon A is split over a plane defined by a face of B.

With some luck, or a good choice of first plane to split by, shape A will quickly be reduced to a much smaller shape than the original, containing little more than the vertices that are actually overlapping B, which will speed up the completion of the process. After all faces of B have been tested against the progressively smaller remains of A, we will produce the intersection volume.

This is not the most efficient method around, but it is fairly simple and produces the intersection volume, which in itself has a valuable information that can be used for high precision collision handling.

8.3.2 Closest point calculation with the GJK algorithm.

The Gilbert-Johnson-Keerthi algorithm, GJK for short, is an efficient and popular solution for collision detection [70]. It does not produce the intersection volume, but rather finds the closest points of two convex polyhedra. If the result of the last test between the two shapes is saved and used as starting point, it can be extremely fast.

Ericsson [4] gives a fairly mathematical description of GJK. Here, I will attempt to explain it from a more intuitive view.

GJK is based on *support mapping*, which is the task of finding the extreme point of a shape in a specified direction. In the figure below, the support mapping of the shape A along the vector $\mathbf{v}$, $S_A(\mathbf{v})$, results in the point $\mathbf{p}$. It should be obvious that this can be calculated by the dot product, so that for a shape where the vertices are p_k for a certain range of k, See Figure 99.

$$S_A(\mathbf{v}) = p_i \text{ where i maximizes } \mathbf{v} \bullet p_i$$

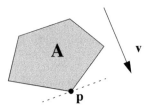

FIGURE 99. The support mapping of the shape A along the vector v is the point p.

Figure 100 is an example case for the algorithm. We wish to test two shapes, A and B, for collision. As you can see from the figure, they do not collide, so this is what the GJK algorithm should result in. But we will now see how it figures that out.

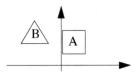

FIGURE 100. The two shapes for our GJK example.

The GJK algorithm implicitly uses the combined shape of two shapes A and B, the dilation of A by the negated (convoluted) B, the Minkowski sum A⊕-B. See Figure 101. We will now, in the figures, follow both the sum and the separate shapes through the search for the closest point.

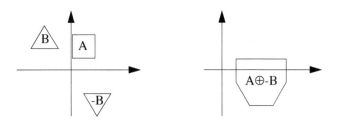

FIGURE 101. The negated shape -B and the Minkowski sum A⊕(-B).

The GJK algorithm should start in some point on A⊕-B. We call that point p_0.
(Figure 102) This point corresponds to one point in each of A and B, called p_{0A} and p_{0B}.
From p_0, a support mapping is calculated towards origin. This corresponds to a support
mapping along the line from p_{0A} to p_{0B}. The support mapping results in the point p_1, corresponding to p_{1A} and p_{1B}. The identity of these two operations can be written:

$$S_{A\oplus-B}(p_0) = S_A(p_{0A} - p_{0B}) - S_B(p_{0B} - p_{0A}) = S_A(v) - S_B(-v)$$

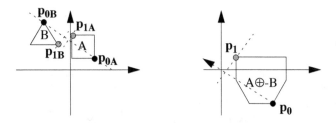

FIGURE 102. The first step of the GJK algorithm, on separate objects (left) and combined (right)

In the following iteration, Figure 103, we take the support mapping of the normal vector to
(p_0-p_1) towards origin, resulting in p_2. Now p_0 is farther away from origin than any of the
other two and can be discarded.

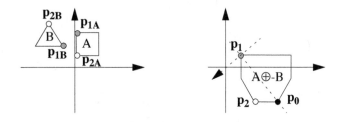

FIGURE 103. The second iteration finds a third point p_2.

One more iteration, Figure 104, using p_1 and p_2, finds p_3.

Rigid body animation   151

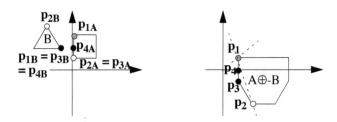

FIGURE 104. In the third iteration we find the last vertex p_3 and from there the final result p_4.

Since p_3 is no better than p_1, we are on a face. As long as we make sure this isn't a face on the opposite side, the final result can be calculated as a point on this face, p_4. The position of p_4 will tell whether A and B collide or not.

As you can see from the example above, the support mappings for A⊕-B corresponds to a walk among the vertices in A and B. We start in two arbitrary vertices, one in each shape, make a support mapping to find another pair. From there we use support mapping again to find new vertices that are good candidates, until we can detect that we have reached the minimum.

The support mapping calculation is a vital part of the algorithm and must be made efficiently. A naive implementation would search all vertices. Doing that kind of search for every iteration would make the algorithm slower than our earlier ones. Instead, it should be found using hill climbing among local neighbors. If the connections to the actual neighbors are complemented by well chosen "artificial neighbors" [4] then we do not only find the desired vertex faster, but we can also use that to get out of local minima on the backside (although that is not really an issue when used for GJK).

Another important aspect is to re-use the result from last time. For the example above, let us consider the next frame, looking something like Figure 105:

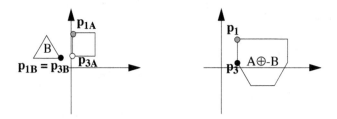

FIGURE 105. Next frame for A and B, where p_1 and p_3 are excellent starting points.

B has moved, so the closest point will change, but unless A or B rotates violently, p_1 or p_3 will provide very good starting points, often making the algorithm finish in a single iteration, that is constant time. This is called *vertex caching*.

GJK will make the collision detection very fast indeed, and provide one closest point. This point is still not necessarily well chosen as a representative for the whole collision when two objects meet face to face, but for other kinds of collisions it is sufficient. A modification that outputs a whole face in the case of planar collisions can help somewhat, but we may still need to extract better information.

It can be noted that GJK is easy to extend to handle moving objects. It is simply a matter of sweeping the volume covered by the movement. This holds for many other algorithms as well.

8.3.3 Other methods

There are, of course, other advanced methods, like the full k-DOP method that breaks up the shapes in sub-shapes. Hierarchical subdivision of models has growing popularity and may become the winning solution. So even if I almost skip this problem completely here, it is well worth studying. Did I mention that you can create image-space collision detection algorithms? You can make collision test using the Z buffer. Etc...

8.3.4 Non-convex shapes

It should be noted that most collision detection algorithms work for convex shapes only. Non-convex shapes are a lot more complicated to handle. Three ways to handle them include:

- Calculate the convex hull of the shape and use only that, thus making it convex.

- Subdivide the shape into a number of convex shapes, and use the algorithms for convex shapes on the parts.

- Represent the shape by a progressive hierarchy of spheres, as outlined in Volume 1.

8.4 Collision response

Once we have detected a collision, we need to make a response. This is a topic where I was brief in Volume 1, so I will discuss this a bit more than collision detection.

There are many ways to deal with collisions, so I will try to list alternatives and discuss the implications. Many questions boil down to whether we allow objects in our simulation to *overlap* or not. Obviously rigid bodies should not overlap during extended time, and not even for short periods, but unnoticeable overlap can be acceptable. Allowing overlap is simple, but clearly less exact.

A related question is the *time of collision*. When allowing overlap, we can happily use *constant time steps*, and if objects overlap we do our best to separate them. Constant time steps may also disallow overlap, but then it has to separate objects immediately on overlap, and that will often cause other objects to overlap. In any event, constant time steps imply that the time of impact is the time when we detect the overlap.

Another option, for higher precision, is to *back up time* to the time of the first collision that occurred. This is often not possible to do exactly (due to complex shapes and/or complex movement) so it can be done by approximations and subdivision of the time step.

Perfection is hard to achieve, though. What happens if complex objects move fast? We can miss some collisions, and when we back up time, the missed collision causes an overlap in the denser time scale. Can that be detected, is it worth the price?

Now we have a time of impact. What about the actual response, change of positions and velocities? There are three options:

- Kinematic response
- The penalty method
- Impulse force calculation

Kinematic response is simple. It involves no forces. In its simplest form, we just separate objects. We can also change velocities in the way that I suggested in Volume 1: split the velocity vector in a parallel and perpendicular part, and play with the perpendicular part. While this is not at all incorrect for certain situations, it is not a full simulation that covers all cases.

The penalty method is a force-based method for simulations allowing overlap. When a point is found to penetrate another object, that point is "penalized" by a force that pushes it outwards. The force is proportional to the depth of the overlap, which effectively makes the penalty force act as a kind of spring force.

This method is a very heuristic method where the magnitude of the penalty force is not rooted in physics, but rather arbitrary. I would argue that it should not be applied separately on every separate point (vertex) since that can make a multi-vertex collision result in a very big force while a single-vertex collision would result in a much smaller. Using a combined response, it is possible to give the penalty force a reasonable dependency of the mass and speed of the objects. It would even be possible to derive a suitable impulse that would be correct... but then we are straying into the third response method.

Impulse force calculation is the third, and most ambitious method. It is most suitable for the back-up-time method for time of collision. This method is highly realistic. A physically based impulse is calculated from the state of the colliding objects, and if correctly applied it should push the two objects apart.

This is not entirely trivial though. Complex, non-convex objects are dangerous. It is all too easy to find positions where even a well calculated impulse will rotate the object right into a new collision. To simplify the following discussion, we look at *frictionless* collision.

The impulse is a momentary change of momentum. It is defined as a force F during a time Δt. In its continuous form, Δt is infinitesimally small, but in the discrete time of a computer simulation, it is simply the time step of the simulation.

Momentum should be preserved, and for every force there must be an equal force in the opposite direction. Both these facts state that a collision should result in an impulse on each object with the same magnitude but opposite direction.

$$Imp = F\Delta t = m \cdot a \cdot \Delta t = m \cdot \Delta v = \Delta P$$

Thus, the change in velocity is

$$\Delta v = Imp/M$$

The impulse also produces a torque:

$$\tau_{impulse} = r \times Imp$$

where r is a vector from the center of mass to the point of impact.

Take two objects, A and B, with mass m_A and m_B, that have been found to collide as in Figure 106. The point of impact is **p**. For each object we form the vector from the center of mass to the point of impact:

$$r_A = p - x_A(t)$$

$$r_B = p - x_B(t)$$

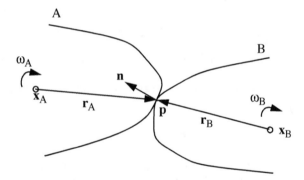

FIGURE 106. The rigid bodies A and B in collision in the point p.

We need the speed in the point of impact **p** for each object to find the relative speed.

Since the change we wish to do is momentary, we look at the speed before and after the collision, denoted v^- and v^+:

$$v_{pA} = v^-_A + \omega^-_A \times r_A$$

$$v_{pB} = v^-_B + \omega^-_B \times r_B$$

$$\mathbf{v}_{rel} = (\mathbf{v}_{pA} - \mathbf{v}_{pB})$$

Since we stated that the collision should be frictionless, the impulse will be along the normal vector in the point of impact. (Finding the normal vector is a problem of its own, but assuming a vertex-to-surface collision it is the normal vector of the surface. We can also use the separating plane approach.)

Then we write the relative movement projected on the normal vector as:

$$v^-_{rel} = \mathbf{v}_{rel} \bullet \mathbf{n} = (\mathbf{v}_{pA} - \mathbf{v}_{pB}) \bullet \mathbf{n}$$

The impulse can now be written

$$Imp = j\mathbf{n}$$

where j is a scalar that we wish to find. We can find it by calculating the resulting relative velocity with j as unknown variable.

$$\mathbf{v}^+_A = \mathbf{v}^-_A + j\mathbf{n}/m_A$$

$$\mathbf{v}^+_B = \mathbf{v}^-_B - j\mathbf{n}/m_B$$

$$\omega^+_A = \omega^-_A + I_A^{-1}(\mathbf{r}_A \times j\mathbf{n}) = \omega^-_A + jI_A^{-1}(\mathbf{r}_A \times \mathbf{n})$$

$$\omega^+_B = \omega^-_B - I_B^{-1}(\mathbf{r}_B \times j\mathbf{n}) = \omega^-_B - jI_B^{-1}(\mathbf{r}_B \times \mathbf{n})$$

Note the negative contribution for the B parts, since the opposite impulse works on B.

These four equations all include j as a factor in one of the terms. The relative velocity must change from the collision according to

$$v^+_{rel} = -\varepsilon \cdot v^-_{rel}$$

where ε is the *coefficient of restitution*, the elasticity factor, which can be anywhere from 0 (plastic collision) to 1 (elastic collision). It should be determined from the materials of A and B. The relative velocity before impact, v^-_{rel} was given above and can be written:

$$v^-_{rel} = (\mathbf{v}_{pA} - \mathbf{v}_{pB}) \bullet \mathbf{n} = (\mathbf{v}^-_A + \omega^-_A \times \mathbf{r}_A - \mathbf{v}^-_B - \omega^-_B \times \mathbf{r}_B) \bullet \mathbf{n}$$

Similarly, the relative velocity after impact is written:

$$v^+_{rel} = (\mathbf{v}^+_A + \omega^+_A \times \mathbf{r}_A - \mathbf{v}^+_B - \omega^+_B \times \mathbf{r}_B) \bullet \mathbf{n}$$

$$= (\mathbf{v}^-_A + j\mathbf{n}/m_A + (\omega^-_A + jI_A^{-1}(\mathbf{r}_A \times \mathbf{n})) \times \mathbf{r}_A - \mathbf{v}^-_B + j\mathbf{n}/m_B - (\omega^-_B - jI_B^{-1}(\mathbf{r}_B \times \mathbf{n})) \times \mathbf{r}_B) \bullet \mathbf{n}$$

Rigid body animation

$$= v\bar{}_{rel} + j(\mathbf{n}/m_A + I_A^{-1}(\mathbf{r}_A \times \mathbf{n}) \times \mathbf{r}_A + \mathbf{n}/m_B + I_B^{-1}(\mathbf{r}_B \times \mathbf{n}) \times \mathbf{r}_B) \bullet \mathbf{n}$$

Insert this in $v^+_{rel} = -\varepsilon \cdot v\bar{}_{rel}$ and you get

$$-(\varepsilon + 1)v\bar{}_{rel} = j(\mathbf{n}/m_A + I_A^{-1}(\mathbf{r}_A \times \mathbf{n}) \times \mathbf{r}_A + \mathbf{n}/m_B + I_B^{-1}(\mathbf{r}_B \times \mathbf{n}) \times \mathbf{r}_B) \bullet \mathbf{n}$$

$$= m_A^{-1} + m_B^{-1} + j(I_A^{-1}(\mathbf{r}_A \times \mathbf{n}) \times \mathbf{r}_A + I_B^{-1}(\mathbf{r}_B \times \mathbf{n}) \times \mathbf{r}_B) \bullet \mathbf{n}$$

which gives us the final formula:

$$j = \frac{-(\varepsilon + 1)v\bar{}_{rel}}{\dfrac{1}{m_A} + \dfrac{1}{m_B} + \mathbf{n} \bullet (I_A^{-1}(\mathbf{r}_A \times \mathbf{n}) \times \mathbf{r}_A + I_B^{-1}(\mathbf{r}_B \times \mathbf{n}) \times \mathbf{r}_B)}$$

This is the same final formula as in [8] and [9]. As usual, check out Baraff for a more detailed work.

The formula may seem complex at first glance, but when you think about it, it is just a few simple cross products with known parameters.

This described a case where the two objects play on equal terms. Maybe you want to use this with fixed objects that are not allowed to move even a little? One way to make a fixed object is suggested by Baraff. You set the mass to infinity, thereby m^{-1} to zero, and you set the inverse inertia matrix to all zeros too.

8.5 Friction

In the formulas above, we did not take friction into account. As noted above, any impact on a surface that is not perpendicular to the surface should not be projected on the normal, but split into normal and tangent parts.

The tangent part may or may not result in sideways movement. I will here cover the basic rules for friction, so you can apply them as appropriate in your situation.

Consider an object resting on a surface. If a sideways force is applied to it, it would start moving unless there was an opposing force. If there is any friction at all between the surface and the object (and there always is) there will be an opposing force, the friction force.

So up to a limit, the friction force and the pushing force will be the same. This limit is can be fairly well approximated by a friction coefficient $\mu_s \cdot F_n$, where F_n is the force between the object and the surface. This force is in reaction to any other force applied to the object, like the force F_g due to gravity, as in Figure 107. F_n and F_g must be equal and with opposing direction, just like the pushing and friction forces, to sum up to zero, or else the object would accelerate.

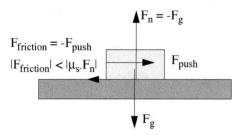

FIGURE 107. A static object generates a friction force limited by its force against the surface

This becomes slightly more complicated if several forces are applied to the object, but it is really only a matter of summing them.

If the pushing force is bigger than $\mu_s \cdot F_n$, as in Figure 108, then the friction can no longer keep the object still and it starts move. There will still be a friction force, but now it is approximately constant, using another friction coefficient: $\mu_k \cdot F_n$ (where k stands for kinetic).

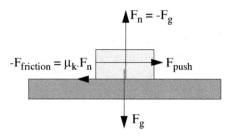

FIGURE 108. A moving object (in this case accelerating) generates a friction force proportional to the force against the surface

We note that if the surface is slanted (Figure 109), the reaction to F_g will be split along the surface into F_n and F_{push}, so in that case the push comes from gravity, a popular special case of applying friction. Given $\mu_s = 0.5$, at what angle will the object start sliding? (Wait, will I not need F_g too? Why not?)

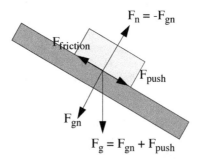

FIGURE 109. A slanted surface; When will F_{push} overcome $F_{friction}$ so the object moves?

In the case where F_g is constant, thereby also F_n, the friction force varies with the pushing force according to the curve in Figure 110.

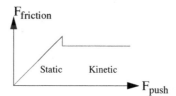

FIGURE 110. Typical friction force for varying pushing force

Thus, static friction will be proportional to the pushing force, while kinetic friction will be constant (again, approximately). The bump at the border between the two parts is due to the difference between the static friction constant μ_s and the kinetic friction constant μ_k, where the latter is generally smaller than the former. That is, it takes a certain force to get an object moving, but a bit less to keep it moving. We know that intuitively but it is true and can be measured.

When applied to the impulse calculations above, this will affect the force along the tangent of the collision, limiting it depending on the normal force and the friction coefficients.

8.6 Resting contact

A different case where friction also plays a part is *resting contact*, but the subject is about even more important things. Detecting whether two object are in contact so that they lie on top of each other rather than bounce off, it is important for two reasons:

- The work on collision detection and impulse calculations can be reduced significantly.
- Objects that should come to rest do that instead of making small jumps all the time.

We define that two objects are in resting contact if their relative velocity is below a certain treshold. When that happens, we can stop calculating their forces towards each other but instead consider them constant, and even stop moving them until some new force appears that changes the situation.

This is not as simple as it may seem. While momentary collisions can be handled well one contact point at a time, a resting contact will have many contact points.

In particular, we can not just pick the first vertex that we find that overlaps, and apply an impulse there. If an object lands on another, say a cube on a plane, all four corners will overlap, but if we calculate the entire collision on the first one found, an impulse will be calculated for that corner alone, and the result is that the cube starts "dancing". If, instead, the center of the overlapping volume was used, or all the overlapping vertices were found and a center point was calculated from them, the cube would get an impulse to its center and the collision would be more gracefully computed.

There are a number of rules to follow, that are harder to handle in this case:

- Non-interpenetration constraint. The objects must be prevented to moving into each other. Note that this may happen slowly if we don't explicitly stop it, due to numerical errors.

- Forces must be repulsive, they may never move objects together, only push them apart.

- When objects separate, the force between them must go to zero.

Solving this strictly requires handling all the contact points at the same time while fulfilling the constraints. See Baraff [9] for details.

Is it possible to simplify this seemingly simple problem? Yes, to some extent, but the conclusion of most attempts is that there tend to appear tricky cases where you get unstable or otherwise unwanted behavior.

8.7 Constraints and joints

An important part of a physics system is the possibility to connect objects together, to apply constraints to their motion.

The most basic constraint on objects' movement is disallowing them to move into each other. If objects are in contact, a force or impulse must push them apart, and this force must go to zero when the are no longer in contact.

Other kinds of constraints are joints, who connect objects more or less permanently to each other. Typical joints include:

- Ball-socket joints, allowing free rotation, although with constraints on how far it may rotate.

- Hinge joint, allowing rotation in one direction only.

- Slider joint, allowing (and controlling) distance between the objects.

A constraint can be hard or soft. A hard constraint should be fulfilled immediately if at all possible. A soft constraint, like a spring, will introduce force to move the connected objects to the desired distance/direction, but other forces may successfully oppose it. Hard constraints can come in direct conflict, while soft constraints in general can not.

A particularly popular example of a constraint system is the *ragdoll*. You can make a fairly nice ragdoll system with a few particles and hard distance constraints. See further

Every particle needs its position, velocity and mass. According to verlet integration (chapter 10.2) you can replace velocity by the previous position. It must also have storage for accumulating all forces it may be affected with.

Every joint needs to know two particles and its length.

Create a stick figure with particles as hands, elbows, shoulders (possibly one particle), head, hips (one particle), knees and feet. Connect them pairwise by joints.

Then you can run animation like this:

- Update all particles according to their mass and velocity.
- For all joints, make sure the distance between them is as specified.
- Accumulate forces for the next pass. (Add forces to make it fun here, like user controls. Being able to pull a particle with the mouse is a common control.)
- Render the ragdoll according to the positions of the particles (possibly using skinning).

Updating the length is really the only part of the system that isn't trivial by now, and it isn't hard. The vector between the two particles is modified to the right length simply by moving the two particles along the vector, depending on their mass.

This is really just a first draft to a ragdoll animation system, but it works surprisingly well. In Figure 111, you see a frame of animation from a ragdoll system that is based on this.

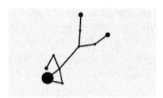

FIGURE 111. A simple ragdoll animation

Testing all joints sequentially is cheating, it will create significant errors, but despite that, the result of this simple scheme will give you a pretty nice ragdoll animation, which tends to be remarkably stable. There are many steps left, collision detection and handling, and rotational constraints, and when you add these, you will find that you need to be more careful in order to keep the system stable.

A system for joints and constraints is a vital part of *physics engines*, our next subject.

8.8 Physics engines

Obviously, collision detection and handling for rigid bodies is not quite as simple as one may hope. However, since the physics is so well-known and general, it is feasible to package that into a library, a *physics engine*. There is a pretty large number of physics engines available, both commercial and free.

Freely available physics engines include

- ODE (Open Dynamics Engine) [24]
- Newton [25]
- True Axis [26]
- Bullet
- NV Physics
- Opal
- BRL-CAD
- Tokamak
- Chipmunk

and commercial engines include

- Havok
- Novodex
- PhysX
- Vortex

Since this book is written with course projects in mind, I choose to focus on the free alternatives, without for a moment ruling out the commercial ones for bigger projects. The most popular free alternative is without doubt ODE. Newton and True Axis are other alternatives that have been recommended. As always, your mileage will vary, so you should always check out more than one and consider how well it fits both your coding style and your needs.

Cross-platform capabilities is always worth considering. ODE, Newton and Chipmunk are all cross-platform, supporting MS Windows, Linux and Mac OSX. The Chipmunk engine is 2D, which limits its usage but it is quite popular for 2D games.

I base this text on the diploma thesis by Henrik Hansson [13], a study comparing and evaluating physics engines.

8.8.1 What is a physics engine?

Physics engines in general handle rigid body motion. Deformable bodies are not necessarily treated at all. A fast and accurate collision detection is vital. A good engine should be able to handle objects piled on each other and resolve collisions in a realistic way, as in the screen shots in Figure 112.

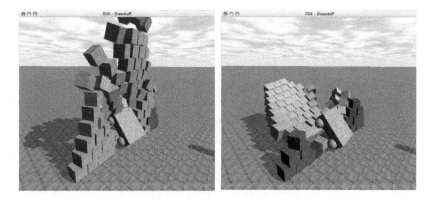

FIGURE 112. The demo "crash" from the ODE distribution.

The physics engine will deal with the following tasks:

- Integrating motion.
- Collision detection and response.
- Constraints, joints.

These points are all what this chapter has been about up to now. What a coincidence!

8.8.2 Summary of an evaluation of physics engines

Hansson [13] evaluated a number of physics engines a coarser level. He found that the included functionality was very similar in primitives, joint types and data types, although Bullet and Tokamak supports fewer joint types than most. True Axis has relatively poor precision, sacrificing that for performance.

Hansson made the conclusion that ODE and Newton were the strongest players and focused his study on them. He made several experiments. The most interesting one is this: A cube dropped between a vertical chute formed by two planes, similar to Figure 113.

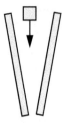

FIGURE 113. Chute test, a box dropped into a narrowing space.

This is a hard problem, and neither of the physics engines did a perfect job. A poor physics engine will fail miserably, possibly with wobbling, vibrations, and accumulating energy. Hansson did several tests with a small and large box, with varying friction settings. Newton did generally not perform very well, with the box getting stuck with significant penetration and bouncing around in non-realistic ways. ODE did better in most cases, except small box with maximum friction, which spinned and bounced around in strange ways.

Other tests included a gravity test, where ODE was closest to ideal, but neither had any major problem. There was a friction test with an object sliding on a slope, where both engines did very well with Newton being slightly better. Finally, there was a constraints test, with a pendulum hanging in a string (a hinge joint). In this case, Newton was the clear winner since ODE drifted badly.

All in all, Hansson concluded that neither engine was clearly better. It seems from the tests that ODE should be better for complicated collision situations while Newton is better at joints. In the end, Newton was chosen for better documentation and additional features that are not in the tests.

9. Representing rotation by quaternions

As mentioned in the previous chapter, interpolation of rotations is an important problem, for which quaternions[1] can be useful. Although there are other ways to represent rotation, interpolation of rotations is one case where quaternions are particularly good.

This chapter is based on lecture material by Peter Johansson, and written in cooperation with him.

9.1 Representing rotation

Rotations can be represented in a number of ways:

- Euler angles
- Orthonormal matrix
- Rotation axis and angle
- 3-component vector where the length is the angle
- Quaternion

With *Euler angles*, the rotation is given as three angles, yaw, pitch and roll. This representation is very intuitive, but is hard to work with. Interpolating between rotation is tricky, will result in non-linear behavior. Also, the representation has the *gimbal lock* problem.

The *orthonormal matrix* is the standard representation in computer graphics. It has many big advantages, such as easy concatenations of operations, including other operations than rotations. It also holds important information that can be read straight out of the rotation matrix, like the forward vector.

---

1. "Kvaternioner" på svenska

Interpolation, however, is harder to do. Making several successive rotations is easy, but how can we find the rotation step? Actually, it is not impossible to interpolate matrices. It is possible to do it through a definition of exponential functions of matrices. However, that is beyond the scope for the moment.

With a *separate rotation axis and angle*, the problem again is that it is not obvious how to interpolate between different axes.

With a *3-component vector* where the length is the angle, interpolation works fairly well with straight linear interpolation. This representation is pretty close to quaternions.

9.2 Definitions

The theory of quaternions is a generalization of complex numbers. It is a skewfield, a rational algebra concept, which works mostly like ordinary numbers (real or complex) except that commutativity is not fulfilled ($xy \neq yx$).

While complex numbers work with one complex unit (usually called i or j), a quaternion is based on three. They are called $\mathbf{i}, \mathbf{j}, \mathbf{k}$.

$$\mathbf{i}^2 = \mathbf{j}^2 = \mathbf{k}^2 = \mathbf{ijk} = -1$$

Using these units, we can defined a quaternion as

$$q = w + x\mathbf{i} + y\mathbf{j} + z\mathbf{k}$$

where w, x, y, z are real numbers. It can also be written

$$q = (w, \mathbf{n})$$

where $\mathbf{n}$ is the three-dimensional vector (x, y, z).

The three units $\mathbf{i}, \mathbf{j}, \mathbf{k}$ each correspond to one of the base axes. Consequently, multiplication of them work exactly like the cross product:

$$\mathbf{ij=k, jk=i, ki=j, ij=-ji, jk=-kj, ki=-ik}$$

Multiplication of two quaternions work as follows. Take two quaternions:

$$q_1 = (w_1, \mathbf{n_1})$$

$$q_2 = (w_2, \mathbf{n_2})$$

Then their product is

$$q_1 \cdot q_2 = (w_1 w_2 - \mathbf{n_1} \bullet \mathbf{n_2}, w_1 \mathbf{n_2} + w_2 \mathbf{n_1} + \mathbf{n_1} \times \mathbf{n_2})$$

The *conjugate* of the quaternion $q = (w, \mathbf{n})$ is

Representing rotation by quaternions

$$q* = (w, -\mathbf{n})$$

The *inverse* of q is

$$q^{-1} = \frac{1}{|q|^2} \cdot (w, -\mathbf{n})$$

The product of the quaternion by its conjugate defines the *magnitude*:

$$|q|^2 = qq* = w^2 + |\mathbf{n}|^2$$

The following rule holds for multiplication and conjugates:

$$(q_2 q_1)* = q_1* q_2*$$

The *unit quaternion* has the norm $|q|=1$, which can be written as

$$q = (\cos(v/2), \sin(v/2)\mathbf{n}), \text{ where } |\mathbf{n}|=1$$

For unit quaternions, $q^{-1} = q*$.

Now you have enough definitions to implement a quaternion module if you like, and it is time to apply it to rotations.

9.3 Rotation using quaternions

A unit quaternion can be rewritten as

$$q = (\cos(v/2), \sin(v/2)\mathbf{n})$$

thereby representing a rotation by the angle v around the axis $\mathbf{n}$.

A position vector $\mathbf{p}$ can be represented by a quaternion as $p = (0, \mathbf{p})$, that is a quaternion with the real component $= 0$. Then the vector can be rotated by q like this:

$$p' = q \cdot p \cdot q*$$

Rotations can be concatenated by multiplication of the quaternions representing those rotations.

A unit quaternion $q = (w, (x, y, z))$ can be converted to a rotation matrix as

$$M = \begin{bmatrix} 1 - 2(y^2 + z^2) & 2xy - 2wz & 2xz + 2wy \\ 2xy + 2wz & 1 - 2(x^2 + z^2) & 2yz - 2wx \\ 2xz - 2wy & 2yz + 2wx & 1 - 2(x^2 + y^2) \end{bmatrix}$$

Expand to a 4x4 matrix as needed. That only requires filling the extra row and column with zeroes, and a 1 in bottom-right.

You can also convert a rotation matrix to a quaternion. Let the following matrix be the rotation matrix (i.e. an orthonormal base):

$$\begin{bmatrix} a & b & c \\ d & e & f \\ g & h & m \end{bmatrix}$$

Then the quaternion $q = (w, (x, y, z))$ is found as follows.

The "trace" of the matrix is a sum of the diagonal components:

$$T = a + e + m + 1$$

If $T \neq 0$, then we get the quaternion as

$$w = \frac{1}{2}\sqrt{a + e + m + 1} = \frac{1}{2}\sqrt{T}$$

$$x = \frac{h - f}{4w}$$

$$y = \frac{c - g}{4w}$$

$$z = \frac{d - b}{4w}$$

Actually, you can pick the positive or negative root of T as you please. All you get is the rotation axis pointing in one way or the other, which does not matter.

If $T = 0$, then we have a special case. T near zero is also bad, since we will get precision problems. This happens, for instance, at a 180 degree rotation around X.

To handle this case, we need to identify the major diagonal element and use a different formula for each case:

```
if a > e and a > m
    S = sqrt( 1.0 + a - e - m ) * 2
    qw = (f - h) / S
    qx = 0.25 * S
    qy = (b + d) / S
    qz = (c + g) / S
else
if (e > m))
    S = sqrt( 1.0 + e - a - m ) * 2
    qw = (c - g) / S
    qx = (b + d) / S
    qy = 0.25 * S
    qz = (f + h) / S
```

```
else
    S = sqrt( 1.0 + m - a - e ) * 2
    qw = (b - d) / S
    qx = (c + g) / S
    qy = (f + h) / S
    qz = 0.25 * S
```

This is a rather clumsy method, with a total of four different solutions for different cases. But there is a more elegant solution that I adapted from www.euclideanspace.com, that handles the special case automatically:

$$w = \text{sqrt}(\max(0, 1 + a + e + m))/2$$

$$x = \text{sqrt}(\max(0, 1 + a - e - m))/2$$

$$y = \text{sqrt}(\max(0, 1 - a + e - m))/2$$

$$z = \text{sqrt}(\max(0, 1 - a - e + m))/2$$

For these four, the max() is not mathematically needed but included for avoiding roundoff problems. Then we need the following sign corrections:

$$x = \text{copysign}(x, h - f)$$

$$y = \text{copysign}(y, c - g)$$

$$z = \text{copysign}(z, d - b)$$

where

$$\text{copysign}(a, b) = a \cdot \text{sign}(a) \cdot \text{sign}(b)$$

This is merely a recipe, which is something I personally don't like, but deriving the conversion between quaternions and matrices does not seem like the most important thing we need to do in this context. Visit www.euclideanspace.com for the derivation.

So far, what we have is a representation of rotation that is more compact than a rotation matrix (4 scalars instead of 9 or 16), but on the other hand it is also less capable in some ways. I will now explore the area where quaternions have their most important strength: interpolation of rotation.

9.4 Interpolation of rotation

Quaternions can be interpolated using SLERP (spherical linear interpolation). This gives the shortest path on the 4-dimensional sphere of unit quaternions.

To interpolate from q_1 to q_2 using a parameter t that is varying from 0 to 1, you can do like this:

We define the operation q^t. For a quaternion $q = (\cos(v/2), \sin(v/2)\mathbf{n})$ it is defined as

$$q^t = (\cos(tv/2), \sin(tv/2)\mathbf{n})$$

Thus, it is a linear scaling of the rotation. Then we can perform SLERP between the quaternions q_1 and q_2 as

$$q = (q_2 q_1^{-1})^t\, q_1 = q_1(q_1^{-1}q_2)^t = q_2(q_2^{-1}q_1)^{1-t} = (q_1 q_2^{-1})^{1-t}q_2$$

So we define the "slerp" function as any of these expressions. We can pick the first:

$$\text{slerp}(t, q_1, q_2) = (q_2\, q_1^{-1})^t\, q_1$$

The SLERP will interpolate between the rotations with constant speed.

9.5 Exponential functions of quaternions

Now, why did we use the notation q^t for some kind of scaling? It looks like an exponential function. That is because it is just that! Above, we only used them for unit quaternions. In this section, we will have a look at the concept in more general terms.

For $q = (w, t\mathbf{n})$, where $|\mathbf{n}|=1$, we define

$$\exp(q) = e^w\, (\cos(t), \sin(t)\mathbf{n})$$

From the definition of the exp() function, we can see that a quaternion q can be written

$$q = R \cdot \exp((0,\mathbf{n})t) \text{ with } |\mathbf{n}|=1$$

Then we can define

$$\log(q) = (\log(R), \mathbf{n}t)$$

It is also possible to define

$$q^t = \exp(t \log(q))$$

which is the same as the previous definition.

This is a polar representation, similar to complex numbers ($r \cdot e^{i\phi}$). The "angle" is here a 3D vector. For unit quaternions, $R = 1$. Then, $\log(q)$ will have a real part 0. Then $t \cdot \log(q)$ has real part zero, too, and $\exp(t \cdot \log(q))$ is a unit quaternion.

9.6 Squad

When interpolating between several quaternions using SLERP, we will get discontinuities in the speed when switching from one pair of quaternions to another. This is because we interpolate with constant speed. A similar problem appears if you do linear interpolation of positions between pairs of points, and the problem is related to the discussion of continuity in Volume 1. Just like a spline can fulfill G^0, G^1, G^2, a rotation interpolation can be described in a similar way.

And the solution is indeed related to splines. We can do something that reminds of Bezier or hermite splines.

With $slerp(t, q_1, q_2) = (q_2\ q_1^{-1})^t\ q_1$ we get

$$squad(t,a,p,q,b) = slerp(2t(1-t), slerp(t,a,b), slerp(t,p,q))$$

For continuity, we should choose

$$q_i = a_i\ exp(-(\log(a_{i+1}\ a_i^{-1}) + \log(a_{i-1}\ a_i^{-1}))/4)$$

and interpolate using

$$squad(t, a_i, q_i, q_{i+1}, a_{i+1})$$

9.7 Final remarks

There is much more to say on these topics, at least from a mathematics point of view, but my ambition has been to provide a tool, together with a decent understanding of what the tool does. I would like to end this chapter by stressing that the quaternion concept is just that, a tool. You should use it when it is a good way to solve a problem, but there is no reason to think that it is better than other representations in every way. Just like with other tools, the best engineer is one who can handle many and switches between them smoothly. The quaternion may be a bit more challenging to understand than matrices or Euler angles, but as a representation for rotation it is pretty straightforward.

10. Numerical methods for stable integration

One of the greatest challenges with game physics and other physically based animation is not physics at all, but numerical integration. The problem is that the simulation runs in discrete time, simulating continuous processes. So, all parameters of the animation are calculated at discrete time intervals, using functions that can not always be described analytically. This is often true for basic things like speed and acceleration.

This chapter is a brief introduction and an overview of some common methods. For a more thorough treatment, I recommend books or courses on numerical methods.

Everybody perform their first physically based animation experiments using Euler integration. It is simpler than anything else so of course you do. For simple cases, like particle systems with little interaction and few constraints, it works nicely. However, the more constraints you need, the more unstable the system will be due to the simple integration.

I will primarily consider the case where you integrate position from velocity and acceleration. As mentioned in other chapters, integrating and interpolating rotations is a significant problem, but I will leave it for the parts where it is central.

The most fundamental rules of physics tell us that the position is the integral of velocity, and velocity is the integral of the acceleration. With Euler integration, the integration is performed by adding the first derivate multiplied by the time step for every time step.

$$x_{i+1} = x_i + v_i * dt$$

$$v_{i+1} = v_i + a * dt$$

This gives a rough approximation, illustrated by Figure 114, that will only be exact for a constant function!

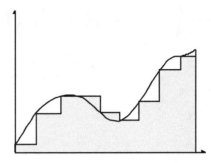

FIGURE 114. Euler integration

The errors of Euler integration implies that there is a significant risk that the system being simulated becomes unstable. The faster a function varies, the bigger the error and the bigger the risk.

A typical system that can become instable is mass-spring systems. The errors of the integration may introduce energy, which can make the system oscillate and explode.

The smaller the step length is, the smaller the error becomes. In practice, this means that higher frame rate is needed, or that several simulation steps are performed per frame.

10.1 Taylor expansion of the function

The Taylor expansion of the function is convenient as a tool for analytically finding better integration methods.

$$x(t+h) = x(t) + h \cdot \frac{dx}{dt} + \frac{h^2}{2} \cdot \frac{d^2x}{dt^2}$$

Euler integration only uses the first two terms. This leaves an error on the order of $O(h^2)$, which is a big error. But there are several other methods to consider:

- Verlet integration
- Adams-Bashforth
- Predictor-corrector
- Runge-Kutta
- Adaptive step length

10.2 Verlet integration

Verlet integration may at a glance seem like a meaningless rewrite of the Euler integration, but it turns out to be something much better. By taking one step forward and one step backwards we get the following Taylor expansions:

$$x(t+h) = x(t) + h \cdot \frac{dx}{dt} + \frac{h^2}{2} \cdot \frac{d^2x}{dt^2} + \frac{h^3}{6} \cdot \frac{d^3x}{dt^3} + O(h^4)$$

$$x(t-h) = x(t) + -h \cdot \frac{dx}{dt} + \frac{h^2}{2} \cdot \frac{d^2x}{dt^2} + -\frac{h^3}{6} \cdot \frac{d^3x}{dt^3} + O(h^4)$$

Combine these two and you get

$$x(t+h) = 2 \cdot x(t) - x(t-h) + h^2 \cdot \frac{d^2x}{dt^2} + O(h^4)$$

That's a simple sum of two positions and the acceleration! The first and third order terms nicely cancels out, and we get an error of $O(h^4)$. From the $O(h^2)$ error of Euler integration, this is a huge improvement! Note, however, that the precision refers to the local error, the error in each step. The global error, the error in position, is bigger, so the method can be outperformed by more precise methods like fourth-order Runge-Kutta.

But isn't $2x(t)$ - $x(t$ - $h) = x(t) + v(t)$? Yes, in a way (when you forget that the underlying function is continuous), but it is a question of taking the velocity in the right time step.

A problem with the method is that it requires two previous positions. This is not a major problem. If the system starts in rest, you simply set the two positions to the same. If not, you can take one step back by the velocity.

The method can be rewritten to explicitly include velocity. It is then called *Velocity Verlet*.

10.3 Adams-Bashforth

The Adams-Bainsforth method includes one more term in the Taylor expansion:

$$x_{i+1} = x_i + 1/2 * h(3v_i - v_{i-1})$$

This demands that we know the speed in the two previous iterations. Thus, the method is not "self-starting"; it can not start from zero. Instead, it is started by a step of Euler integration, the first order.

This results in an error of $O(h^3)$ instead of $O(h^2)$

10.4 Predictor-corrector

In the predictor-corrector method, we make a preliminary calculation, the prediction. Then we calculate the gradient in the prediction. Based on the change in the gradient, a new calculation is made using the two gradients. See Figure 115.

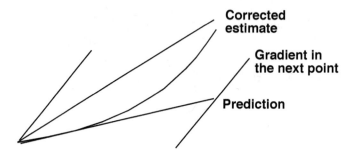

FIGURE 115. Predictor-corrector

10.5 Runge-Kutta

The Runge-Kutta integration methods are probably the most famous integration methods. They can be described as extensions of the predictor-corrector method. The interval can be divided into several, so several intermediate gradients are used. There are several Runge-Kutta variants, and the fourth-order is the most popular, so popular that it is sometimes carelessly referred to as *the* Runge-Kutta method.

Consider the position/function $x(t)$ to be integrated, that is, we want to estimate the next position $x(t+h)$. The first derivate x' is a function both of t and x, so we can write $dx/dt = x'(t, x)$.

Now, why did we get a two-dimensional function? Even in the simple case where we just work with a speed and a position, different estimates of $x(t+h)$ imply that we should also change the estimate of $x'(t+h)$, thus adding that x parameter. And modifying the estimate several times is what the Runge-Kutta method is all about.

Four different estimates are calculated of the derivate. The first one, k1, is simply the slope in the starting point:

$$k_1 = x'(t, x)$$

Then, we follow the slope k1 to a point half-way over the interval, and use the x value for that point for a new estimate.

$$k_2 = x'(t+h/2, x + h/2*k_1)$$

Same thing one more time, we follow the k_2 slope to yet another point.

$$k_3 = x'(t+h/2, x + h/2*k_2)$$

We use the third estimate to jump to the end of the interval and take a last sample there

$$k_4 = x'(t+h, x + h*k_3)$$

Finally, all these four samples are weighted together to a resulting estimate of x:

$$x(t+h) = x(t) + (k_1 + 2*k_2 + 2*k_3 + k_4)/6$$

Figure 116 illustrates what happened.

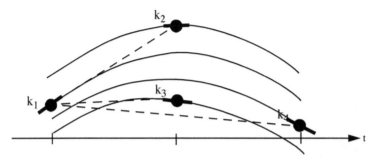

FIGURE 116. The fourth-order Runge-Kutta method

In the figure, each of the four blobs with a short line illustrate one of the four estimates. Each estimate from k2 and up are on a helper line with the same slope as the previous estimate. The four solid curves are all the same function, but different slopes depending on the x value (the height in the figure).

As mentioned above, this is merely one of the Runge-Kutta methods, but the most popular one. Proving its precision and studying variants must be left to other courses.

10.6 Adaptive step length

The error varies with the function in question. The step length h directly affects the error, as so does the amount of variation in the higher derivates of the function.

A very simple way to reduce the errors is to vary the step lengths depending on the function. We must, obviously, calculate an estimate of the error to control this.

10.7 Practice

After all these principles, I feel that we want to get it running too, with a simple demo. Now, a trivial demo is not entirely trivial to find. There are countless implementations around, but I wanted one that you can understand and play with quickly, where I can easily integrate it in an OpenGL based demo. This is what I came up with. It is based on the description on the web [72]. The full demo includes a simple animation , a ball hanging in a rubber band.

```
// derivative of x, ie change in position/speed
float dx (float x, float v )
{
    return v;
}
```

```
// derivative of v, ie change in velocity/acceleration
float dv (float x, float v )
{
    return (-stiffness/mass) * (x - rest_length) - (damping/mass) * v;
}

void rk4 ( float *t, float h, float *position, float *velocity)
{
    // step 1
    float x = *position;
    float v = *velocity;

    float k1x = dx(x, v); // k1 for x, that is x'(t, x), = v in our case
    float k1v = dv(x, v); // k1 for v, that is v'(t, x, v)

    // step 2
    x = *position + ( h / 2.0 ) * k1x; // Follow slope k1 a half step
    v = *velocity + ( h / 2.0 ) * k1v;

    float k2x = dx(x, v); // k2 for x = x'(t+h/2, x+h/2*k1x)
    float k2v = dv(x, v); // k2 for v

    // step 3
    x = *position + (h / 2.0) * k2x; // Follow k2 a half step
    v = *velocity + (h / 2.0) * k2v;

    float k3x = dx(x, v); // k3 for x
    float k3v = dv(x, v); // k3 for v

    // step 4
    x = *position + h * k3x; // Follow k3 a full step
    v = *velocity + h * k3v;

    float k4x = dx(x, v); // k4 for x
    float k4v = dv(x, v); // k4 for v

    // now combine the derivative estimates and
    // compute new state
    *position += (h / 6.0) * (k1x + k2x * 2.0 + k3x * 2.0 + k4x);
    *velocity += (h / 6.0) * (k1v + k2v * 2.0 + k3v * 2.0 + k4v);
    *t += h;
}
```

As usual, the full program is of limited interest in print but I will make it available on-line.

This code follows our previous algorithm fairly well, with some exceptions. The weights k1, k2, k3, k4 exist in two sets, one for v and one for x, since both are integrated. Since x and v are not expressed as functions of time, the dx (x') function doesn't take the same arguments.

10.8 Conclusion

This short chapter has given an overview of a number of integration methods that can be useful for games, especially physics simulations. It is not exhaustive by a long shot, but includes the most popular and practical choices. All in all, I believe that we end up with two primary choices, namely Verlet and fourth-order Runge-Kutta. Both are highly accurate. The Verlet integration method often wins for its simplicity.

11. Body animation, skinning

Rigid bodies are clearly insufficient for many purposes. We do expect certain objects to be deformable. In particular, animals and humans should be able to move their limbs. Since we have a skeleton, this movement is constrained to the bone movements.

In this chapter, I will first discuss body animation in general, but the main topic is skinning, the popular technique for making a surface mesh deform after the movement of an inner skeleton.

Note: This chapter is partially based on lecture notes by Johan Hedborg.

11.1 The skeleton

The skeleton (Figure 117) is the archetype for a hierarcically structured 3D model. It can easily be modeled as a tree structure, typically using the spine as its root. A set of significant bones such as upper and lower leg bones and upper and lower arm bones each for nodes in the tree. Each node holds a transformation relative to the parent, with translation and rotation. This means that each node has its own coordinate system, with origin in the joint to the parent, which is also where it has its rotational freedom. See Figure 118.

FIGURE 117. Skin and bones. The bones are a set of joints. The skin is a single mesh.

Each node must thus contain a transformation representing translation and rotation relative to its parent. It must also have some kind of identification, like an ID number. This is needed in order to identify what parts of the skin, the model mesh, that follows each bone. It must also have a reference to all children.

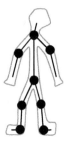

FIGURE 118. Joints connecting the bones. Each connection is a transformation to the next joint.

There may also be constraints on the allowed movement for the joint. The constraints may depend on classifications of joints. Ball joints allow rotation in all directions, but may include limitations in how far it may rotate. An example of a ball joint is the hip joint and shoulder joint. Other joints may only allow rotation around a specified axis. This is true for the elbow and knee.

11.2 Animating a skeleton

Given the skeleton structure, there are two problems: performing the animation and calculating the shape of the skin. Let us start with the animation and return to the skin later.

All kinds of animation dealing with human bodies are very hard to perform since we are so well trained at analyzing such movement. The human body is a very complex structure with over 200 degrees of freedom and 600 muscles. We need a very detailed model over its movement to make a convincing animation, but there is no such model that is truly well-defined. As an additional problem, there is also personal differences. All humans move slightly different, and we can to considerable extent identify humans from their way to move. The movement should also reflect their mood and physical condition, the so-called body language.

There are three popular methods for animating bodies:

- Keyframe animation
- Inverse kinematics
- Physically-based animation

11.2.1 Key-frame animation

In key-frame animation, positions are pre-defined at certain times, the *keyframes*, and then positions between the keyframes are interpolated. The keyframes are either set manually

Body animation, skinning

in a 3D modeler or set using *motion capture*. The manual method is tedious and the quality is poor. It typically results in animation of the kind you see in old japanese horror movies. With motion capture, real human positions are recorded and the motion becomes much better. The physical constraints on the body are implicit by the motion of the live model and thus the motion can be highly realistic.

This is not always entirely true, though. Motion capture is only realistic when the motion is applied to a model that is similar to the human whose motion is being captured.

As mentioned above, motion capture is the best way to pre-record keyframe tracks. A motion capture system records the movements of a living model, and is translated to transformations for the needed body parts and converted to a keyframe track that can be used for animation.

A motion capture system can be built on different principles. It can use electromagnetic transmitters placed on the body, sending out signals that are recorded by sensors, and their exact positions are calculated by triangulation. Such a system was used in the Swedish TV show "Tödde" with Sven Melander in the 90's. An advantage of such systems is that they output 3D data immediately, and thus are useful for real-time use.

Another possibility is a visual system, where the motions are recorded by an ordinary camera. This usually involves special optical markers on the body, to simplify image analysis of the images. Doing motion capture without optical markers is hard, and remains a field of research. [48]

The system may use several cameras, in order both not to miss any markers and to be able to determine the depth. A visual motion capture may include as much as eight cameras! [8]

If we save all data for all frames, the total amount of data will be very large. Thus, it is common to save data at certain times, the *keyframes*. Since keyframes are only a fraction of the frames that will be generated, frames between the keyframes must be interpolated.

If interpolation is performed by linear interpolation between the two closest keyframes, the results may be visible momentary speed changes at the keyframes. A better solution is to interpolate the transformations using splines. The Catmull-Rom spline is particularly nice for this. (See Volume 1.)

When interpolating rotations, the statements made previously apply: Don't interpolate matrices by interpolating their values. You should interpolate the represented rotation instead, using either 3-component vectors or a quaternions.

Even with quaternions and vectors, you have the choice between linear interpolation (LERP) and spherical linear interpolation (SLERP). If you interpolate between two rotation vectors, a linear interpolated position will be shorter than the two endpoints, thereby rotating less. This will cause the interpolation to take a detour slightly closer to the non-rotated orientation. See chapter 9 for details about rotation with quaternions.

11.2.2 Inverse kinematics

Kinematics is basically the art of placing things. Forward kinematics is the next to trivial case where the transformation in each joint is controlled directly. With inverse kinematics, we start with the goal instead and calculate a position that match the goal. This works fairly well for modeling robots, but its use for modeling humans is limited.

Inverse kinematics is an optimization problem. For complex cases, it may not be feasible to calculate the solution analytically, but it must be done by iterative methods. One such method is Cyclic Coordinate Descent (CCD). In CCD, you start with the outermost joints, the leaf nodes, aim them towards the target, and then continue towards the root.

It is important to have good constraints on allowed positions, to prevent the model to move to a position that is physically unreasonable. The constraints are usually given as angles on the unit sphere, Euler angles.

11.2.3 Mixing and blending animations

In keyframe animation, an animation consists of a "track" for each joint that it controls. It does not necessarily contain a track for every joint. Different parts of a body can be controlled by different tracks, there can be tracks blending into each other, and some parts can be controlled by inverse kinematics instead.

An example of such animation can be a character who is running and shooting and the same time. In the past, games were unable to combine animations, so the character had to choose between actions. In Quake 2, there was a bizarre case where a running character switched to standing animation if shooting when running, which caused the character to slide over the floor while shooting.

Instead, the body is split into several parts, controlled by different tracks. The legs can be controlled by walking and running animation, while the upper body concerns itself with other things. A shooting animation can either be a separate keyframe track, or the gun arm is controlled by inverse kinematics to aim in the desired direction.

A keyframe animation can be combined with inverse kinematics. The keyframe animation decides on preliminary positions, but then some positions are adjusted to keep within limits. For example, a character can be made to walk a stair by pushing the legs upwards to fit the shape of the stairs.

The choice of animation for each part of the body will also vary over time. Walking turns into running, aiming turns into lifting an object and so on. This is not only a matter of blending between keyframe animations. You may also want to mix between keyframe animation and physically based animation, to avoid jumps.

11.2.4 Physically-based animation

In physically-based animation, classical physics laws are applied to the skeleton. This sounds good but is hard to apply to a human body when it is active. Modeling a walking character that was is a very complex task. It is possible, and we have some results from our group combining learning and physics, but the possibilities are still limited.

In current games, the most popular use of physically-based animation of human bodies is *ragdoll animation*. In ragdoll animation, keyframe animation is used as long as the character is conscious. Only when the character turns unconscious, its animation gets controlled by physical laws. Then the body becomes limp and it will fall down, possibly fall down stairs and similar things, in very realistic ways.

11.3 Skinning and stitching

Once you have decided on positions for the skeleton, the next problem is to coat the bones with a skin, with the desired mesh for the character. This process is called *skinning*.

In order to do this, you need the bone structure and the mesh, but also information on what parts of the skeleton that controls what parts of the mesh.

In the past, body animation was performed using a separate rigid body following every bone. This was fairly common at that time, used in games like MechWarrior and Weekend Warrior. The body is organized hierachically, typically using some point on the spine as global origin and root for the hierarchy. The animations are described by a transformation from every node to an underlying one, and all the vertices in each sub-model follows the movement of the transformations from its position in the hierarchy to the root. This kind of animation is called *parenting* [63].

For objects like robots and insects, this is excellent, but for mammals and anything else with a soft skin we get visible artifacts in the joints which were quite disturbing. Thus, games soon moved to skinning. According to the author of Nanosaur, Brian Greenstone, skinning turned out to be easier than separate body parts in the long run, since each character no longer needed many models. Only a single mesh had to be handled, which simplified things.

Skinning is somewhat tricky to read about, since the literature has not agreed on terminology. According to Lewis [61], the fundamental skinning algorithm is unpublished. Thus, there is no obvious main reference, and we see different terms in different sources. Lewis calls the method "Skeleton-Subspace Deformation". Another name is *enveloping*. I will stick to the common *skinning*, used by e.g. Maya [62].

The background of skinning may explain why the textbooks often handle the problem pretty loosely. Despite the common use of the method, even some of the strongest textbooks give little more than a brief introduction.

The simplest kind of skinning is called *stitching*. [64] In stitching, every vertex follows only a single bone, but vertices can be connected to the same polygon and follow different bones. See Figure 119.

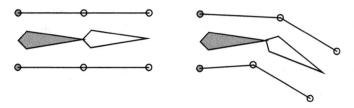

FIGURE 119. Stitching - every vertex follows only one bone

Stitching is remarkably good in many cases. This happens when the joints and the vertices fit the method well, with low-polygon models and relatively small rotations.

This is pretty good, up to a point. As long as the movements are small relative to the density of the vertices, the results are pretty nice (see Figure 119). When movements get too large, however, neighbor vertices belonging to different legs may overlap, and we get visible artifacts, as illustrated by Figure 120. This gets more likely the more detailed models we use.

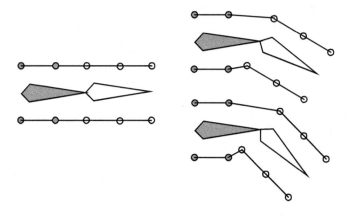

FIGURE 120. With a higher detail mesh and more rotation, stitching is not as good.

The solution to this problem is to allow vertices to belong to more than one bone. Vertices near joints will have different weight for each bone, which will make the joint smoother, as we can see in Figure 121. The weighting of vertices is called *vertex blending* and the whole process is *skinning*.

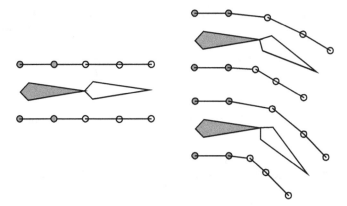

FIGURE 121. Skinning with vertex blending.

To perform skinning, every vertex must carry a number of weights, with the total sum of 1, and every weight refers to one bone. Most vertices will be controlled by one or two bones, and the number is rarely higher than 4.

Given a transformation (which we will return to shortly) that moves a vertex with the movement of a specific bone, we perform the vertex blending like this:

$$v' = \sum_{i=1}^{n} w_i M_i v$$

where

$$\sum_{i=1}^{n} w_i = 1$$

This will render much better results, but it still is not a perfect method. It has a number of shortcomings, described by Lewis [61] (Figure 122). The most obvious ones include "collapsing elbow" and "twist" problems.

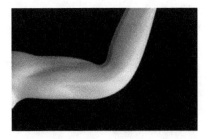 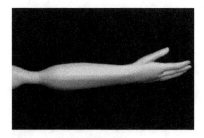

FIGURE 122. Skinning problems, "collapsing elbow" and "twist". Images from [61]

Thus, even more advanced skinning methods are called for. Such methods include using several models that you blend between, or to add constraints that enforce volume preservation. The easiest way to improve things is probably to add bones, to use more than one joint in a joint. There is no physiological explanation for doing so, but this is not a problem. The skeleton, with or without extra joints, tend not to be based on human skeletons at all.

But this is not the place to go deeper into advanced methods. First, we must know how to get the matrix M_i above.

11.4 Coordinate systems and transformations for skinning

The most fundamental problem in skinning is how to calculate the modified position of a vertex following a bone. This important and not necessarily trivial problem is often ignored in literature. It is, of course, a straight linear algebra problem, but we should still properly define the coordinate systems. Once we do, the problem gets easier.

All vertices are given by a single polyhedra model, a mesh, placed in its default, resting position, for which all bones are in known position. This is *model coordinates*, from where the root bone has a model-to-world transformation.

Every leg defines a coordinate system of its own. These coordinate systems are further to "the right" than the model coordinates. (See the transformation discussion in Vol 1.) Thus, I claim that these transformations should be given right-to-left, transforming towards model coordinates (and from there onwards to world and view coordinates etc).

For clarity and simplicity, let us consider a simple example, with one root node (bone) followed by two underlying bones, as in Figure 123.

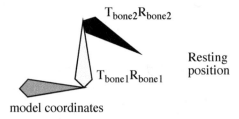

FIGURE 123. Example model, root (grey) and two bones (light grey, black) in resting positions.

The resting position of each leg is defined by a transformation, $M_{bone2} = T_{bone2}R_{bone2}$.

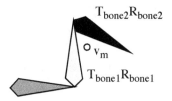

FIGURE 124. A vertex v_m (white circle) given in model coordinates.

Consider a vertex $\mathbf{v_m}$ defined in model coordinates (Figure 124), and we want to find its position in the local coordinate system for a certain bone. Then we must multiply it with the transformations for all bones between the root and the target bone (Figure 125). Since these transformations are defined in the other direction, we must apply the *inverses*!

$$\mathbf{v_{bone2}} = M^{-1}{}_{bone2} M^{-1}{}_{bone1} \mathbf{v_m}$$

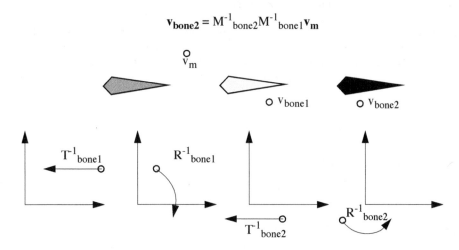

FIGURE 125. The vertex is transformed between the coordinate systems.

If, on the other hand, we know the vertex defined in bone relative coordinates, we can find the model coordinates as:

$$\mathbf{v_m} = M_{bone1} M_{bone2} \mathbf{v_{bone2}}$$

When animating the skeleton, the transformations are modified, so the positions are defined by the modified transformations M'_{bone1} and M'_{bone2}. To transform a vertex $\mathbf{v_m}$ from model coordinates to its modified position $\mathbf{v'_m}$, also in model coordinates, the total transformation is

$$\mathbf{v'_m} = M'_{bone1} M'_{bone2} M^{-1}{}_{bone2} M^{-1}{}_{bone1} \mathbf{v_m}$$

Obviously, the two bones bone1 and bone2 are replaced by whatever bone sequence you have.

Thus, the entire process is, in more general terms:

- Transform the vertex to the local coordinate system for the bone, using the inverses of the resting positions for the bone transformations.

- Transform back to model coordinates using modified transformations, describing the current pose of the skeleton.

Just like in the bump mapping and shadow generation, the most important thing is to have good control over your coordinate systems. Once you have that, many problems suddenly become fairly easy. What can make skinning unnecessarily hard is that these transformations are so seldom explained. All too often, you will find them by analyzing code.

Note that the order of operations is important for performance. The multiplications of the matrices are done *for every bone*, while the final multiplication by the matrix are done *by vertex*. So don't multiply all matrices for every vertex.

It is possible to optimize the process somewhat by applying all inverse transforms beforehand, so all vertices are available in bone-local coordinates. [64] When performing skinning on the CPU, this is no problem. When doing it on the GPU, in a shader, the situation is different. The amount of available memory is much smaller, so we need to optimize its usage.

11.5 Vertex blending

The sequence of matrices in the example above, $M'_{bone1}M'_{bone2}M^{-1}_{bone2}M^{-1}_{bone1}$, corresponds to the matrix M_i in the formula

$$v' = \sum_{i=1}^{n} w_i M_i v$$

For our example, assume that the vertex is affected by the bones bone1 and bone2. Then,

$$M_1 = M'_{bone1}M^{-1}_{bone1}$$

$$M_2 = M'_{bone1}M'_{bone2}M^{-1}_{bone2}M^{-1}_{bone1}$$

and the blending will be

$$v' = \sum_{i=1}^{2} w_i M_i v = w_1 M_1 v + w_2 M_2 v$$

11.6 Animation parameters

For every bone, there is a transformation matrix M_{bone} which defined the transformation from the bone coordinate system to a level closer to the root. The animation is achieved by modifying this transformation. In particular, we tend to apply *rotations*. We can write the resting position of a bone as a rotation and a translation:

$$M_{bone} = T_{rest} \cdot R_{rest}$$

Rotation of the bone using the rotation R_{anim} is applied as

$$M'_{bone} = M_{bone} \cdot R_{anim} = T_{rest} \cdot R_{rest} \cdot R_{anim}$$

Let us express the blending in more general terms. The total calculation of a vertex position thus is as follows. The matrix for transforming model coordinates to bone coordinates is, for a sequence of bones indexed by i

$$M_{mb} = \prod M^{-1}_{bone,i}$$

and the transformation back to model coordinates is

$$M_{bm} = \prod M_{bone,i} \cdot R_{anim,i}$$

so we get

$$v' = M_{bm} \cdot M_{mb} \cdot v$$

11.7 Implementation in a shader

It is possible, and under certain circumstances advantageous, to implement skinning in a shader. The big advantage is that the entire model can be resident in VRAM, uploading only animation parameters for every frame.

In order to implement skinning in a shader, a relatively big amount of data must be updated and passed to the shader for every frame. They should, if at all possible, be sent as attribute or uniform variables, since they are accessed more efficiently than data stored in textures. Note that it is possible to pass entire arrays of data to attribute and uniform, but the amount of memory for attribute and uniform variables is limited.

Since all transformation matrices are pre-multiplied, what should be implemented in the shader is the following formula, which appeared above:

$$v' = \sum_{i=1}^{n} w_i M_i v$$

Again, this formula is what is left after multiplying all transformation together. The matrix multiplications should be done on the CPU, not in the shader.

The resulting matrices M_i are passed as *uniform* variables. The weights w_i varies per vertex and are sent as *attribute*.

11.8 Representation of rotation

Above, it has been implicit that rotations are represented by matrices. Depending on the animation situation, it may be suitable to represent rotations by quaternions, in order to make interpolations of rotation easier. This is, however, an entirely different problem, another layer, and has therefore been ignored here.

11.9 Conclusions

In this chapter, the skinning algorithm has been described as the main feature. We choose not to go deeper into the advanced skinning algorithms, but encourage the reader to look them up in research papers.

12. Deformable objects

In the previous chapter, we have looked at one very common way to handle deformable bodies. There are, however, many shapes that need a different solution. Such shapes include:

- Cloth
- Foam rubber
- Jelly
- Balloons
- Clay

and many others. There are several methods to handle such shapes.

12.1 An overview of the subject of deformable bodies

I have been involved in several diploma theses on this subject, and have based this material on two of them: "Simulering av mjuka kroppar för spel" by Roger Johannesson [11] and "Physical Simulation and Visualization of Cells" by Johannes Nilsson [12].

The following approaches of deformable body animations will be covered:

- Pre-generated deformations
- Mass-spring systems
- Finite element method
- Shape matching
- Pressure model
- Implicit modeling
- Point-based animation

12.2 Pre-generated deformations

In older games, it is common to find pre-generated deformations. This is not least true for driving games like Midtown Madness or Driver. When a car, or other object, is hit by a large force, the model is simply replaced by another, slightly deformed model. There can be several different models each representing various amounts of damage. Obviously, the deformation will have no direct relation to the collision it is response to, so it is quite unrealistic. It is also of no technical interest, a designer-level solution.

12.3 Mass-spring systems

In a *mass-spring system*, the deformable shape is modeled as a set of particles, point masses, interconnected by springs, generally springs that only work on the distance between the points, as in Figure 126.

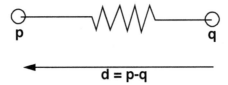

FIGURE 126. Mass-spring model

Let us look at two particles connected by a spring. The distance between them will give the force from Hooke's law.

The spring has a rest position, which is a distance denoted r, the distance where the spring force is zero.

The distance is the difference in position:

$$|\mathbf{d}| = |\mathbf{p}\text{-}\mathbf{q}|$$

Then the force, in the direction of the spring, is

$$f = -k_s(|\mathbf{d}|\text{-}r)$$

In order to map the force in the direction of the spring, we multiply by $\mathbf{d}$ and get the forces for each of the two points $\mathbf{p}$ and $\mathbf{q}$:

$$\mathbf{f}_p = -k_s \cdot (|\mathbf{d}| - r) \cdot \frac{\mathbf{d}}{|\mathbf{d}|}$$

$$\mathbf{f}_q = -\mathbf{f}_p$$

This simple formula is an undamped spring. With damping, we get a slightly more complicated formula. Most importantly, the relative speed between the points must be taken into account, in order to add a force component that will reduce it. See Figure 127.

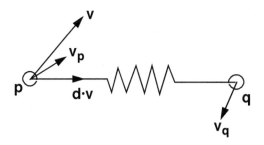

FIGURE 127. Mass-spring system with damping

The damping depends on the speed difference:

$$v = v_p - v_q$$

The speed difference is projected onto the direction of the spring by the dot product d•v.

The force now is

$$f_p = -\left(k_s \cdot (|d| - r) + \frac{k_d \cdot (d \bullet v)}{|d|}\right) \cdot \frac{d}{|d|}$$

A suitable number of particles can be connected by such springs. The particles can be organized in many ways, but of course a 2D or 3D grid is easiest. Then a 2d grid might look like in Figure 128.

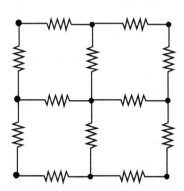

FIGURE 128. An insufficient mass-spring system with nine particles.

Alas, with this few springs there is no reason for the system to keep its shape. It will collapse like in Figure 129.

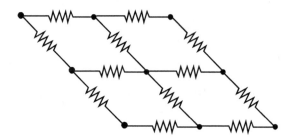

FIGURE 129. The mass-spring system will collapse with too few springs

The problem is that there simply is no reason for the system to keep its shape with this few springs. We must add more springs, as in Figure 130.

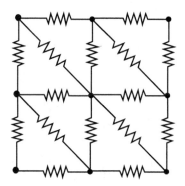

FIGURE 130. Better mass-spring system.

Even this is not enough, we should add the other diagonal too. And this is just for 2D! In 3D, the number of springs will be considerable. You can make a fully interconnected square with 6 springs. Doing the same for a cube requires 28 springs!

The algorithm for running the mass-spring system is very simple. In its simplest form, it can be written as follows:

- Sum all forces for each particle.
- Calculate acceleration from the forces.
- Update speed and position (Euler integration).

The method has a few pretty important weaknesses.

- As mentioned above, too few springs will make the system unstable. This is a design issue, but also a question of computational burden.

Deformable objects

- It only works with distances and has no way to know if a point is on the "right side" of another. If a large force is applied on a mass-spring system, it might turn inside-out.

- Since there are so many interacting forces, Euler integration is insufficient. The system will easily be unstable, oscillate and explode. Smaller integration steps or better integration methods can improve the situation.

- The method can not prevent self-intersection (without non-trivial extensions).

Mass-spring systems have found some use for cloth animation. [58] Due to the large number of springs needed, they are less popular for 3D objects. The stability problems makes it unsuitable for a general solution for deformable bodies. It is best for objects that are not affected by large and sudden forces.

In my courses, there have been several projects based on mass-spring animation, mostly in 2D. In 2D, we have seen cloth animation, simulation of a soccer goal, flags and more. There have also been a few bold groups working in 3D, experiencing models turning inside-out, oscillating etc.

12.4 Finite element method

The *finite-element method* (FEM) is a general method for approximating solutions to boundary-value problems over non-regular grids. The domain that it works on is divided into a finite number of elements and the equations approximated over these elements.

This method has found its way into simulating deformable bodies. A good way to do this is to subdivide the shape entirely into *tetrahedrons* (Figure 131). For complex models, the number of tetrahedrons can be pretty large.

FIGURE 131. A tetrahedron, the building block in FEM-based deformable body animation

With a tetrahedron as building block, it is fairly easy to calculate the volume of the element, which is an important component in calculating the interaction with neighbor elements. In contrast to the mass-spring method, this will make it impossible to turn elements inside-out.

Every element can be assigned all material properties desired, possibly unique for that element. Through these parameters, we can design the entire object in a fairly simple way, through physical facts rather than fine-tuning. This will also give a more exact result that the mass-spring method.

Furthermore, the FEM method is stable, can even be guaranteed stable. It handles interpenetration, so parts of the same object can collide with each other.

Clearly this is an attractive method, not least for 3D models. On its negative side, it is relatively computationally demanding, and it requires that we break down the entire model to a volumetric mesh. This is moderate drawbacks, so the method can be recommended as a safe and capable approach to deformable body animation.

The computational load can be reduced somewhat by mapping a detailed surface mesh onto a coarser set of finite elements, tetrahedrons. This method is similar to the skin & bones method (chapter 11) but the skin follows the tetrahedrons rather than bone structure. See Müller & Gross [55] for more details.

12.5 Shape matching

Shape matching is another method that gives good results with good stability. It was presented by Müller et.al. in 2005 [56]. Roger Johannesson [11] studied this method in his diploma thesis.

This is a particle system method, just like mass-spring systems. The idea with the method is that instead of having springs striving to restore the shape locally, each particle will, independently of each other, strive towards its proper position in a global sense.

The shape is defined at rest as a set of points, the positions of each particle. We call this set of points A. When forces act upon the point masses, they will move to new positions. The current positions is another set of points which we call B.

Using A and B, we can calculate a rotation and translation that will match them onto each other as well as possible. Using these transforms, we transform A to A'. Thus, A' and B will be placed on top of each other, differing only in internal individual movements for the particles. See Figure 132.

Then each point B_i in B is attracted by the corresponding point A'_i in A', as in Figure 132. As long as the attraction force is small enough not to move B_i past A'_i, the system will be stable. This can be done as follows.

$$v_i(t + h) = v_i(t) + \partial(A'_i(t) - B_i(t)) \cdot h^{-1}$$

$$B_i(t + h) = B_i(t) + h \cdot v_i(t + h)$$

where $v_i(t)$ is the velocity of the particle at the time t. The constant ∂ should be between 0 and 1.

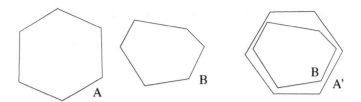

FIGURE 132. The original shape A is translated and rotated to a best fit on the current shape B.

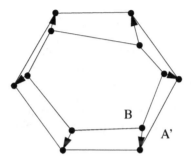

FIGURE 133. The current shape B is attracted to A'.

One problem is how to calculate the transformations from A to A'. The translation is trivial, it is simply the difference between the centers of mass, which I call A_{cm} and B_{cm}. The rotation should be one that minimizes the following sum:

$$\sum_i m_i \cdot (R(B_i - B_{cm}) - (A_i' - A_{cm}))^2$$

See [11] for details on how this can be solved.

12.6 Pressure model

The *pressure model* was proposed by Matyka [57]. Matyka was guest student at the University of Linköping and worked on this model as part of courses here, giving very impressive presentations. The method has become increasingly famous since then. Recently, Johannes Nilsson did his diploma thesis using this model as a central tool [12].

Instead of using a complex inner structure like the mass-spring system or FEM method, the pressure model uses a 2D surface mesh without an inner structure. The pressure is calculated from the ideal gas law:

$$PV = nRT$$

In the equation, P is the pressure, V is the volume. The constant n is the mol number of the gas. R is the ideal gas constant and T is the temperature. For practical purposes, nRT can often be considered constant, so $k_p = nRT$. Then we can rewrite the formula to:

$$P = k_p/V$$

From the pressure we can calculate the force on a surface patch, that is a polygon in the mesh. Let the area of the surface patch be A_i and its surface normal $\mathbf{n}_i$. Then the force acting on this surface patch is:

$$\mathbf{f}_p = PA_i\mathbf{n}_i$$

Since we rather work on vertices than polygons, we distribute this force to all vertices. The total force on each vertex is then a force from the pressure on each of its neighbor polygons, plus the spring forces to each neighbor.

The result is particularly suitable for objects that, just like the model, has a distinct, elastic shell and a fluid or gas-filled inside. Balloons filled with gas or water, as well as cells [12] have been simulated with this model.

On the negative side, the model can have problems with self-intersection, and it is not very suitable for non-convex objects.

12.7 Implicit modeling

In implicit modeling, we use continuous functions to represent the surface rather than a mesh.

An important implicit method is the *level set method*, where the continuous function is also implicit. We have no analytical formula for the function, but a sampling, typically in a Cartesian grid.

The level set can, for example, represent the density in each sample. Then we can find the surface of objects at the points where the density it at a treshold value. The surface is conveniently extracted by the marching cubes algorithm, well-known from visualization of volume data.

The level set method has been successfully applied to applications like simulating water and smoke.

12.8 Point-based animation

Point-based animation is a fairly new field in computer graphics, where the availability of the big processing power in modern GPUs is used for running models that have no mesh. This is the case for implicit modeling too, but while implicit modeling rely on functions, point-based animation works from sets of points. (You may argue that the set of points can define a function.)

The shape is represented by a set of point samples, dubbed *phyxels*. (Pixels, voxels, texels... Everybody want their own names on things. It is a *point*, OK?) Instead of connecting vertices by a fixed grid, each point is connected dynamically to the closest points by a weight function.

Since there is no fixed connections, the points can move more freely. The shape of the object is generated from the points. This can be done by blobs, where a weight function is mapped onto every point, and the surface is assigned a certain treshold.

The computational load is considerable. On the positive side, breaking a point-based object is easy. The model is suitable for materials like clay.

12.9 Breakable objects

A problem related to deformable objects is the problem of making objects breakable. How hard it is to break up a model depends very much on the kind of model. Breaking polyhedra objects is pretty hard. It can be done, of course.

For a deformable body, we tend to calculate many inner forces anyway, which makes the breaking a feature on the top which has pretty good support to begin with. Breaking rigid bodies is different. We do not have any measures of the forces inside the shape, so we much make such calculations from the ground up.

A mass-spring system can detect when a spring is overburdened. At that time, it makes sense to break the spring in two, create two new vertices somewhere at the middle of the spring (not the exact middle, add some randomness). For a 2D mass-spring system this is pretty manageable. A 3D system is, as always, more complicated. Then we can not just split a vertex, but must also create new polygons to introduce the edges of the crack, and we may need to modify remaining springs, as shown in Figure 134. An alternative could be to remove the springs altogether, but then we must also identify what polygons to remove. When should a polygon be removed? When any spring in it breaks, or the last one? Again, in 3D we must be more sophisticated than that.

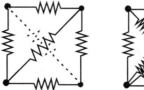

FIGURE 134. Breaking a mass-spring system can be complicated.

While mesh objects are somewhat hard to break, the situation is very different for point-based methods and FEM.

Point-based methods are very good at making breakable objects. A point-based object can be made to break apart almost effortlessly since the points are only attracted to each other, as in Figure 135. Thus, there are no firm connections to break.

FIGURE 135. Point-based shapes easily break apart.

FEM models, which I have already mentioned as a good approach to deformable bodies, is also suitable for breakable objects, as long as we are happy breaking it into the finite elements (Figure 136). It is pretty straight-forward to assign a treshold for how large the forces working on a certain vertex may be. When the forces (not the sum but rather the sum of the magnitudes) are above the treshold, we may split the vertex in two, separating parts of the model from each other.

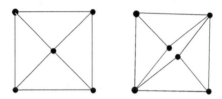

FIGURE 136. Breaking up a FEM model is relatively simple, only needs duplicating vertices.

12.10 Simulating liquids and smoke with the Navier-Stokes equations

There are several approaches to simulating liquids and smoke. On a high detail level, they can be simulated with particle systems, as mentioned in chapter 12.8 and chapter 12.9. Other approaches to liquids is to only simulate the surface of the liquid, e.g. by sets of harmonic functions.

Another approach, which is popular not least for its ability to model swirls, flow and other effects, is implementations based on the Navier-Stokes equation. It has been used successfully to model fluids, smoke and fire, both in 2D and 3D.

The most central Navier-Stokes equation can be written as follows.

$$\frac{\delta v}{\delta t} = -(v \bullet \nabla)v + \gamma \Delta v - \frac{1}{\rho}\nabla p + f$$

This equation certainly requires some explanation.

Deformable objects

The whole expression tells how the velocity is affected by various local properties of the fluid, that is an expression for the acceleration. Let me remind you of the symbols. The symbol ∇ is the gradient of the argument. In 2D, you can write this as a vector $(\partial/\partial x, \partial/\partial y)$. The symbol Δ (often written ∇^2) is the Laplacian, $\partial^2/\partial x^2 + \partial^2/\partial y^2$.

Now, let us look at each term.

The term $-(v\bullet\nabla)\cdot v$ is the *advection* term, the divergence of the velocity. It describes that the divergence of the velocity will affect the velocity itself. Essentially, when the flow narrows, it goes faster, and vice versa.

The term $\gamma\Delta v$ is the viscocity γ times the gradient of the velocity. This is the *diffusion* term, where the velocity is affected by the velocity variation within the neighborhood. If viscocity is high, the material is thicker, so neighbor particles will move more like its neighbors, while low viscocity materials will move more freely.

The third term, $1/\rho$ times ∇p, is the gradient of the pressure times one over the density. This term simply models that high pressure areas will produce a flow towards low pressure areas, an obvious fact, and the effect is lower for high density materials.

Finally, we have the sum of all external forces **f**.

Implementing this is a matter of discretization, but also a matter of finding a stable model Taking the gradient and Laplacian in a discrete domain is simple enough, while discrete time can cause more trouble, as discussed in chapter 10. There are several approaches to this, and stability is an important issue. An often cited paper on the subject is by Stam [98]. His implementation is available on-line.

12.11 Further comments

Deformable models is a challenging topic, but can be very amusing and really quite manageable if you choose a suitable representation. The processing power needed for bigger deformable bodies is large, but not more than what modern computers can handle.

There are some related subjects, like ragdoll physics and body animation, which we sort under other chapters in this book since they are not about fully deformable bodies but rather about systems of rigid parts (with a more or less soft skin). Another related subject is face animation, which is also a combined problem where rigid parts play a big role. [48]

13. Fundamental AI for games

Artificial Intelligence used to be a too ambitious word for describing the behavior of game entities. Therefore, I avoided it when I wrote the AI chapters for a game programming book in the 90's. Since then, the concept "game AI" has matured as a concept that gamers know well. Since they, unlike the customers of bigger systems, do not expect a system that is truly intelligent, the term "game AI" gives lower expectations. This is actually a good thing, not only for game AI but for the AI concept as such. Even simple behavior systems can be "AI" today.

There are some concepts that are inevitable when dealing with game AI, concepts that are also central in general AI like state machines and path finding. However, beyond that, game AI is a subject with many disconnected ends and limited possibilities for general methods. In all too many cases, game AI is simply hacked. In this chapter, I will give an overview of the most fundamental concepts. That will not make this chapter very exciting for an experienced game programmer or a CS student with experience of AI courses. However, in the next chapter I hope to break some new ground.

13.1 Game AI, geometry and physics

It is really impossible to discuss AI, geometry and physics for games as entirely separate problems. Game physics is a straight-forward application of classic physics, but its interaction with decision making (AI) is non-trivial. In many games, we can see poor AI where the game entities make poor decisions since they do not understand the physics or even the geometry of the game world.

So the game level gives the geometry, the physics describe the results of movements, and AI plans and makes decisions based on the others. And the result of this interaction is the animation, as in Figure 137.

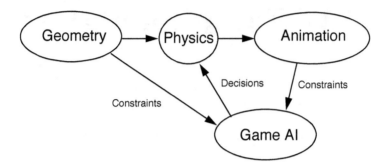

FIGURE 137. Physics and AI interacts

Typical AI problems include:

- Path planning
- Behavior
- Decision making

There are two different kinds of game AI:

- Agents: opponents and other computer controlled objects
- Abstract control systems, overall behavior of higher level entities like an army or a flock of sheep

The former controls agents that are easy to understand, so we often expect a certain behavior from them. We expect a knight to patrol, defend, attack, an ape to climb trees and a sheep to move in flock. Thus, the behavior should match the expectations to a reasonable degree. The latter group contains all kind of abstract control systems, from the opponent in Chess to the general of an army.

There are many problems that the game AI should (or at least may) take into account. As already hinted, spatial information, the geometry of the game world, is important. On a small scale, this includes line-of-sight, visibility.

The entities often need to have memory, or they will be so short-minded that they become too easy to outsmart. But how should we save that memory?

The analysis of the situation, in order to make a decision, is often done with very simple methods. Decisions can be taken with primitive rule-based systems.

What decisions that need to be taken may be more interesting than how to make the decisions. The abilities of the agent is important. What can it do? Can it move, use different poses, hide, fire...?

Finally, we have the subject of cheating. Do we want the agent to be able to cheat? What do we mean by cheating? An agent can be allowed to know a bit more than its line of sight really should allow it to. We can give it extra information to compensate for other short-comings.

13.2 Behavior

The most basic form of game AI is to control the behavior of agents. Common methods include:

- Finite-state machines
- Rule-based systems
- Planning and problem solving
- Biology inspired AI, optimizations on parameter sets, learning systems

A simple and common problem is to make agents for action games. They have a set of pretty well-defined behaviors:

- Hunting
- Evading
- Random movement
- Follow a path
- Rest

The *hunter* is your average action game opponent, moves towards you as its only behavior. But it can also be a part of a more complex behavior, and it does not necessarily "hunt" the player, it can have other goals.

The *evader* is in its simplest form the opposite of the hunter. It can be an opponent that runs away when badly hurt (at least a first sign of "intelligence"), or civilians running away from the baddies. But again, it can also be part of a more complex picture.

Random movement sounds more dull than it is. Purely random changes in position is certainly not a good behavior other than for some small insects, but changes in speed and direction can be very good, especially when mixed with other behaviors. Remember what I said in Volume 1: Noise is beautiful. And that goes for behavioral noise too.

Following a path is great for a lot of things. Patrolling opponents will seem a lot smarter than idiots that wander aimlessly or just stand still until they notice the player. Paths can be pre-generated, but can also be the result of path planning.

Resting, finally, is not much of a behavior, but again it can be mixed in with others. For example, imagine Dr. Frankenstein in his lab. You can't really simulate all that is going on, we don't know exactly what he is doing, but we can fake it pretty nicely. You can make him follow a path between a number of places, and rest at each place to represent "work". Without resting, he would be running around all the time.

So mixing behaviors is important. The agent may switch between different behaviors depending on game events. Such events include:

- Sound nearby
- The player or other interesting objects within sight
- The agent is hurt, attacked etc.
- Communication
- Other events, like reaching the end of a path

Thus, the behavior is determined by the current state of the agent, represented by some kind of state parameters stored in the agent. Changes of state can cause changes of behavior. This can be represented by a *finite-state machine* (FSM). A simple game FSM can look like Figure 138:

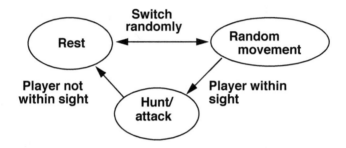

FIGURE 138. Simple finite-state machine

This looks simple and understandable, but the agent will be a total idiot. We can try to make a slightly more advanced example (Figure 139 on page 207).

This is a nicer, smarter entity, but it is a lot more complicated, and it is not even complete; the "Ally" state should probably be several states, hunting the player when too far away, attacking anyone attacking the player... If the player should have any possibility to communicate with it, things get even worse. And it will still not appear very smart at all.

So maybe the FSMs are not so perfect after all? They can be unnecessarily formal and rigid. A possibility to handle this is to use parallel FSMs, where several FSMs work in parallel on the same agent. This makes it possible to model multiple behaviors separately. We must, of course, resolve situations where the states imply multiple behaviors, but that can be solved.

Another option, which is a lot less formal and suitable for "hacking" solutions is to use *rule-based systems*. We may skip the states and state switches, but rather use a few simple rules. The simple FSM above will turn into something like this:

- If no player is visible, move randomly
- If the player is visible, hunt

- If the player is close, attack

This is just as fine, and is easier to expand.

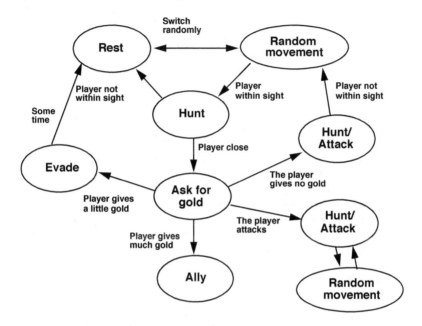

FIGURE 139. A somewhat more advanced finite-state machine

13.3 Data representation of entities

The data representation of the game entities is mostly a trivial problem. A game entity should be represented by a data structure (object). In simple games, the game entities can be organized as a single linked list. In larger games, the entities need to be grouped in several lists, e.g. one per room or similar. It is important to be able to turn off entities that do not affect the player.

A minor issue that can cause problems is the disposal of game entities. When can an entity be removed from the list(s) of game entities? If you can unlink and dispose at any time, then what happens when an entity disposes itself, or an entity disposes an object that is queued as the next to process? This is really just an issue of fixing bugs, but the bugs can sometimes be hard to understand.

When I wrote the 2D game engine "Sprite Animation Toolkit", my solution was that the game entities (sprites) could only be marked for disposal in the game loop, they could not be disposed. That way, entities could "kill" each other as much as they wanted. The actual disposal was done in a separate stage.

13.4 World representation

The representation of the game world is vital for most aspects of a game. For graphics, the representation of the visual content has importance for quality as well as performance. The same holds for physics. For AI, the world representation affects the possibilities of the agents.

A very simple example of world representation is Pac-Man. The world is a grid, which is easily represented by an array. We need boolean information that says whether a space is open or blocked, but there is more. We need to decide on the representation of the markers that we collect as well as power-ups.

What is interesting with this case is that there can be an additional array, which exists for the AI alone, an array that saves information that affects the movement of the agents (the ghosts). The player can leave tracks, a kind of "scent" that the ghosts will follow. Without that information, the ghosts may either move towards the player on the shortest route, which makes them too smart, or they only move towards the player when they have a free line of sight, which makes them incapable. By following the "scent" they will appear to have some memory. Add some randomness to make them make mistakes and their behavior can be very nice. See Figure 140.

In the Pac-Man clone "Bachman", I used this kind of "scent grid", mixed with randomness, so every time a tomato (ghost) reached a fork in its path, the path with the best "scent value" had a higher probability to be chosen, but there was a fair chance that it took the wrong way. This added a randomness that made the game a lot more fun.

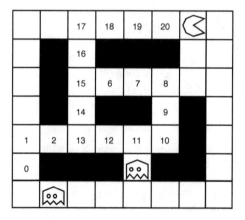

FIGURE 140. Pac-Man can have a "tracking" grid for assisting the game AI

The scent grid is only one kind of extra data for the AI. Other extra data can include influence maps (see chapter 14.1), and information about physics. The latter is particularly important. It is hard for the AI system to predict the outcome of the physics engine. It is easier to pre-generate such information. For example, a slope can not only include information about the direction that the gravity will bring you, but also inform the AI where it will end up if it slides down the slope, information that will make it easier to make proper decisions.

Other games may benefit more from polygonal representations, especially when the geometry is polygonal to begin with, e.g. most 3D games. Consider a game like Robowar. We can represent the world as a mesh of triangles. All triangles carry references to all neighbors, for easy searching of neighbor areas. They also have a pointer each to a list of objects that are located in the triangle.

Visibility is vital for a game like this. For this particular representation, visibility can be calculated by using the triangle edges as portals. See Figure 141.

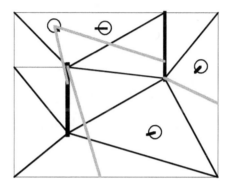

FIGURE 141. Robowar-style game with polygon world

A polygonal world is a lot more awkward to search. Thus, many games combine the two. It is common that games use three or more resolutions of the game world for different purposes. The highest resolution is for graphics. GPUs are powerful and can pump many polygons through its pipeline per frame. A lower resolution is used for physics, with simplified bounding shapes for collision handling. Finally, a fairly rough grid-based sampling can be used for AI, sampling the continuous game world to discrete positions that makes it easier to run AI algorithms. Thus, a detailed 3D scene can be reduced to a simple 2D grid. Making the grid unnoticeable in the game is a challenge, though. Entities that always move from grid position to grid position may reveal the trick.

13.5 Distance in game worlds

Since game worlds are so often discrete, at least on the AI level, the problem of measuring distance is non-trivial. What we expect is that the distance between two points is the Euclidean distance, so that the distance between two points $p_1 = (x_1, y_1)$ and $p_2 = (x_2, y_2)$ is

$$D(p_1, p_2) = \sqrt{(x_1^2 - x_2^2) + (y_1^2 - y_2^2)}$$

or, with $\Delta x = |x_1 - x_2|$ and $\Delta y = |y_1 - y_2|$

$$D(p_1, p_2) = \sqrt{\Delta x^2 + \Delta y^2}$$

For most people, this is the "true distance", but for a mathematician, or someone working with digital geometry, it is one *metric* out of many (although the "finest" one that you often want to achieve). A metric is a distance measure, a concept often used for other distances than geometrical distances. In our game related applications, it is usually geometrical distance, but in the field of AI there are other options.

A metric is a measure that fulfills a few conditions:

$$D(p_1, p_1) = 0$$

$$D(p_1, p_2) > 0, p_1 \neq p_2$$

$$D(p_1, p_2) = D(p_2, p_1)$$

$$D(p_1, p_3) \leq D(p_1, p_2) + D(p_2, p_3)$$

From top to bottom, this means that

- A point is always at distance zero to itself.
- The distance between two different points is larger than zero.
- The distance is the same in both directions.
- The distance between two points does not get smaller by taking a detour over another point.

Any measure that does not fulfill these criteria is not a metric, and is thus not a *distance* measure but something else. A measure that take slope into account may be useful but it is by definition not a metric. Thus, we should discern between metrics and movement cost. However, many problems are valid for both and a movement cost can often be the distance multiplied by terrain factors.

When working with a discrete grid, it becomes awkward or even impossible to use Euclidean metric all the time. If an agent walks from p_1 to p_2 but has to make every move between neighbor grid spaces, then the path becomes longer and the effect is that we get a different metric.

Take the chessboard for instance. It takes the king exactly 7 moves from any corner to any other corner, so the distance is the same - even the diagonal. This metric is known as the *chessboard distance* and is very common in games. It is defined like this:

$$D_{chessboard}(p_1, p_2) = \max(\Delta x, \Delta y)$$

Fundamental AI for games

The chessboard metric is what you get when allowing movement one step at a time in all 8 directions on a Cartesian grid. Another common metric is the *City Block distance*, which is what you get by disallowing diagonal moves. It is sometimes called *Manhattan distance*, as if Manhattan was the only city with streets in a regular grid.

$$D_{cityblock}(p_1, p_2) = max(\Delta x, \Delta y) + min(\Delta x, \Delta y)$$

With both these metrics, the difference from Euclidean distance is disturbing. Both have a maximum error of 40% (square root of two). For example, when playing Sid Meier's Civilization (that is, the computer game), you can walk in zig-zag, covering extra ground, for no extra cost.

This can be remedied by using pseudo-Euclidean metrics. The simplest pseudo-Euclidean metric is the *Chamfer 2-3 distance*. What we do is to assign different movement costs for different moves, so horizontal/vertical moves cost 2 and diagonal moves cost 3. This is a very good approximation. It can be proven that Chamfer 3-4 distance is even better, but the difference is marginal. It is tempting to believe that floating-point weights, 1 and the square root of 2, would be perfect. It is indeed good, but it is only perfect on the axes. If you take a move of $(1, 2)$, the metric is still an approximation.

It is also possible to make even better approximations by handling larger steps, in particular to have a separate weight for moves like $(1, 2)$. Chamfer 5-7-11 distance is proven a good integer metric, and again we can also consider floating-point measures.

Another method for getting better metrics is to use hexagonal distance. This is what you get if you represent your world by a hexagonal grid instead of a Cartesian one. The hexagonal grid is very popular in strategic board games, and has been used in many computer games, like XConq. Adapting games created on the Cartesian grid to hexagonal grid is interesting and often result in twists on the original that make them more or less all-new games. Such adaptions include Tetris (Hextris and Bikaka), Mines (Hexmines) and Snake (Hexnake). However, the Cartesian grid is much easier to work with, so hexagonal games will remain a curiosity niche.

13.6 Path finding with variations

A common problem for game AI is to decide how an entity should move. When an entity is not following a path, but moving towards some goal without a known path, it needs to find the path itself. Sometimes it finds a path that is certain to work, and sometimes it should find a path that *might* work, but that can change over time.

Finding the path in a scene with no obstacles is plain silly; just move towards the goal. When there are obstacles, this approach does not work at all, but you can still find it in games. One example is the game Bugdom, where opponents (ants and others) move straight towards the player entity. The player can easily take advantage of this by making opponents run into objects or even into dangerous areas. This has a point in terms of game mechanics, but it lacks realism.

A simple but quite usable movement algorithm is the *crash and turn* algorithm. It can be described like this:

- Move towards the goal.
- If you run into an object, move in a random direction for some time, then continue.

At first glance, it looks as stupid as the straight hunter, but it works a lot better. The entities will run straight into obstacles, but unlike the Bugdom ants, they will not just stop at the obstacle, but will try again and again to get out of it. It will still be possible to trap them, if there are dead ends that are big enough, but at least they won't get trapped by running into a tree or a chair. This also makes the method work well in environments where many objects are moving.

The algorithm is illustrated by Figure 142. An agent moves towards a goal (left). When it hits an obstacle (middle) it turns to a different direction and moves some distance in that direction. Then (right) it turns towards the goal and tries again.

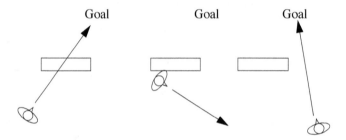

FIGURE 142. The Crash and turn algorithm

There is one parameter to play with, and that is the length of the random moves. There is also a possibility to increase the random component over time, make the random moves both longer and in more than one direction at a time, in order to "shake" the system out of a deadlock. However, the agent will not really appear to have a very intelligent behavior, so it is best used in environments where short, simple random moves are likely to work.

A more exact method is Dijkstra's algorithm. It is defined on a graph with movement cost weights, but fits well on the Cartesian grid as well. In the latter case, the algorithm is called the *constrained distance transform*. [45]

The algorithm works like this: The grid is filled with infinite distance (the highest that you can represent), except for one endpoint which is zero, and obstacles that are assigned a special blocking symbol. Starting at the endpoint that we gave distance zero, a breadth-first search propagates distance values over the grid. We keep a list of active points in the propagation front, which initially only contains the starting point.

```
for all points in the list p
    for all neighbors n
        if D(n) > D(p) + 1 then
            D(n) := D(p) + 1
```

```
      put n on the list
remove p from the list
```

With 8 neighbors, this algorithm uses Chessboard distance, and with 4 neighbors it uses City Block distance. It is easily updated to other distances like Chamfer 3-4, but including moves longer than one step is not advisable since it will jump over thin obstacles.

The algorithm is run either until the other endpoint is reached (a good pick when using Chessboard distance since the shortest path is always the first to reach the goal) or until no changes occur in the image. Then we find the path by walking "downhill" from the other endpoint. See Figure 143.

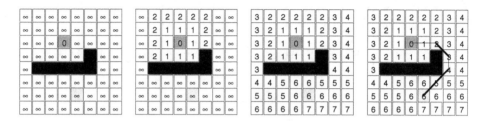

FIGURE 143. Path finding with constrained distance map a.k.a. Dijkstra's algorithm

A drawback with Dijkstra's algorithm is that it propagates uniformly in all directions. It can be optimized to do most work in the areas that are most likely to matter. A very popular algorithm with this feature is the A* algorithm.

With A*, a heuristic function is added, which should be some kind of estimate for how many steps there can be left from that point. This is usually as simple as the distance to the goal as the bird flies. This is combined with the distance value of the point in question (the distance already traveled), say by addition. The sum is an estimate of the total path length.

The heuristic function is used to decide which list element to process next.

A* can be applied to many problems other than path finding in a grid. Some of them are just as valid for games. For example, you can search state-spaces by distance functions in similar ways, which can be a way to make an agent solve seemingly harder problems.

For example, you can solve the Towers Of Hanoi game using A*. The state space can be a 3-dimensional grid where each axis is a bit array with all pieces on each stick. From each state, a maximum of three moves are possible. A* will search the state space efficiently and output a solution. However, even though the Towers Of Hanoi is a game, the solution is not a game problem but an optimization problem. You rarely need a puzzle-solver in a game. The player solves the puzzles.

The same goes for path-finding, at least partially. Path-finding is indeed important for deciding on movement for agents, but is the shortest path necessarily what we want? There are several alternatives to following the shortest path! Some other approaches include:

You can switch between random movement and moving towards the path. This will generate a movement that is a bit absent-minded, as if the agent is insecure or distracted by other things. It will find its way as well as "crash&turn", but it will not seem as stupid since it will not find itself with the nose in the wall over and over again.

You may follow not the shortest but the *safest* path. Why go through narrow spaces, squeezing through narrow passages, when you can take a little detour and go somewhere where the path is more spacey. This can be achieved by reducing the area a bit, for example by binary erosion, a concept from *mathematical morphology*. Basically, every open space that is neighbor to a wall is set to blocking. As long as a solution is found and it is not much longer than the original one, we may use that. It is also possible to add a penalty function that makes the agent avoid edge spaces when possible but does not forbid it to go there, for example using an influence map (see chapter 14.1).

Figure 144 shows a scene with obstacles, where two paths are suggested: one that is shortest, and one that is "safer". The "safer" path is wider.

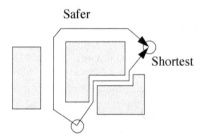

FIGURE 144. The shortest path is not always the safest. The broader path is "more comfortable".

You can find both paths by performing mathematical morphology operations and running the path-finding algorithm several times. After one step of dilation (expansion) on the obstacles, which is the same thing as erosion (shrinking) of the open areas, we can get the shapes in Figure 145.

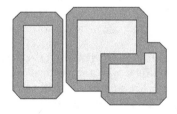

FIGURE 145. By dilating the obstacles, that is eroding the open space, the narrow passage is blocked.

As desired, the narrow passage is now blocked, and we will find the broader passage. Note that this kind of operations can be useful not only for agents who wish good margins, but it

---

can be downright necessary for agents that simply have a large physical size! In order not to get stuck in collision detection, the agent needs to stick to passages where it fits!

Yet another case is to find paths in scenes with moving obstacles. If there are moving obstacles, such as other agents, the path will often get blocked while the agent is walking it. When that happens, the agent can wait for a while to see if the path gets clear again, it can use "crash&turn" to try to get around it, or it can plan a new path. We can see this in action in The Sims. The sims often run into conflicting paths. If they are in open areas, they quickly re-plan and move on, while in narrow spaces (like doors) they may stop and wait. This game is particularly good at using emotion animations in such situations, so when obstructed, they make irritated gestures, a very nice touch.

Finally, there are many cases when the agent should not follow the optimal path since it simply can not know it! An agent can not know the path to an object that it does not know the exact location of (e.g. the player), and it can not know the path if it does not know the terrain. In such cases, the agent should use a search algorithm instead, using a special map that tells where it has been, and when. If it has looked into a certain room recently, it should not go there again in some time but rather search in other places. But don't make it perfect. A real human will not make an optimal search, but may forget about some locations and over-search others. A path-planning algorithm will be a good component in such a behavior, but only a component.

Only when these considerations are properly taken into account, you will get an agent that has a human-style behavior rather than moving around like a robot.

13.7 State-space search: Minmax and other turn-based game algorithms

A classic part of game AI that should not be ignored is the study of turn-based games, to make computer players for boardgames. This is the topic that has the attractive name *game theory*. I will only briefly introduce this since I assume that it is well known.

A board game player needs to find the best move it can make. It needs to search the possible moves and select one from some goal function. For simple games, like tic-tac-toe, it is possible to make an exhaustive search of all moves all the way to the end of the game. For more complex games, this is not possible and the goal function must somehow evaluate the position to a quantitative measure.

This is analyzed by a *minmax* (or minimaxing) algorithm, where we recursively search the state-space of the game, searching for the best moves. The function returns a value that tells how good the state is, a heuristic function that typically is positive if the player making the first move has an advantage, and negative if the other player has the advantage.

With every move, we are looking for the move that is best for the player who makes it. From one player's perspective, the best moves that the player can make, and the *worst* moves that the opponent can make.

Simple games can apply this with a full breadth-first. A simple case is the game Ägga-schack ("egg chess"), which is a creative twist on tic-tac-toe. It was published in Ny Teknik a few years ago (around 2000). I made an implementation called MacÄggaschack (for MacOS, obviously), shown in Figure 146, which was complete with a computer opponent. This was a very straight-forward and simple case of the minmax algorithm.

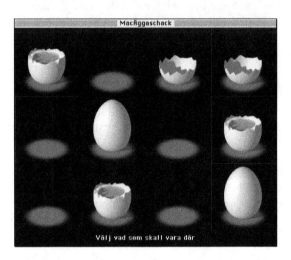

FIGURE 146. MacÄggaschack, a game that uses a simple Minmax game AI. (Artwork by Susanne Ragnemalm.)

The rules are as follows:

The game board is 3x3 spaces, and is initially empty. The players take turns with one move each. A move can be one out of

- Placing an egg in an empty position.

- Eating a full egg to half, a full egg to empty or a half egg to empty.

A player wins when he makes a move that makes three in a row of equal eggs, that is three of the same kind out of full, half or empty.

The recursive evaluation function returns -1 if the opponent won, 1 if the player won and 0 if no victory is found.

By doing the search with varying search depth, the result was a pretty impressive computer player (for anyone who didn't know how simple it was). "Dumb as the hen" only checked if it could make a winning move, and otherwise picked randomly. "Fast as the dog" went one level deeper, avoided to give the player a straight win. "Sly as the fox" and "Mean as the cat" were each a level deeper. (I thought I was really funny making up the names for the AI levels. Still, it is more amusing than "1", "2", "3", "4", right?)

Negamax is a simplifying trick for minmax algorithms, where the heuristic function value is negated at each call, to simplify the calculations. Then no special code is needed for keeping track of whose turn it is, that is whether we should maximize or minimize.

Highly compact pseudo code for minmax/negamax can look like this (adapted from [59], modified to be somewhat more complete):

```
function minimax(node, depth)
    calcnodevalue(node)
    if node.value=win or node.value=lose or depth = 0
        return node.value
    else
        value := MAX
        for each child of node
            value := max(value, -minimax(child, depth-1))
        return value;
```

"Each child" means "each possible move from node". Note the minus on the second to last row. It simplifies the code and is what makes it "negamax".

For more complex games, the search space can be too large for a breadth first search. By *alpha-beta pruning*, we can avoid moving down branches that can not possibly be useful. This is done by passing a limit for how good (or bad) the state value can be until we know that we are in a hopeless case. In particular, we can discard any branch where the opponent can find a too good value; we don't want to go there.

Also, consider the possibility to perform such a test before doing any deep searches. In MacÄggaschack, it makes perfect sense to check the result of *one* step to see if there is a winning move, and if there is, we don't have to do any deep searches whatsoever.

Minmax works well for games like Chess, Othello and others, where the opponent's state is known. For some games, like card games, Stratego and Mah-Jong, we do not know the opponent's state. There are various hints about what the opponent can do, but it is not possible to know what move is the best or worst for the opponent. In games like Mah-Jong, you do not even know exactly what tiles are in play. In Bridge, you know that all cards are in play, but not on what hand. For such games, the AI must be based on heuristic evaluation functions.

Take the case of Mah-Jong (not the silly tile-matching solitaire game but the real thing). You have your hand, you pick up a tile and must choose one to discard. Look at the hand in Figure 147. (Example blatantly stolen from [5] because it is OK to steal from yourself. Tile images from Wikipedia.)

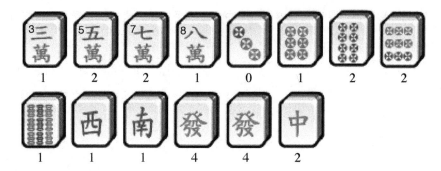

FIGURE 147. A Mah-Jong hand to be analyzed.

If you know Mah-Jong, you can probably suggest some tiles that are good candidates for discarding. The green dragons should be saved unless two are already in the discard pile. There are some good candidates for chow's. There are four tiles that can not combine with any others. The one that is not a honor tile, circle 3, is a good pick. There are plenty of circles but far from enough to go for a circles-only hand.

This evaluation can be turned into numbers like this:

- Add one point if the tile is an honor tile, that is 1, 9 or wind.
- Add two points if the tile is a dragon or your own wind.
- For every tile of the same kind, add two. (Chance for pong.)
- For every tile of the same suit one or two steps away, add one. (Chance for chow.)

This is a really, really simple Mah-Jong evaluator function, which needs additional rules to deal with discarded tiles, complete or conflicting combinations etc, but it is a good start.

The circle 3 got the lowest score, and is indeed a good pick for discarding.

So, since this kind of games can not be analyzed in many steps, we work with these quantitative measures, and every move is a new move.

13.8 Summary

Although we try to make fundamental game AI into an interesting subject, it can often be described in only two sentences:

- Figure out a suitable representation
- Hack a behavior

Now comes the question: What is advanced game AI?

14. Methods for behavior and learning

In this chapter, we will move into some more involved game AI methods. Hopefully, we can find some methods that you don't consider as much common knowledge as the previous chapter. No guarantees, of course. What you will find here are introductions to influence mapping, flocking and learning, all from the game programming perspective.

14.1 Influence maps

Influence maps is a powerful game AI technique for analyzing the situation in a complex scene. Its classic use is in strategy games, but as we shall see it is useful for many things.

The basic principle of influence maps is that the presence of a game entity is recorded in the proper place in an array, the influence map, by some value. In strategy games we may record friends and foes with different sign. More about that later.

Then the influence map is filtered by a low-pass filter. This will smear out the mark to the surrounding area. This makes it easier to analyze proximity and presence. If an area is zero, you only need to inspect your current position to know that nobody is near. (If your own value is written in the influence map, you know what value it gives you.)

If the value is different from expected, someone else is near. If you use different signs on friends and foes, a value higher than expected signifies friends and a lower foes.

The influence map can be used for many things:

- In a strategy game, the influence value may be directly used to determine ownership or supply routes.

- It can be used to alert the agent that someone is near so that appropriate action can be taken.

- It can be used to analyze the strategic value of a space. In a sports game, you can compare players in the same team to determine who is in the best position (e.g. suitable to pass the ball to). If a player has a bad influence map value, he is likely to be guarded by opponents.
- It indicates weak spots in the defense to attack or strengthen.
- It indicates "safe" areas where we can send weak units that should not be attacked.

An example is shown in Figure 148.

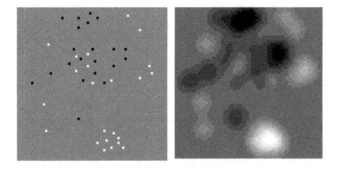

FIGURE 148. Influence map example.

All members of a black and a white team are marked in the left figure. Then the image is filtered, resulting in the right image.

This example is a "flat" map. It is also possible to make the map terrain dependent, so a unit's influence does not pass through walls and is influenced by height difference and rough terrain.

We can also introduce different strengths for different units, so a "pawn" has a low value and a "queen" higher.

And this is still only a simple influence map with a single scalar for each space. An advanced influence map can hold multidimensional information. You can analyze distribution of resources as a separate dimension, to find good places for certain structures. You can analyze history data, showing where there have been many battles in the past.

An influence map does not have to be made in a single resolution. It has been proposed [38] to make influence maps as resolution pyramids, similar to mip-mapping.

But it all boils down to the same thing: low-pass filtering is an effective way to make data easier to analyze, when we want to find overall (low frequency) features. See [37] for more information. I would conclude that influence mapping is one of those techniques where you start with a simple principle and then find that it can be used in many different ways. By mapping your data into an image, you can apply image analysis algorithms on it and the options are numerous.

Methods for behavior and learning

14.2 Flocking

Flocking is a large-scale behavior method that is pretty effective for simulating group dynamics. As such, it is as much an animation method as an AI one, and is described in books for both subjects [8][60]. A particularly significant example is the *boids* algorithm invented by Craig W Reynolds [53]. Although originally designed for special effects in movies, it has found itself into games where it is used for flocks of animals as well as soldiers.

The boids algorithm is marvelously simple. The principle is described by three rules (illustrated in Figure 149):

- Separation
- Alignment
- Cohesion

The separation rule states that if two individuals come too close, they must try to move away from each other to avoid collision. Since boids work on speeds and direction, separation is not enforced by pushing them apart by force but by changing their directions.

The alignment rule states that the individuals should try to aim in the same direction. Either they mimic the closest member's directions, or they try to follow the movement of the center of gravity of the group.

Finally, the cohesion rule states that the members of the group should aim toward the center of the group, towards the center of gravity.

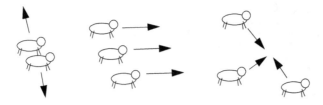

FIGURE 149. The three rules of boids, separation, alignment and cohesion

These three rules will conflict with each other to varying degrees all the time, so they must work with different priority or be weighted together.

You can implement boids in a few different ways. The simplest way is really a rather straight-forward particle system, with the rules above used for having the particles affect each other. Thus, each boid is a particle with no particular direction or shape, only a speed vector. The only thing that makes it different to a particle system is that it follows the three rules that give it group dynamics rather than just the rules of physics. All boids within a certain distance are inspected, and for each of the three rules, an offset to the current speed vector is calculated.

Separation: This is the most complex of the three. For all nearby boids, make a vector pointing away. This can be made for the closest boid or for all within a distance. This rule may be applied on a much smaller neighborhood than the others, preferably with a falloff so it creates a stronger force the closer the other boid is.

Alignment: Calculate the average difference in speed between the current boid and all other boids. Add a fraction of this to the speed of the current boid.

Cohesion: Calculate the average position of all boids within a certain distance. Take this position minus the position of the current boid. Add a fraction of this vector to the speed of the current boid.

The algorithm is not quite as simple as it sounds, because you must first calculate all the contributions to the speed to every animal, and then add that contribution as a second step. in that way, the change for one animal can not affect the others in the same iteration. The effect is that we apply the changes in parallel.

Here is the algorithm summarized in pseudocode:

```
// Double loop for accumulating contributions from other boids
for all boids i
    count := 0
    i.speedDiff := 0
    i.averagePosition := 0
    i.avoidanceVector := 0

    for all boids j
        if i ≠ j then
            if |j.position-i.position| < kMaxDistance then
                // for alignment:
                i.speedDiff += j.speed - i.speed
                // for cohesion
                i.averagePosition += j.position
                // for avoidance
                i.avoidanceVector += CalcAvoidance(j.position - i.position)
                count += 1
    if count > 0
        // Divisions
        i.speedDiff /= count
        i.averagePosition /= count
        i.avoidanceVector /= count

// Second loop for adding the resulting contributions
for all boids i
    i.speed +=
            i.speedDiff*kAlignmentWeight
          + i.averagePosition * kCohesionWeight
          + i.avoidanceVector * kAvoidanceWeight
i.position += i.speed
```

This implements a point-based flocking, which will work nicely given the proper weights and a good avoidance function. It should be obvious that a large system should use a space subdivision method, like quad trees or BSP trees, to optimize the search for nearby boids, reducing the complexity of the double loop from the current $O(n^2)$ to $O(n \cdot \log n)$.

Methods for behavior and learning

An alternative is to implement it in a direction-based way, where not the speed but the rotation of each boid is affected by the neighbors. Such an implementation is harder to make stable, but that is not necessarily a drawback.

Above, I assumed that we select neighbor boids by distance only. We may adjust that to include boids in view only. Reynolds [53] suggests including boids within a certain angle, as in Figure 150.

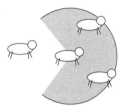

FIGURE 150. A boid may ignore other boids out of view, i.e. behind them.

There are some variations to this that you might want to add. For example, if the group is split in two, it should start behaving as two groups. This comes for free when only dealing with boids within a given distance (kMaxDistance in the pseudo code). The same holds for individuals that are separated from the group. Rather than searching the world for boids in the vicinity, influence maps can be used to make similar flocking decisions.

To this, add heuristic reasons for movement. Sheep may run away from dogs or wolves, or walk towards food. Soldiers may like sticking near resources that should be guarded, or attack enemies, or weak units may avoid enemies. Obstacles may be nicely avoided by contributing to the avoidance vector. There can also be a global force, a "wind", affecting the boids (especially of they are flying or swimming), and there can be attractors that pull the flock to certain desirable positions, including a flock leader, explicitly leading the flock.

Boids is an example of A-life, the art of mimicking lifelike behavior. As you add additional rules and constraints to your boid, you are really turning it into the A-life system you need for your game.

Tom Scutt [69] suggests that simple swarms can be a viable alternative to boids. A swarm is more similar to a conventional, basic particle system, simplifying the problem by not using any avoidance between the particles. While this is clearly unrealistic for small flocks of large animals, it can work well for large swarms of smaller animals.

There are many variations on the theme, but one thing holds for much behavior coding: The code isn't necessarily very complex. The system can have a behavior that is by far more complex than the code defining it. Interesting behavior is often coded with very simple means. Well selected rules based on perception and vicinity checks can create very lifelike systems, at least as long as you are modeling simple creatures like insects.

14.3 Learning, function approximation

Machine learning is one of the most fascinating topics in computer science, but also one of the hardest to master and do something meaningful with. At a distance, machine learning sounds like exactly what you need to create a good game AI. The truth is, however, not so simple.

First, we have the question of how the learning takes place. Is it on-line, while the game is played, or off-line, as part of the design? Off-line, it can be used for training the AI system to produce a desired behavior that is fixed when the game reaches the customer. On-line learning, however, is matter of making games adapt to the behavior of the player, to provide dynamics and new challenge when the player has mastered the original behavior.

Then there are many methods for learning. Some may seem trivial, others advanced, and some look very different from each other at first glance, but that is mostly a question of context. You see, learning is really a question of *optimization* or *function approximation*. You have some kind of parameter set describing a behavior, and you want to optimize the parameters to get the most desired behavior, to find a good approximation to the desired function. No, you can't just "teach" your AI, you need to identify the parameters, one way or the other, and feed them to the system, and provide information on what behavior you want.

Suddenly the problem doesn't seem at all that magical.

There are a number of learning (optimization) algorithms, including:

- Neural networks
- Genetic algorithms
- Hill climbing
- Simulated annealing

The methods above solve two different problems. Neural networks is primarily a representation model for the state space, while the others are algorithms for performing the search of the search space.

Neural networks is a structure for representing the state space, mimicking neural networks in biology. This is done by a network of interconnected nodes, neurons. Each node has a number of inputs and outputs, where there are weights mapping inputs to the outputs, a simple function. These weights are the parameters of the optimization, which are updated, again using a goal function. The actual updates can be made using several search algorithms, including hill climbing, simulated annealing or genetic algorithms. The actual structure of the network comes in many variants, most notably feed-forward and backward propagation networks.

In *genetic algorithms* (Figure 151), the parameters are considered "genes". A number of sample points are randomized, tested against a goal function. Then new ones are calculated from the first ones, mixing "genes" between pairs of samples. Good points are promoted by keeping them and letting them "breed" more than bad points. As iterations run, the algorithm will explore areas in parameter space where the goal function has high values. The algorithm should also include randomness, "mutations", in order to not get stuck in limited choices.

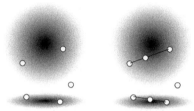

FIGURE 151. Genetic algorithms example. The best samples are combined to find new positions in promising areas.

Hill climbing (Figure 152) is the simplest there is, where you take a single sample and move to nearby points wherever the goal function is higher. Running hill climbing from one single stating point will often get stuck in local minima, but by running this algorithm not from one but from many starting points, a decent coverage of the state space can be achieved.

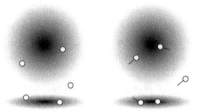

FIGURE 152. Hill climbing example. Several starting points are needed to explore the goal function properly.

Simulated annealing (Figure 153) is very similar to genetic algorithms. Instead of combining pairs of samples, random offsets are made, again promoting good samples. The length of the random steps are determined by a "heat level", and that level is gradually decreased, shortening the random steps, until it reaches zero and the system stops, and we hope that we have found an optimum. The difference to genetic algorithms is twofold. Simulated annealing has more freedom to move in all direction of parameter space, it is not restricted by positions of two samples. Genetic algorithms, on the other hand, will reduce unnecessary search of bad points along directions in parameter space where the function does not get better, e.g. on a ridge in the function.

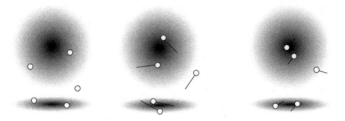

FIGURE 153. Simulated annealing example. The step length is decreased over time to make the system stop.

The step length shortening in simulated annealing is readily applied to hill climbing and genetic algorithms.

Learning can also be achieved by non-formal methods, heuristic methods based on the problem and a simple solution for that, like making some simple statistics about the player behavior and modifying computer agents from that in some hard-coded way. If the player then perceives the system as intelligent and adaptive, the problem is solved.

A good overview over these and other methods are given by Millington [60]. Millington also makes an important statement: *Learning is not very important in games*!

This is a bit disturbing if you find machine learning interesting, but it is a fact. Machine learning is useful for things like training image processing systems, but where does it fit in a game? There have been attempts to use learning for animations and for game entity behavior, to train them at the design stage, but the cost is high and the results usually limited. Games have been created with learning, most notably Black & White, where you can train your own "creature" to help you playing – but players soon found out that they were better off ignoring the creature and play the game as the updated Powermonger that it was. So the learning was wasted since it was not important enough for the game goals.

I am not saying that learning can not be useful, but machine learning is a small and over-hyped topic in game AI (unlike topics like machine vision where it has grown extremely hot recently). Thus, I choose to leave it as such. There are other game AI methods that are much more rewarding. Learning may be the answer, but first we need to know what the problem is.

14.4 Final remarks

The game AI subject is a challenging one, not least since it is so diverse and not trivial to apply. It ranges all the way from heuristic hacks to formal methods, and what can be used in games varies.

If you want to go deeper on AI, as always research papers are important. If you want a book, I believe that Millington [60] is a good choice, covering lots of non-trivial things in non-trivial depth.

Methods for behavior and learning

15. Other topics

15.1 Sound effects and music

Music and sound is not one of the main topics of the course, despite the title of the book. However, it is a great importance for games, and far from trivial.

Simple sound effects and music are mainly a question of finding a playback API. This is not as simple as it may seem, and we will discuss that further below.

Advanced sound effects start with stereo placement of sounds, to indicate the position of the sound source. The sound effects get even better if you can filter the frequency content depending on direction, distance and location. And that is where we move into the really advanced sound effects. Advance sound effect systems can analyze the geometry of the surroundings and accurately calculate the impact on the sound, creating echoes as well as frequency filtering.

Music is generally not dependent on the environment, except for the special case where there is an explicit source for the music, like the music in Lara Croft's living room. However, music can vary in time rather than room. Making different music tracks for different parts of the game is easy. A lot more challenging is to change the music in a smaller scale, to vary the mood of the music with different situations. Fading in and out such changes is far from trivial.

15.1.1 Playing sound effects with OpenAL

Finding the right sound playing library is surprisingly difficult. There are many libraries available, but few will do what you need out of the box. Among the popular libraries are FMOD and SDL Mixer. One library that is powerful and freely available is OpenAL by Creative Labs. It does not only play audio, it also includes functionality for representing 3D location and speed of the sound sources, so stereo and volume can be calculated from position, and even doppler effects.

A surprising omission in OpenAL, similar to the lack of texture loading in OpenGL, is that OpenAL can not load sounds from files. The add-on library ALUT (c.f. GLUT) will provide a loader for WAV files. However, since that is the only really meaningful thing that ALUT provides, and ALUT may complicate installation, I would recommend you to use your own WAV loader, as source or static library. Such code can be found on Internet.

Granted that you have a WAV loader, your OpenAL code is quite simple. I will leave discussions about stereo placement and doppler, and just briefly show how to get a sound effect to play.

The central concepts in OpenAL are the *listener*, *sources* and *buffers*.

The listener is the output device. We can ignore that for now, which means that we use the default listener with default settings, but a full OpenAL program will specify the position, speed and even direction of the listener.

The sources are sound playing channels, capable of playing one sound each at a time. You will typically use several sources, so you can play many sounds simultaneously. A source is created like this:

```
alGenSources(1, source);
```

You may set various attributes of a source. The most obvious ones are these:

```
alSourcef(source, AL_PITCH, 1.0);
alSourcef(source, AL_GAIN, 1.0);
```

but just like for the listener, we may also specify position and velocity.

The buffers may hold audio data, which can be played by sending it to a source. A buffer is created and assigned data like this (granted that you have a loader for the data):

```
alGenBuffers(1, buffer);
alBufferData(buffer, format, data, size, freq);
```

This is strikingly similar to how you create a texture object and upload a texture to it in OpenGL!

Finally, let us use the buffer and source to play a sound! It is done like this:

```
alSourcei(source, AL_BUFFER, buffer);
alSourcePlay(source);
```

When writing your first OpenAL test program, you will also want to keep the program running until the sound has stopped. You may inspect

```
alGetSourcei (source, AL_SOURCE_STATE, status);
```

to know if the sound has stopped playing. (The variable status is AL_PLAYING while the sound is being played.)

It should be noted that you can not use several buffers in one source, and you can not abort an old sound merely by specifying a new buffer. To switch sound in one source, you first stop the old sound using

```
alSourceStop(source);
```

and then you can specify a new buffer and play as above.

There is also a small number of needed initialization calls, with which your program should start:

```
device = alcOpenDevice(NULL);
context = alcCreateContext(device, NULL);
alcMakeContextCurrent(context);
```

and to be really nice, you should end your program by stopping all sources and tidying up using

```
alcDestroyContext(context);
alcCloseDevice(device);
```

but we usually don't need to be *that* nice to the system.

I hope this brief introduction can help you get started. The next step from here is to start using the source and listener position and velocity data.

15.1.2 Playing music

Playing music is rather different from sound effects. While sound effects can be stored as uncompressed audio (e.g. WAV), music takes much space and must be compressed. Typical formats include mp3 and Ogg Vorbis.

There are plenty of audio players out there, but still it is not easy to find one that is easy to use. One that is fairly simple is Apple's QuickTime, available for Mac OS X and MS Windows. While QuickTime is primarily a movie playing library, it is very useful for playing music as well, not least for its capability of decoding a wide range of formats.

Simple OSX code for playing music can be found on my web pages as "SimpleAudio-Movie", in C and FPC versions.

Unfortunately, Apple has not kept the Mac and Windows versions in perfect synch, so you may have to resort to coding styles that are considered old-fashioned on the Mac to make the code portable. This problem makes QuickTime less attractive, and you may want to look into other options. Furthermore, its cross-platform capability only is across two platforms, and there is little hope to ever see it running elsewhere.

A different approach would be to use a decoder for mp3 or Ogg Vorbis, and stream the data to an OpenAL source. Available libraries for this change a lot over time. A popular option is SDL_mixer.

15.2 Special input and output devices

When Sony and Microsoft were hunting performance, the seemingly weaker player Nintendo grabbed all attention and big market shares with the Wii. That event is very significant. A performance increase only makes a difference once you do something interesting

---

(entertaining) with it. What Nintendo realized was that their efforts were better spent on something that really made the platform more interesting, the new hand control.

The most obvious follower is Apple, who makes both MacBooks and iPhones capable of more by putting in motion sensors. More recenly, Microsoft's Kinect has been a considerable success, and not only as a gaming device. The conclusion is that you don't make it fun by trimming numbers but by making something different. This is true in many other ways.

On the output side, we are currently experiencing a revival of 3D (stereo) displays, both in cinemas and consumer products. The products have matured, and the need for them, in order to provide novel experiences have grown.

In times when software is running into the problem that all special effects have been made, special devices will widen the borders of the imaginable. That will create new products, new opportunities for profit, and because of that, we will see more and more such products. Jumping on the right "device train" will be as important as releasing your game for the right platforms.

15.3 User interface issues

If there is one aspect of program design where games are notoriously poor, it is the user interface. While other programs usually follow the user interface for their platform very well, games follow no standard, and their user interfaces more often than not looks like something slapped together as being a triviality that is no concern. We will frequently see the following:

- Non-standard keyboard shortcuts.
- Selections (menus etc.) are equally non-standard.
- Tedious sequences of spinning logos when launching the game.
- Strange limitations due to poor user interface design. Example: A limited list of player names or save files due to fixed lists.
- Lack of protection of user data.
- "Pause" function not always easy to find. On-line games often have none. Some games can't survive a task switch.

Many of these issues seem deeply rooted in the game industry, and seem to be considered more state-of-the-art than the user interface mistakes that they really are. The non-standard look on menus is a minor problem, that ironically is an advantage when porting between platforms. Many of the other issues, however, are annoying for the users and make it unnecessarily hard to get into new games.

I conclude that user interfaces are significantly worse in games than in other software. This is obviously a minor issue for game programming companies. The obvious question is: can one gain revenue, more sales, by making a good UI? In the past, apparently not. But today? Maybe. I believe that the big difference is that as long as sales were one-shot and games cost $50 in a store, this simply was not a problem. If you buy a full-price game, you will not give up that easy, you learn the quirks. And if you got it from the bargain bin, you just put it aside and forget about it. Is this changing? Maybe. We live more on-line, some games have more longevity than past games had, and the simpler games are web-based. I admit that I am speculating, but if nothing else, I wish that the time has come for game programmers to spend a little more time to make the user interfaces *good* instead of something between bearable, frustrating or confusing.

15.4 Game mechanics

One of the most essential things with a game is the *game mechanics*, which is really the rules of the game. In the computer game market, there are many games without any unique rules, with no apparent game mechanics of its own. However, many seemingly similar games have subtle differences that give implicit game mechanics, so the problem is not as big as it may seem.

Ever since the first computer games, there have been too many games with the rules so nicely summarized by MacBugs!, one of the first Mac games (that means early 80's):

* Shoot everything
* Don't get hit

Isn't that a bit too trivial? However many games are a lot more complex. The most advanced games in terms of game mechanics are probably strategy games, but even simple games like Tetris and Mines are way above the MacBugs! level in terms of game rules.

Now, game mechanics, game rules, is about logic, the explicit or implicit rules of play. Even a shooter has more rules than MacBugs! lists. Here is a short summary:

* Number of lives
* Scoring system
* High score system - how are we rewarded for good play?
* Score for extra lives
* Power-ups
* Movement options
* Movement and armament of opponents
* Intelligence of opponents

And this is just what you have in a trivial shooter! Modern first person shooters tend to have a rather delicate balance of health and shield points, availability of powerups, different kind of damage by different opponents, different weapons...

All these things are part of the game design, but note that the graphics have little or nothing to do with it. Physics and AI, however, are much more closely connected to the game mechanics, so close that they are often an integral part of it. Networking may unintentionally be part of the game mechanics; when it works perfectly, you should not notice it.

A simple example of when the physics is an important part of the game mechanics is when you throw grenades. Grenades are usually allowed to bounce off walls, so you can bounce them into inaccessible places, clearing mines or attacking unseen opponents. Thus, the physics simulation becomes very important, and the player will take advantage of the physics simulation, regardless of whether it is realistic or not.

Likewise, the intelligence and perception of computer controlled entities is essential. When can they hear you? In games like Noone Lives Forever, sneaking past enemies is part of the game, while other games are simpler and opponents react on distance or line-of-sight.

These examples are game mechanics coming from the simulation of physics and intelligence/perception. Since these "game rules" mimic reality, we do not need to describe them much to the player, the player will, in varying degree, expect things to work that way. Other rules are different.

Thus, game mechanics is the sum of many "game rules", in all parts of the game. Physics, AI, graphics, networking, and even sound, they all contribute to the flow of information, to the success or failure of the player. Some rules are explicit, but more often than not, most rules are implicit.

And that is really why so much of this book is about all those other parts, and so little about game mechanics. You can take just about any chapter in this book and take something there and make that a central point in your game. And when you do, you take that vital decision that makes a game out of a concept.

16. Final words

Writing this book has been an adventure, at least as big as arranging the course past years. It mixes knowledge from many fields, and still it is mostly written by one single person (with some advice and help from my colleagues). Is it advanced enough in each area, is it interesting? Well, I hope so. I have been working from the point of view of putting in what I find interesting and that I think you might find interesting, while trying to keep within the limits of the subject and the size of the course.

With this book my two-volume project was completed (although I consider extending it with more). In a way, I have done what I wanted to do with the "Tricks" book back in the 90's. That book was great in some ways, but it was lacking in others. Now I just might have done the book that *really* screams!

Now it is your turn, go out and make them scream! Start with a project. Do what I did, make the project that you always wanted to do!

17. References

[1]   OpenGL ARB, "OpenGL Programming Guide", (known as the "Red Book") fifth edition, Addison-Wesley 2005.

[2]   R. Rost, "The OpenGL Shading Language", second edition, Addison-Wesley 2006.

[3]   Paul Martz, "OpenGL Distilled", Addison-Wesley 2005.

[4]   Christer Ericson, "Real-time Collision Detection", Morgan Kaufman/Elsevier, 2005.

[5]   McCormack, Ragnemalm, Celestin, "Tricks of the Mac Game Programming Gurus", Hayden Books/MacMillan, 1995.

[6]   D. Astle, "More OpenGL Game Programming", Thomson, 2006.

[7]   I. Ragnemalm, "Polygons feel no pain", 2008.

[8]   R. Parent, "Computer animation", second edition, Morgan Kaufman/Elsevier 2008.

[9]   Andrew Witkin and David Baraff, "Physically Based Modeling", SIGGRAPH course notes, 2001

[10] Johan Sjöstrand, "A communication system for a pluggable game engine", LiTH-ISY-EX--07/4004--SE, 2007.

[11] Roger Johannesson, "Simulering av mjuka kroppar för spel", LiTH-ISY-EX--06/3772--SE, 2006

[12] Johannes Nilsson, "Physical Simulation and Visualization of Cells", 2008

[13] H. Hansson, "Craft Physics Interface", LiTH-ISY-EX--07/3887--SE, 2007.

[14] D. Astle, K. Hawkins, "Beginning OpenGL Game Programming", Thomson 2004.

[15] M.J. Kilgard, "Shadow mapping with today's OpenGL hardware", CEDEC 2001.

[16] D. S-C Dalmau, "Core Techniques and Algorithms in Game Programming", New Riders, 2003.

[17] J-M. Hasenfratz, M. Lapierre, N. Holzschuch, F. X. Sillion: "A survey of real-time soft shadows algorithms", Eurographics 2003.

[18] Markus Fahlén, "Illumination for Real-Time Rendering of Large Architectural Environments", LiTH-ISY-EX--05/3736--SE, 2005.

[19] Erik Häggmark, "Nighttime Driving: Real-time Simulation and Visualization of Vehicle Illumination for Nighttime Driving inn a Simulator", LiTH-ISY-ED--04/3676, Linköping University, 2004.

[20] Erik Pettersson, "Signal- och bildbehandling på moderna grafikprocessorer", LiTH-ISY-EX--05/3761--SE, 2005.

[21] K. Perlin, "An image synthesizer", Computer Graphics 19(3), pp 287-296, 1985.

[22] Harris and Lastra, "Real-time cloud rendering", Proceedings of Eurographics, pp 76-84, 2001.

[23] John Nilsson, "3D-visualisering av moln", LiTH-ISY-EX--05/3664--SE, 2005.

[24] ODE (Open Dynamics Engine), http://www.ode.org

[25] Newton, http://www.newtondynamics.com

[26] True Axis, http://www.trueaxis.com

[27] Tom McReynolds, David Blythe, "Advanced Graphics Programming Using OpenGL", Morgan Kaufmann, 2005

[28] Miguel Gomez, "Integrating the Equations of Rigid Body Motion, in: DeLoura, "Game Programming Gems", Charles River Media, 2000, pp 150-160.

[29] Andrew Witkin and David Baraff, "Physically Based Modeling: Principles and Practice", 1997, www.cs.cmu.edu/~baraff/sigcourse/ (especially the "d" notes)

[30] Pharr, "GPU Gems 2", Addison Wesley, 2005.

[31] Emil Jansson, "Matematisk generering och realtidsrendering av vegetation i Gizmo3D", LiTH-ISY-EX-3487-2004, 2004.

[32] Eric Chan, Fredo Durand, "Rendering fake soft shadows with smoothies". In: Rendering Techniques 2003, ACM Press, 2003.

[33] Tomas Akenine-Möller, Ulf Assarsson, "Approximate soft shadows on arbitrary surfaces using penumbra wedges". In: Rendering Techniques 2002, pages 297–306. ACM Press, 2002.

[34] OpenGL.org, "Survey Of OpenGL Font Technology". http://www.opengl.org/resources/features/fontsurvey/

[35] Ryan Woodland, "Filling the Gaps – Advanced Animation Using Stitching and Skinning", in: Game Programming Gems, Charles River Media, 2000, pp 476-483.

[36] Alan Watt and Fabio Policarpo, "3D Games Volume 2", Addison Wesley, 2003.

[37] Paul Tozour, "Influence Mapping" and "Strategic Assessment Techniques", in: Game Programming Gems 2, Charles River Media, pp 287-306.

[38] Game Programming Gems, Charles River Media, 2000, page 403.

[39] William Donnelly, "Per-Pixel Displacement Mapping with Distance Functions", in: GPU Gems, Addison Wesley 2005, pp 123-136 (also available on the Internet).

[40] Fabio Policarpo, "Real-Time Relief Mapping on Arbitrary Polygonal Surfaces", http://www.inf.ufrgs.br/~comba/papers/2005/rtrm-i3d05.pdf

[41] Fabio Policarpo, Manuel M Oliveira, "Relaxed Cone Stepping for Relief Mapping", in: GPU Gems 3, pp 409-428, http://developer.download.nvidia.com/books/gpu_gems_3/samples/gems3_ch18.pdf

[42] T. Kaneko et al, "Detailed Shape Representation with Parallax Mapping". In: Proceedings of ICAT 2001, pp. 205-208. http://vrsj.t.u-tokyo.ac.jp/ic-at/ICAT2003/papers/01205.pdf

[43] Jonas Lindmark, "Tredimensionella detaljer på plana ytor", projektrapport TSBK10, 2007.

[44] Jason Zink, "A Closer Look At Parallax Occlusion Mapping", http://www.gamedev.net/columns/hardcore/pom/

[45] Ingemar Ragnemalm, "The Euclidean Distance Transform", PhD thesis, 1993.

[46] Per-Erik Danielsson, "Euclidean Distance Mapping", Computer Graphics and Image Processing 14, pp 227-248, 1980.

[47] Lena Klasén, "Image Sequence Analysis of Complex Objects", PhD thesis, 2002.

[48] Jörgen Ahlberg, "Model-based coding", PhD thesis, 2002.

[49] Robert L. Cook, "Shade trees", SIGGRAPH '84: Proceedings of the 11th annual conference on Computer graphics and interactive techniques, 1984

[50] Greg James & John O'Rorke, "Real-Time Glow", in: GPU Gems, Addison Wesley, 2004, pp 343-362

[51] Jason Weber, Joseph Penn, "Creation and rendering of realistic trees", SIGGRAPH '95, 1995

[52] Oliver Deussen, Pat Hanrahan, Bernd Lintermann, Radomir Mech, Matt Pharr, Przemyslaw Prusinkiewicz, "Realistic modeling and rendering of plant ecosystems", SIGGRAPH '98, 1998

[53] Craig Reynolds, "Boids, Background and Update", http://www.red3d.com/cwr/boids/

[54] Masaki Kawase, "Frame Buffer Postprocessing Effects in DOUBLE-S.T.E.A.L (Wreckless)", Game Developer's Conference 2003, http://www.daionet.gr.jp/~masa/archives/GDC2003_DSTEAL.ppt

[55] M. Müller, M. Gross, "Interactive Virtual Materials", ACM International Conference Proceeding Series, 62:239–246. 2004.

[56] Müller, M., Heidelberger, B., Teschner, M., and Gross, M. "Meshless deformations based on shape matching", ACM Transactions on Graphics, 24(3). 2005.

[57] Maciej Matyka, "Practical Animation of Soft Bodies for Game Development: The Pressurized Soft-Body Model", in: Game Programming Gems 5, Charles River Media, 2005, pp 435-448.

[58] Juan Cordero, "Realistic Cloth Animation Using the Mass-Spring Model", in: Game Programming Gems 5, Charles River Media, 2005, pp 421-433.

[59] Wikipedia on Minimax, http://en.wikipedia.org/wiki/Minimax

[60] Ian Millington, "Artificial Intelligence for Games", Morgan Kaufmann, 2006.

[61] Lewis, Cordner, Fong: "Pose Space Deformation: A New Unified Approach to Shape Interpolation and Skeleton-Driven Deformation", SIGGRAPH, 2000

[62] Gould, "Complete Maya Programming", Morgan Kaufmann 2003

[63] "The Art Of Maya", Alias learning tools, 2005

[64] Game Programming Gems 1, Charles River Media, 2000

[65] D. Hearn, M. P. Baker, "Computer Graphics with OpenGL", third edition, 2003.

[66] E. Angel, "Computer Graphics with OpenGL, a Top-Down Approach"

[67] Mike Reed and Konstantin Othmer, "Curves Ahead: Working With Curves In Quickdraw", in: Develop 8, 1991. Available online as: http://www.mactech.com/articles/develop/issue_08/Reed_text.html

[68] NeHe lesson 15, http://nehe.gamedev.net/data/lessons/lesson.asp?lesson=15

[69] AI Game Programming Wisdom, Charles River Media, 2002.

[70] E. Gilbert, D. Johnson, S.S. Keerthi, "A Fast Procedure for Computing the Distance Between Complex Objects in Three-dimensional Space", IEEE Journal of Robotics and Automation, vol 4, no 2, pp 193-203, 1988.

[71] Fabien Sanglard, "ShadowMapping with GLSL", http://www.fabiensanglard.net/shadowmapping/index.php

[72] MyPhysicsLab, http://www.myphysicslab.com/runge_kutta.html

[73] W.E. Lorensen, H.E. Cline, "Marching cubes: A high resolution 3d surface connstruction algorithm", SIGGRAPH 21(4): 163-169, 1987

[74] F. Schlaug, "3D modeling in augmented reality", LITH-ISY-EX-ET--10/0379--SE, 2010

[75] Mihai Aldén, Andreas Andersson and Fredrik Salomonsson, "Cloudy", project report from TSBK03, Linköping 2011

[76] Carl Symborski, "Scalable User Content Distribution for Massively Multiplayer Online Worlds", IEEE Computer Society "Computer", vol 41, no 9, pp 38-44.

[77] Xinbo Jiang et al., "Latency and Scalability;: A Survey of Issues and Techniques for Supporting Networked Games", 13th IEEE International Conference on Networks, vol 1, 2005.

[78] 9th Annual Workshop on Network and Systems Support for Games (NetGames), 2010.

[79] Saurabh Ratti et al., "FizzX: multiplayer time manipulation in networked games". In: Proceedings of the 8th Annual Workshop on Network and Systems Support for Games, 2009.

[80] Tom Ching Ling Chen, ‚ÄúA protocol for distributed collision detection‚Äù. In: 2010 9th Annual Workshop on Network and Systems Support for Games (NetGames), pp 1-6, 2010.

[81] Zsolt Kenesi et al., "Optimizing Multiplayer Gaming Protocols for Heterogeneous Network Environment ". In: ICC '07 - IEEE International Conference on Communications, pp 1606-1611, 2007.

[82] Philip A. Branchet et al., "A Markov Model of Server to Client IP Traffic in First Person Shooter Games". In: ICC '08 - IEEE International Conference on Communications, pp 5715-5720 , 2008.

[83] Yand Yu et al., "Network-Aware State Update For Large Scale Mobile Games". In: ICCCN 2007 - Proceedings of the 16th International Conference on Computer Communications and Networks, pp 563-568, 2007.

[84] Preetam Ghosh et al., "A cross-layer design to improve quality of service in online multiplayer wireless gaming networks ". In: BroadNets 2005. 2nd International Conference on Broadband Networks, vol 2, pp 813-822, 2005.

[85] Johnny Chung Lee, Carneige Mellon University, "Head Tracking for Desktop VR Displays using the WiiRemote", YouTube video, http://www.youtube.com/watch?v=Jd3-eiid-Uw

[86] NVidia GPU Programming Guide, http://developer.download.nvidia.com/ GPU_Programming_Guide/GPU_Programming_Guide.pdf

[87] Jens Ogniewski, 3D display presentation, http://people.isy.liu.se/icg/jenso/

[88] Jens Ogniewski and Ingemar Ragnemalm, "Maximizing User Comfort & Immersion: A Game Designer's Guide to 3D Displays", Game And Entertainment Technologies 2011, pp 145-148.

[89] Yen Tran, "Utvärdering av rörelseparallax i datorspel", LITH-ISY-EX--10/4426--SE, 2010.

[90] Eric Dubois, "A Projection Method to Generate Analglyph Stereo Images", IEEE Computer Society, 2001.

[91] Jonas Andersson Hultgren, "Metoder för förbättrad rumsuppfattning i körsimulatorer", LITH-ISY-EX--11/4442--SE, 2011.

[92] Zhukov, S., Iones, A., Kronin, G. "An Ambient Light Illumination Model", Rendering Techniques '98 (Proceedings of the 9th EG Workshop on Rendering), 45-56, 1998

[93] Shanmugam, P., and Arikan, O., "Hardware accelerated ambient occlu- sion techniques on gpus", In I3D '07: Proceedings of the 2007 symposium on Interactive 3D graphics and games, ACM, pp 73—80, 2007.

[94] Mittring, M. "Finding next gen: Cryengine 2", In SIGGRAPH '07: ACM SIGGRAPH 2007 courses, ACM, pp 97—121, 2007.

[95] Simon Fenney, "Texture compression using low-frequency signal modulation", HWWS '03 Proceedings of the ACM SIGGRAPH/EUROGRAPHICS conference on Graphics hardware, pp 84-91, 2003.

[96] Jacob Ström, Tomas Akenine-Möller, "iPACKMAN: high-quality, low-complexity texture compression for mobile phones", HWWS '05 Proceedings of the ACM SIGGRAPH/EUROGRAPHICS conference on Graphics hardware, pp 63-70, 2005.

[97] Joel Jansson, "Ambient Occlusion for Dynamic Objects and Procedural Environments", LITH-ISY-EX--13/4658--SE, 2013

[98] A. Kaufman, D. Cohen, R. Yagel, "Volume Graphics", IEEE Computer, Vol. 26, No 7, july 1993.

[99] Johan Serebrink, "Detection of Primitive Shapes in a Voxel Grid", LITH-ISY-EX--15/4903--SE, 2015

[100] Henrik Bäcklund, Niklas Neijman, "Automatic Mesh Decomposition for Real-Time Collision Detection", LITH-ISY-EX--14/4755--SE, 2014

[101] Agnes Larsson, "Automatic Mesh Repair", LITH-ISY-EX--13/4720--SE, 2013

[102] E-A Karabassi, G. Papaioannou, T. Theoharis, "A Fast Depth-Buffer-Based Voxelization Algorithm", Journal of Graphics Tools, Vol. 4, Issue 4, 1999.

[103] L. Latta, "Building a Million-Particle System", Game Developers Conference, San Francisco, 2004. www.gamasutra.com/view/feature/130535/building_a_millionparticle_system.php

[104] M. Takeshige, "The Basics of GPU Voxelization", NVidia, 2015, developer.nvidia.com/content/basics-gpu-voxelization

[105] D.E. Muller, F.P. Preparata, "Finding the Intersection of Two Convex Polyhedra", Theoretical Computer Science, vol 7, 1978, pp 217-236.

[106] K. Rutanen, "Half-edge structure", kaba.hilvi.org/homepage/blog/halfedge/halfedge.htm

[107] A. Blackert, "Evaluation of Multi-Threading in Vulkan", thesis to be published 2016.

[108] C. Crassin, F. Neyret, M. Sainz, S. Green, E. Eisemann, "Interactive Indirect Illumination Using Voxel Cone Tracing", Computer Graphics Forum 2011.

18. Index

Numerics

A

B

I

J

K

L

M

N

O

P

Q

R

S

www.ingramcontent.com/pod-product-compliance
Lightning Source LLC
LaVergne TN
LVHW080115070326
832902LV00015B/2591